MW00490745

# THE eXVANGELICALS

# THE
# EXVANGELICALS

Loving, Living, and Leaving
the White Evangelical Church

# Sarah McCammon

ST. MARTIN'S
PRESS
NEW YORK

AUTHOR'S NOTE: Parts of this book are drawn from my experience and recollections. The events here are described as I remember them. Some names have been changed to protect the identity of the subjects.

First published in the United States by St. Martin's Press, an imprint of St. Martin's Publishing Group

www.stmartins.com

Designed by Steven Seighman

The Library of Congress Cataloging-in-Publication Data is available upon request.

ISBN 978-1-250-28447-1 (hardcover)
ISBN 978-1-250-28448-8 (ebook)

Our books may be purchased in bulk for promotional, educational, or business use. Please contact your local bookseller or the Macmillan Corporate and Premium Sales Department at 1-800-221-7945, extension 5442, or by email at MacmillanSpecialMarkets@macmillan.com.

First Edition: 2024

10   9   8   7   6   5   4   3   2   1

*To my sons, for helping me to see that parents, while imperfect,*
*are doing the best they know to do.*

*To Christopher, for making the journey with me*
*through difficult paths.*

*And to Greg, for coming alongside me on this journey,*
*and for your guidance, affection, and love.*

# CONTENTS

# THE EXVANGELICALS

# INTRODUCTION

Jesus stumbled under the weight of the cross. Blood dripped down his face, flowing from the crown of thorns that sat atop his head. A harsh yellow spotlight followed his heavy steps.

"We want Barabbas! Give us Barabbas!" shouted an angry mob of men, preferring to free a hardened criminal, as Jesus haltingly dragged the cross toward his place of death. All were silent in the darkened sanctuary as men spat on Jesus, mocking and cursing.

From one of the middle rows, I stood up on the scratchy, industrial brown carpet that covered the floor, craning to see past the adults in their movie theater–style seats.

Jesus put down the cross. The spotlight focused in on him, and everything else disappeared, except for the angry men who were beginning to spread Jesus, limb by limb, across the wooden beams.

One of them lifted up a hammer and a thick nail, and I began to sob. At about age four, I understood that this man wasn't *really* Jesus—he was in Heaven with God the Father. But those nails, and all of that blood, looked very real. And I was afraid for the man who was portraying Jesus in our church Easter pageant.

*This poor man is dying so we can understand how Jesus died for us,*

I thought. But as I watched, something combusted inside, and I felt panic and horror wash over me, pushing out tears.

"They're killing him," I cried.

I remember my parents comforting me from their seats, assuring me that it was only pretend, that the man would be okay—and that while Jesus had suffered and died for us, this man from our congregation would do neither.

It wouldn't be the last time I would sit in a church sanctuary, at once moved and afraid, and unsure what was real. Uncertain what to believe. But that day, I caught my breath and sat back down on the scratchy carpet. My heart was still pounding as the men hoisted the cross toward the sky, and Jesus cried out in pain. His voice rang out across the high ceiling: "Father, forgive them, for they know not what they do."

I came to understand that of course the violence I believed I was witnessing on that day was not real. Instead, it was meant to illustrate a deeper reality: that lurking beneath the veneer of our comfortable, suburban, midwestern American lives was a threat so severe that God had to send his only son to brutally suffer and die to save us from it. The blood might be fake, but the danger was not.

That threat informed every aspect of my life as an evangelical girl, growing up in Kansas City in the 1980s and '90s. It animated the efforts of the adults around me. The youth pastors who warned young evangelicals about the dangers of premarital sex—and the promise of the reward of a blissful marriage for waiting. The speakers who gave Young Earth creationist seminars in churches, and the teachers who instructed us from alternative textbooks in Christian schools. The religious leaders who warned against the dangers of what they described as "false religions" like Islam or even, according to some, Roman Catholicism. The droves of parents—

including mine—who marched with their children outside abortion clinics, praying for the end of *Roe v. Wade*, and fought against the legalization of same-sex marriage.

For many evangelicals of my parents', pastors', and teachers' era, decades of political activism and careful curation of alternative media and educational institutions culminated with the election of Donald Trump—whom many saw as the unlikely champion of their outsider movement—and the overturning of *Roe v. Wade* in the summer of 2022.

For others, especially many of their children—the Gen-Xers, millennials, and Zoomers who grew up in the shadow of the Moral Majority only to come of age in a far more pluralistic and interconnected world—these years have been a time of confusion and disillusionment. People born into evangelical families during that era have reached adulthood at a time when the country is more diverse than ever, and information is more readily available than ever—making alternative points of view impossible to ignore. It's also a time when Americans are rapidly becoming less religious, a shift that's most pronounced among younger generations.[1]

Now, as they've reached adulthood, those raised in white American evangelicalism have witnessed the realization of many of the most fervent fever dreams of the religious right—the 2016 election, the deterioration of abortion rights, the flourishing of conservative opposition to teaching about race and gender in public schools, and the growing alliance of the Republican Party with right-wing Christian nationalists.

For many, these developments have been a tipping point and have brought to a head years of doubt, discomfort, and trauma that can no longer be ignored. For those who began to "deconstruct" their faith years before the Trump era, this moment has occasioned an opportunity for larger, more open conversations about navigating the "wilderness" that comes after leaving the white evangelical world behind. This coming-of-age, and coming-to-terms, has been particularly traumatic for many who were raised evangelical and who are LGBTQ+, non-white, female, or members of other marginalized identities.

These are the "exvangelicals"—a loosely organized, largely online movement of people who are trying to make sense of the world as it is, and who they are in it.[2] The term emerged as a hashtag around 2016, and is generally credited to Blake Chastain, who launched a podcast called *Exvangelical* that year. Chastain and other former evangelicals began connecting online to discuss their disillusionment with Trumpism, anti-LGBTQ+ sentiment, racism, religious abuse, skepticism of science, and a host of other concerns about white evangelical beliefs and culture. Together, an increasing number of adults raised in conservative evangelical Christianity and other conservative faith traditions including Mormonism are openly navigating what's become known as "deconstruction"—the often painful process of rethinking an entire worldview and identity that was carefully constructed for them. Other former evangelicals are moving away from the movement less publicly, quietly rethinking their beliefs as they listen to podcasts, read scholarly books about theology and church history, lurk in exvangelical and faith-deconstruction online spaces, and engage in private conversations with friends.

Through the power and capacity of the internet and social media, many of these exvangelicals are finally finding each other and discovering that they are far from alone in their personal journeys. Just a few decades ago, people leaving conservative religious communities often found themselves isolated and shunned by former friends and family. Those who leave today are finding ample resources to answer questions that seemed off-limits within the walls of their churches and to fill in gaps left by their Christian school or homeschool education, a widening array of spaces for dialogue around deconstruction, and new opportunities for building communities around this shared experience.[3]

As they leave, exvangelicals are forging a variety of new paths. Some leave religion altogether and ultimately identify as atheists or agnostics. Others are actively working to reform evangelicalism or "reconstruct" a new expression of faith that better aligns with their deepest values and understanding of the world. Some are shifting into mainline Protestantism, Catholicism, or other Christian traditions. Others leave Christianity to explore other faith traditions or spiritual practices, and some simply take an indefinite break from church to figure things out.

Wherever the journey takes them, and however they come to describe their experience, many exvangelicals report feeling relief after giving up the struggle to affirm doctrines that violate their deepest intuitions about morality and, often, reality. Significantly, however, this shift often comes with an accompanying sorrow and a loss: of identity, community, and sometimes family. And in that void, many exvangelicals struggle with new questions about what to believe, how to exist and grow in social and romantic relationships outside the structure of the church, and, very often, how to parent without the structure and prescribed answers of evangelicalism modeled by their parents during their own childhood.

Those who leave are also increasingly catching the eye of powerful evangelical leaders, some of whom are angrily pushing back, delivering pointed sermons and writing caustic essays attacking this movement and warning exvangelicals of the grave danger to their souls. Admittedly, and thankfully, others are taking a gentler approach as they grapple to understand the reasons so many younger evangelicals and other Christians are fleeing their churches. These leaders often urge evangelicals who are questioning their beliefs to "reconstruct" a more authentic Christian faith—and come back to church.

Whatever their new path, a commonality that many deconstructing evangelicals share is a sense that the very tradition they were raised with—the emphasis on seeking ultimate Truth and taking seriously the biggest questions in life—have ultimately led them to an unexpected, often difficult, but more authentic journey.

Tim Whitaker, founder of The New Evangelicals, an organization for former evangelicals rethinking their faith, said many of his followers want to remain Christian in at least some sense.

"Most of us are trying desperately to follow Jesus," Whitaker told me. "And that is what has caused us to deconstruct and to rethink this stuff, because we find it at odds with the evangelical machine that we've been a part of."[4]

Singer-songwriter David Bazan, lead musician and creative force behind the band Pedro the Lion, publicly grappled for years with his own departure from evangelical Christianity. His song "When We Fell" is essentially a Dear John letter to God, in which he describes the irony that aspects of his evangelical upbringing would eventually lead him away from it:

> With the threat of hell hanging over my head like a halo
> I was made to believe in a couple of beautiful truths
> That eventually had the effect of completely unraveling
> The powerful curse put on me by you.[5]

These are the stories of that unraveling: the stories of millions of Americans who are now adults, and who grew up immersed in what was arguably the largest and most influential American subculture in recent memory. It was a subculture that was at once insular and immense: from the movement's peak beginning in the late 1980s and holding more or less steady through the mid-2000s, close to a quarter of Americans could be described as white evangelicals.[6]

The vastness of the very movement I was being raised in was completely invisible to me as a tween in the early 1990s, shyly starting to show up at youth group meetings, believing the world to be a dangerous place that both needed saving, and that I needed saving from. While many of my generation have grown up and stayed in the culture despite misinformation, manipulation, and abuse, others have chosen an often arduous journey out. It's a journey that I, and a host of other adults from evangelical backgrounds, now find ourselves on, for reasons that are at once unique to each person and yet similar, because we are all products of this shared culture.

To describe this experience, I have borrowed the label often attributed to Chastain, "exvangelical"—which I find useful because of its specificity and complexity. To me, the term particularly resonates, signaling both where we have come from, a nod to the reality that the culture and identity of our communities of origin shapes each one of us, and the active decision to separate and leave that world behind.

That separation, however painful, often feels inevitable. It stems from a cognitive dissonance that ultimately becomes overwhelming, compelling many of us to distance ourselves from the community that had been our home, a home that was our source of comfort as well as pain. That leaving creates a breach, forcing a search for a new path forward and a reconceived sense of meaning, purpose, and identity.

I use "exvangelical" loosely, in the same way that "evangelical" is a controversial and often ill-defined sociological term. When I was an evangelical, for example, I would not have thought to describe myself as one—simply as a "Christian." And in retrospect, I was an exvangelical long before I knew such a term existed.

I also use it with the understanding that not everyone I've interviewed would describe themselves in that way. Some who have left evangelicalism shy away from the term, out of a preference not to be defined by what they were, but rather by who they are now and where they are going. Some instead prefer terms like "post-evangelical," "former evangelical," "progressive Christian," or, in cases where it applies, "ex-Christian." Many fall into categories described by religion scholar Isaac B. Sharp as "the other evangelicals"— Christians with identities such as queer, Black, liberal, or feminist, who've found themselves "pushed out, excommunicated, or defined out" of the evangelical movement "or those who simply threw up their hands and left in despair."[7] What the people you'll meet in these pages share, with the exception of a few expert voices from outside the evangelical world, is a theologically and politically conservative Protestant Christian background, and the decision to leave it behind in search of something new.

As a journalist, I'm used to telling other people's stories. But for this one, I'm unable to sit on the sidelines. So in these pages, you will meet many exvangelicals, and learn their stories in conversation with my own. In many ways, this book is my bid to answer a question I am asked often in one form or another: "How did you go from who you were, to who you are?"

By the end of 2016, I had become accustomed to being yelled at by angry crowds of people. Assigned to cover the Donald Trump campaign as a correspondent for NPR, it felt almost routine to those of us in the press pen to huddle over our laptops, rushing to meet deadlines while people passed by to shout insults at us.

However large our egos may be in the national media, I don't intend to compare myself to Jesus here. But there were frightening moments in those angry crowds. It also wasn't unusual to engage in warm, friendly conversations with rally goers, often as they were arriving and Elton John's "Tiny Dancer" blared over the loudspeaker. They might have made a joke about the "liberal media" at my expense, but many were equally happy to talk and tell me why they felt so seen and inspired by this real estate developer from New York City. And then, the music amped up, Trump took the stage, and the atmosphere would shift.

The crowd took on its own energy as Trump pointed toward the risers and cameras at the back of the room, complaining about those "disgusting reporters" who were "the worst people." This quickly became a part of his schtick, a highlight of every rally. Trump would whip the audience into an excited frenzy, as they turned to point at us and laugh. In my reporting for NPR, I often described this moment as very much like a rock concert, in which Trump's attacks on the press functioned like one of his "greatest hits" that the audience would demand to hear before they could leave satisfied.

You could feel the catharsis in the air as these crowds poured out their frustrations—with the economy, with immigrants, with the Washington establishment that they felt disdained them—and directed them at us. Men in red MAGA hats shook their fists and tried to stare us down. I'll always remember one grandmotherly looking woman in Colorado who leaned in toward the reporters' pen, pointing and shouting, "You're disgusting!" We were, it seemed, representatives of the hated establishment, on their turf, and we were more than a sufficient proxy.

But I wasn't part of that—or, I hadn't felt that I was. I had moved to Washington part-time to cover this campaign, and spent months reporting on the Republican Party's evangelical base, leaving behind a spouse and two young children in Georgia, feeling nervous and out of my element after spending most of my life and career in the Midwest and South. These people in the crowds were, in reality, my people: white, largely midwestern or Southern Christians. They looked, sounded, and believed a lot like people in the evangelical community where I'd first learned about God, and about politics. When I interviewed them, they'd often bring up their Christian beliefs, and their fears about the direction in which they felt the country was going. They saw Trump as someone who could get the country back on track.

I'd been away from the church of my childhood for many years, but I watched with curiosity and sometimes confusion as members of the movement and its leaders first wrestled with and then wholeheartedly embraced Trump, in numbers large enough to secure the Republican nomination and, ultimately, the presidency.

By November 2016, I was physically, emotionally, and spiritually depleted. The final weekend before the election was a blur of flights in the small plane chartered for campaign reporters, along with bus rides, tight deadlines, and very little sleep. We crisscrossed the country, documenting the final frenetic push through battleground states. It was at one of those final rallies, in Minnesota, that a man was photographed wearing a T-shirt printed with the ominous words, "Rope. Tree. Journalist. SOME ASSEMBLY REQUIRED."[8]

I was there, though I didn't even see the shirt until it started spreading across social media. But what I did see in those final days of the campaign unnerved me. There was a palpable tension in the air as the clock ticked toward Election Day. At each event, I said a prayer as people crowded close to us, shouting inches away from our faces, pressing their bodies against the flimsy metal gates that cordoned off the press area. After each rally, I breathed a little sigh of relief as we filed back on the bus.

On the morning of November 8, 2016, I wrote on Facebook:

"I'm not a Bible-thumper or much of a churchgoer. But standing in 10 rallies over the past two days, being yelled at again and again in sometimes frightening ways (sometimes by people who were perfectly pleasant 20 minutes before), the only thing that has gotten me through is meditating on these verses which I learned as a child."

I quoted the passage in Matthew 5, where Jesus tells us, counterintuitively, to love our enemies, turn the other cheek, and "pray for those who persecute you."

And then he goes on to say the most difficult, and frankly kind of annoying, thing:

"If you love those who love you, what reward do you have? . . . And if you greet only your brothers, what more are you doing than others?"

I've always thought this was a bit naive. I don't like to think of myself as the sort of person who sticks around so that you can feel free to take another swing at me. And yet, when I needed it most, it was a truth that rose up from somewhere deep inside and gave me the strength to feel, for a moment, something almost like compassion for these angry crowds. Maybe all of their anger was really a lot of pain. That recognition felt like the only thing keeping me standing on both feet in the cold Michigan amphitheater or the packed Pennsylvania auditorium in the days before the election.

This, I was taught growing up, is what we are called to do: to try to mimic Christ, to love generously, even at great cost. Even when people don't deserve it. Even when they hurt us.

I was taught to pray, "Father, forgive them, for they know not what they do." And I was taught to speak the truth.

I was taught this, and much more, by evangelicals.

# 1

# PEOPLE NEED THE LORD

D ear Lord," I prayed. "Thank you for this food and for this day. And I pray that Grandpa will get saved. In Jesus's name, Amen."

Every night, the six of us—my parents, two sisters, my brother, and me—gathered around our antique wooden kitchen table, and someone prayed a version of that prayer for my grandfather. I didn't know much about him, only that his house was filled with interesting objects and artwork and books, that he played classical music on the grand piano in his living room, that the kitchen smelled of garlic and sherry from his beloved cooking projects, and that he always had at least one cat lurking around the house. I knew that he was a brain surgeon, and I understood that was something we were proud of. But I couldn't understand why he didn't love Jesus—the man with the gentle face surrounded by the herd of fluffy sheep in the tiny framed painting on my bedroom shelf.

What I did know was that Grandpa, and my aunts and uncles, were going to Hell. Like everyone who didn't believe in Jesus, their souls were in great danger. We had to pray for them, my parents told us, and whenever we saw them, we had to "be a witness"—be friendly, respectful, and well-behaved, so as to show them the light of Jesus. Being evangelical meant *evangelizing*—sharing the news of Jesus with everyone we could, before it was too late. And this was especially urgent for the people we loved most—our family. If they could see Jesus shining through us, they might be drawn to him, and understand that they were lost in the darkness, and that if they would simply believe and pray to receive him into their hearts, they could become better people here on Earth, and then, when they died, go to Heaven with us.

Though we feared an eternity of separation from our family members who would be in Hell while we were in Heaven, my parents seemed cautious about spending time with them while we were together here on Earth. Grandpa lived only a few miles away, but we didn't see him much. Mostly at holidays and major family gatherings. No sleepovers, no group vacations, no hanging out at Grandpa's house. We probably spent more time there for the few years of my life when my grandmother, whom I called "Mee-Maw," was alive, but that's only a fuzzy memory of a memory; she was gone not long after my third birthday.

So on the occasions we visited Grandpa's house, I was on my best behavior. The stakes could not have been higher. My childish disobedience, even my failure to exhibit the "joy of Jesus" that should be clearly radiating from my heart, could cost my relatives their very souls. Carrying that heavy truth, I put on a smile.

I was the oldest of the four kids. We were the kind of family of blond, well-behaved children that strangers complimented in restaurants: "What a beautiful family," they'd tell my parents, who would beam at us. Three girls, spaced three years apart, in smocked dresses and shiny black patent leather Mary Janes, and the youngest, a little boy with thick glasses and a shock of white-blond hair in front, and cheeks like those Hummel figurines we sometimes saw in antique stores.

We knew that our neat appearance, and our obedient behavior in public, was one small way that we could be a witness for Jesus, by displaying what a family could—and *should*—be like: a father and mother, four obedient children, fresh from church, eating apple pie together. Everywhere we went, everything we did, we were told we must be ambassadors for Christ.

*"This little light of mine, I'm gonna let it shine,"* we sang in Sunday school. Or, *"Be a missionary every day/Tell the world that Jesus is the way/The Lord is soon returning; there is no time to lose, so!/ Be a missionary, God's own emissary, be a missionary today!"*

We all felt the urgency. And as the oldest, I held a position of honor and had a special responsibility to shine my light, "set an example," and help care for each of the babies as they came, one after another.

Most of the time, I loved that role. I watched with excitement as my mother's belly grew each time, slowly over the months. I read, a bit vicariously, her copy of *What to Expect When You're Expecting*, stuffing my T-shirt with blankets or stuffed animals as I pretended to expect my own little baby—something I dreamed of doing one day, something I'd learned was the highest calling for a woman. I enthusiastically watched as my parents prepared the nursery and attended birthing classes; as my mother neatly folded the cloth diapers she painstakingly washed for each child. When the time came, my parents rushed me to the home of a family member or a friend from their Bible study group, and I waited for the phone calls in the middle of the night, informing me, "You have a sister," and then again, "A sister," and then—oh no!—"A brother!" *What is that?!*\*

---

\* I want to stipulate that I eventually came to terms with having a brother, and that today, I love all three of my siblings very much.

Each child was a blessing, a reflection of God's favor: "'Children are a heritage from the Lord, offspring a reward from him,'" my mother would say, quoting from Psalms. "'Your wife will be like a fruitful vine within your house; your children will be like olive shoots around your table.'"[1]

My parents *were* fruitful, and with each birth came an opportunity to gently evangelize. They selected names from the Bible for each of us, starting with mine, Sarah Elizabeth. To welcome each newcomer, in our charismatic evangelical tradition—unlike in Catholicism and much of mainline Protestant Christianity—babies were not baptized. Baptism was reserved for "believers" who'd actively chosen Christ, and so that would come later.

Instead, the church held a dedication ceremony to honor the baby and pray for God to bless the family. The goal was to set up the new parents to "train up a child in the way he should go. And when he is old he will not depart from it."[2] That passage from Proverbs promised that the right kind of parental guidance would all but certainly achieve the intended result of a devoted Christian adult, who would build a family of her own, and train her own children in the same way. It was an opportunity to invite extended family for a time of celebration, but even more in our case, a chance for them to hear the Gospel and maybe, just maybe, finally "get saved."

I was six when my youngest sister was born. Before her dedication, at home together in our three-bedroom ranch house, we prayed for the souls of the family we'd invited, that God would "speak to their hearts" and that hearing the Word of God from the pulpit might open their eyes—that they might finally repent.

On Sunday morning, we sat near the back of the mammoth sanctuary at Full Faith Church of Love in suburban Kansas City. This was a megachurch in 1987, before many national news outlets were writing trend pieces about megachurches. Instead of pews, we sank into movie theater–style padded seats, upholstered in a brown that complemented the tan hue of the tightly woven, textured carpet. Up front, a full worship band, with drums and guitars and backup singers, led the congregation in praise songs displayed on a giant screen from an overhead projector.

*"Lord, you are more precious than silver; Lord, you are more costly than gold,"* the adults around me sang, swaying as they closed their eyes and lifted their hands up toward the vaulted ceiling. *"Lord, you are more beautiful than diamonds, and nothing I desire compares with you."*[3] The music was beautiful and soothing, and while I felt uncomfortable raising my hands like many of the more enthusiastic adults did, I loved hearing them sing around me, and sometimes joined in myself.

At some point, my dad's younger brother and sister joined us. I watched them nervously, wondering if the Lord might be working, waiting for the moment that the truth of the Gospel might break through and soften their hard hearts. Our pastor, a rotund man with a bald head who reminded me of the pictures of Mikhail Gorbachev on the nightly news, called our family to the front of the room, where he gently took my baby sister from my mom for a moment and displayed her to the approving congregation.

After a prayer, we were back in our seats in time for the sermon when the pastor could speak directly to us and, more importantly, to my aunt and uncle. As we settled in and he cracked open his Bible to begin the sermon, I noticed a motion to my left. My aunt and uncle waved and smiled politely, and quietly slipped out.

In our belief system, while my sister's dedication was important, it was only a symbol. For us, the central question was what we believed in our hearts, not whether we'd participated in the proper rituals. I was probably in high school before I realized that the formal name for the kind of Christianity that typically practiced infant baptism was "mainline Protestantism," not "nominal Christians," or Christians in name only, as I'd sometimes heard them called.

There were frequent warnings against insincere belief, reminders to look deep within and be certain, absolutely certain, that your "heart is right with God." At the end of many church services, the pastor would deliver an altar call, asking anyone in the room who didn't know Jesus to make a decision. "Make it tonight," he'd urge. "If you were to die in a car accident on the way home, do you know where you'd go? I want you to wake up in Heaven!" And for those who'd already prayed that "prayer of salvation" giving their hearts to Christ: Are you really sure? Is your heart truly in the right place? Have you "backslidden"—the dreaded term for someone who once walked with Christ only to "slide back" into a life of sin? There were so many Bible verses, like Jeremiah 17:10, telling us that God was looking closely, scanning for sin: "I the Lord search the heart and examine the mind, to reward each person according to their conduct, according to what their deeds deserve."

Even for children, it was critical to make a personal decision for Christ, as soon as she could even vaguely begin to comprehend it. The summer I was ten, my parents gave me a new Bible, King James Version, bound in lavender leather. On the inside cover, in my mother's perfect, elegant script, was my name and the date: June 8, 1991. On the opposite page, under the blank page labeled "Church Record," in my own wobbly handwriting, I wrote down the two major religious events of my life so far: my "believer's baptism" at age eight and "Saved—age 2 ½."

I would come to understand much later that this version of evangelical 1980s American Christianity was the descendant of a long succession of schisms and divisions and calls for spiritual revival and renewal. We had cast off the rituals of older, more established sects for an individualistic, emotional, relational faith. Those rituals did not bring a child into the church; she must choose it for herself, and freely believe in salvation through Jesus. She must recognize that she's a sinner—that like every other human being before her, she was born with a nature that will make sin inevitable, that no sin is too small to deservedly incur God's anger, and that God is pure and holy and righteous and cannot tolerate even a speck of sinfulness. She must understand that the only just and appropriate punishment for sin is permanent separation from God, in "eternal, conscious torment," as many pastors reminded us, in the fires of Hell, which burn forever but never consume.

This was all very dire, but there was "Good News" in the Gospel: a simple way to avoid this horrific fate. It did not require a pastor or a priest or a splash of holy water or anything else mediated by another person or a church. It required, at minimum, a simple "Sinner's Prayer" of repentance.

Sophisticated theology is beyond the grasp of young children. But I knew who Jesus was. Most Sundays, while my parents stayed behind in the giant sanctuary, I'd walk over to "children's church" down the hall, where we would sing songs and watch puppet shows all about Jesus and his love for us. During smaller Sunday school classes before church, we sat in a circle with other children our age on the carpeted floor, as smiling teachers told Bible stories. They pressed colorful cut-out figures onto the flannelgraph, an easel covered in fabric printed with images of rolling green hills that could transform, with a few scene changes, from the mountainside where Jesus preached about the Beatitudes to Calvary, where he was crucified in between two thieves.

I studied Jesus's face—on the flannelgraph, in picture books, and the little framed painting of the Good Shepherd that I kept in my bedroom. His face looked warm and tender and kind. And, I was told, he loved me and wanted to have a relationship with me that would last my whole life, and then greet me when I went to Heaven. That sounded much better than the alternative.

Though I liked the idea of going to Heaven, I wasn't sure how to imagine it. We'd been promised a place of eternal happiness, with choirs of beautiful angels singing, all of our Christian friends and family dressed in white, walking on streets paved with gold. We'd be reunited with people who died before us, if they knew Jesus, like my mother's parents (who, despite being Lutheran rather than evangelical, were assumed to have been fervent enough to have been granted admission).

But, in quiet moments when I was honest with myself, I thought that Heaven sounded a little bit scary and strange and even . . . boring? I worried that I was doing something wrong that made me feel that way. I'd heard a braver child than me raise the same concern once or twice, in Sunday school or Bible class, and I cringed slightly at their boldness in asking what I sensed was an off-limits question. The response, as I recall, from the teacher was that being in God's presence would be more wonderful than we could ever imagine, and that in our human existence we couldn't begin to fully understand what it would be like.

I did, however, very clearly understand the idea of fire. In cold midwestern winters, I loved evenings when my father would carry in wood from the pile outside and build a warm fire in our brick living-room fireplace. But when I looked into the flames, and felt their heat as I drew closer, I knew that I did not want to burn forever and ever. So, at not yet three years old, I asked Jesus to come into my heart and save me. No child was too young to be saved. After all, we sang, *"Jesus loves the little children."*

I sat in my bedroom with my mother and repeated, line by line, the Sinner's Prayer. And, I was assured, my life was changed at that moment. Jesus had come into my heart and given me the greatest gift possible: eternal life with God and salvation from eternal torment in Hell.

But still, it was hard not to think about it. I tried not to picture Grandpa burning in the Lake of Fire forever and ever. I didn't think I felt any different, and I wondered how I could know for sure that I was saved, that God had definitely heard my prayer. So, two years later, I asked my mom to help me pray it again, just to be safe.

My mom told me about her own fear of this as a child. She would practice repeatedly reaching out to touch the radiator, in an effort to build up a tolerance for heat, in case she wasn't deemed worthy of Heaven. It was only when she truly met Jesus, she said—amidst the energy of the Jesus Movement and the enthusiastic circles of newly converted hippies she joined as a teenager in the 1970s—that she could really give her life to him. And that was when she found true peace.

*"I've got peace like a river/I've got peace like a river/I've got peace like a river in my soul,"* we sang in children's church. We waved our hands to the right, then left, and back again, miming the motion of a flowing river. It was a simple song: we chanted about "joy like a fountain," hands sweeping upward, and "love like an ocean," fingers wiggling like happy little waves. All because of Jesus.

I wanted to feel the peace and joy we sang about, and that my mom talked about, but it was often elusive. And when it did come, it felt more like an unpredictable trickle than a mighty river or an ocean.

If you'd accepted Jesus into your heart, that was supposed to settle it, I thought. But had I really believed, and believed *enough*? What if *I* was among the lost? The stakes were far too high to get this wrong. Alone in my bedroom, I flipped through the pages of my lavender Bible, looking for reassurance. I read the words of Jesus in the book of John: "Peace I leave with you, my peace I give unto you: not as the world giveth, give I unto you. Let not your heart be troubled, neither let it be afraid."[4]

And from 1 John: "If we confess our sins, he is faithful and just and will forgive us our sins and purify us from all unrighteousness."[5]

I'd done it all, confessed my sins again and again: my disrespect toward my parents, fights with my siblings, laziness and reluctance to wash the dishes after dinner. I'd prayed the Sinner's Prayer, more than once. But still, my heart was troubled. At night, after I'd settled into my twin bed with my little sister asleep in the trundle next to me, my stomach tightened and my mind raced.

I was never afraid of monsters. I knew from children's television shows and in books I saw at the public library that other kids were. But monsters seemed kind of silly, especially compared to demons and the Devil himself, which were very real and never far away, trying to steal our souls.

In the darkness and quiet, I wondered if it was all true, and why, if Jesus had come to save the world, so many people apparently would not be saved? Something felt very wrong about that. But to entertain such doubts would be to subject myself to the same fate I feared for them. What if this was the Devil, trying to lead me astray? What if, despite the prayers and the promises in the Bible and the reassurances of my parents and pastors, I wasn't *really saved*?

And even if I was saved, and if it was all true, then what? There was still so much to fear. We lived each day with the knowledge that Jesus could come back at any time to take us to Heaven, in the Rapture predicted in the Book of Revelation. If, and only if, we were ready, Jesus would take us up with him, into the clouds. "The trumpet shall sound," the verse from Matthew promised, and he would gather up his people from all over the Earth. This was supposed to be a joyful hope for the Christian, but I was ashamed to feel afraid when I thought about it. I wondered, if I didn't believe quite enough, could I grab my mother's ankles and fly into Heaven with her? Would God let me in? And if I did believe enough, what would it mean to be sucked up into the air? The sound of a train whistle, or a loud car horn, was enough to send me into a panic, that maybe this was it, the moment of truth.

Our concern for lost souls extended far beyond our own and those of our family, of course. We were taught to share our faith freely and widely, with anyone who might be placed in our path by God, ready for the Good News. God brought people into our lives for a reason, and we always should be looking for "divine appointments"—meetings arranged for us by God, to tell them the Truth that they were blind to. We were reminded of this in sermons at church, and chapel presentations at my Christian school, which met on the campus of a local Bible church. The theology there was slightly different from the church we attended on Sunday mornings—they didn't speak in tongues or raise their hands in worship like we did—but we were all united by our belief in the inerrancy of the Bible and in the necessity of faith in Jesus Christ to secure our eternal salvation in Heaven.

Missionaries—people who dedicated their lives to telling others around the world about Jesus—would come to speak, toting a slide carousel from their travels. One missionary's wife showed us how to wrap an Indian sari. They all offered glimpses of busy markets in Latin America, crowded streets in Asia, and faces of thin brown-skinned children.

During one of these presentations, I remember sitting in the red upholstered pew of the church sanctuary that doubled as our chapel during the school week, watching these faces flash across the screen, as a recording of the Steve Green song "People Need the Lord" played in the background. Through lyrics about passing "empty people" on streets and being able to somehow see their emptiness and internal suffering simply by looking "in their eyes," the idea was that people without Jesus are so lost and without purpose, their desperation is written all over their faces for any devout believer to perceive. The chorus climaxes with the solution: "People need the Lord!" And it asks the listeners, assumedly Christians sitting in a pew like I was, to "give our lives" to help bring the Gospel to people.

The traveling missionaries exemplified the Christian's mandate to evangelize and share this Good News. Secretly, many of us feared receiving such a "call" from God—a call we were told could come mysteriously, even during childhood, in the form of a feeling or a strong impression that we must one day leave our own homes and families, live within a new community somewhere in the world, and learn their language so that we could sufficiently communicate and perhaps translate the Bible for them.

For the moment, the instruction was clear: the least we could do was avoid missing an opportunity to share the Gospel with someone God had placed in our path, right in the middle of our relatively comfortable midwestern lives.

It's difficult to save a world you're taught to fear and are carefully sheltered from. In my early years, my own world revolved around our church—on a sprawling campus a short drive over the Kansas state line into the suburbs—and the K–12 school I began attending at age five, which met in classrooms inside redbrick buildings of a small fundamentalist Bible church in Kansas City, Missouri. Aside from my father's family, I didn't know anyone who didn't know Jesus. Our "mission field" was limited, so every sustained interaction with a potential nonbeliever felt a little guilty, like a shirked obligation, if I stayed silent.

One of those rare opportunities presented itself when I was about eight years old, as my mother correctly determined that I needed to spend several Saturday mornings at what can only be described as remedial skating lessons. At least once a year, my school rented out a rink for a party where we skated to praise and worship songs. Some of the girls would show up with their own beautiful skates from home—in pink or white leather—and seemingly fly around the rink. And I, in my rented brown skates, would cling to the metal bar, scooting a few steps at a time around the circle, and often falling. So my mom found a class where an instructor patiently showed us how to maneuver our skates to slow down and speed up, and how to use toe stoppers to brake.

I didn't know any of the other kids, but I understood that most of them went to public school. There was one girl about my age that I especially liked. She was friendly and chatty and almost as awkward in the rink. We'd stumble through our lessons together, then talk while we unlaced our skates and put on our sneakers to go home.

One week, an unwelcome thought entered my mind: *What if God wants me to witness to her?* My stomach tightened. *What if I'm the only person in her life who can tell her? What if she dies without Jesus because of me?* I couldn't shake the sense of obligation.

The last week of class came, and all I could think about was what to say to her. As we took off our skates and put on our shoes for the last time, I couldn't bring myself to start with the opening line we'd heard in so many sermons: "If you died tonight, do you know where you would go?"

It felt like a little much for Skateland.

We picked up our jackets and I followed her outside. We waited by the front door, watching the car line as each parent pulled up.

Any moment, my parents would arrive, whisking me home to clean my bedroom before spending a lazy Saturday afternoon playing in the backyard. I'd probably never see her again. Eternity hung in the balance, with seconds to spare.

My heart pounded. *Now. This is your last chance.*

"Uhm," I said. "Do you . . . go to church?"

"Yeah, sometimes," she said. "Anyway, my dad's here!"

And that was that. No big sign from God, no literal come-to-Jesus moment. Only me, my skates, and my awkward gesture toward Heaven. I wouldn't try to make another one for a long time.

My memory from Skateland flooded back as I came across artist Stephanie Stalvey's comic book–style drawings on Instagram, where she vividly describes her own post-evangelical journey under the #exvangelical hashtag.

In one frame I particularly resonate with, a young white girl sits on a school bus, clutching a spiral notebook and a folder with a picture of a kitten. Beside her sits another young woman, wearing a hijab.

In the next image, the first girl's thought bubble reads, "God probably placed her in my path because he wants me to witness to her and help her get saved!" She begins to plot her strategy, planning to invite the Muslim girl to church, but not too soon, so as not to appear too "pushy." In one image,[6] her face crumples as she contemplates the dangers of waiting "*too* long" to invite her friend: "This bus could crash at any moment, and if she died she would go to *Hell*. And that would be partly my fault."

Like me, Stalvey grew up hearing that it was her responsibility to help save the world and to share her beliefs with others, without being influenced by theirs.

"Everyone who was not a Christian was either a potential convert or a potential stumbling block," Stalvey told me.[7] "Either you could lead them to Christ, or they might influence you away from Christ."

Stalvey is a little younger. She grew up in the 1990s in Ohio, the daughter of a pastor who led an evangelical mission and church-planting ministry, and she, like me, attended a Christian private school.

"I was kind of always immersed in that parallel universe of American fundamentalist Christianity," Stalvey said. "Every adult in my life, every authority figure, was repeating and teaching me these same things. So that was reality for me as a child."*

She's now in her thirties, working as an art teacher and living in Florida with her husband and their toddler, and processing her evangelical childhood through her art.

"Everything was either black or white," Stalvey writes in one series of images. "Sacred or secular, righteous or unrighteous . . . We were all either saved or lost."

Like mine, her evangelical childhood also was characterized by the push and pull of fearing eternal punishment from God while embracing his love, which was the theme of every church service, every prayer meeting, every hymn. In one of Stalvey's images, a little girl smiles, looking up toward the Heavens and basking in "the early message that I was completely, unequivocally loved by God."[8] The warmth and security of that feeling was belied by what Stalvey describes as an "invisible threat," the ever-present awareness that

---

* I want to acknowledge that Stalvey and I are far from the first, or the only, former evangelicals to describe the world of our childhoods this way. For example, see this 2011 conversation from the public radio program *Talk of the Nation,* "Evangelical Christians Form Parallel Structure," October 20, 2011, https://www.npr.org/2011/10/20/141557124/evangelical-christians-form-parallel-structure.

she was sinful, so sinful she deserved Hell; that were it not for Jesus, she would go there; and that because of her sin, Jesus had to die a horrible death by crucifixion in order to save her soul.

"One of the first things I knew is that I was loved—I was loved by God. But it was confusing because I didn't deserve that love," Stalvey said. "You metabolize the idea that you're inherently bad."

As she got older, Stalvey struggled with evangelical teachings about who was saved and who was lost. As a teen, she remembers talking to other Christian friends about their friends who were LGBTQ+.

"It's like, 'What are we allowed to think about this?'" she said. "It's kind of like pulling on the string and everything starts to unravel."

As she began to explore her deepest questions and express doubts about her beliefs, some evangelical friends, no doubt worried about her soul, told her to trust God, to pray more. It wasn't as if she'd never tried that.

"I have stood in a church singing a worship song that I didn't believe in," Stalvey said, "and kind of feeling this ache and wanting to believe in the words, and it feels like you're the only one. . . . That doubt is really isolating. You're like, 'What's wrong with me?'"

I do know that sense of isolation. But over time, like Stalvey, I've realized I'm not alone. And in the past several years, I've observed a groundswell of other younger adults like us, reevaluating the picture of the world that was painted for them by their evangelical subculture and trying to make sense of how, in the words of the prophet Micah, "to act justly and to love mercy and to walk humbly" with God, or with an altered vision of the divine, as the case may be.[9]

There are signs, particularly in an era that has been characterized by a growing evangelical alliance with white Christian nationalism, conspiracy-theorist thinking, and science denialism, that many former evangelicals are trying to make sense of these questions. In his 2020 book *After Evangelicalism,* the Mercer University ethicist David P. Gushee argues that evangelicalism is in decline largely because of a rapid loss of its young people.

Gushee estimates, based on Pew Research Center data from 2014, that, even before the rise of the Trump era and all of the fallout it brought, some twenty-five million American adults who had been raised evangelical had left the faith. He points to data showing that the white evangelical church is aging more quickly than the population as a whole, as younger generations of Americans rapidly become less and less religious.[10] And he notes, as documented by polling researcher Daniel Cox in 2018, that about one-third of Americans raised in evangelical households leave the tradition as adults.[11]

This, Gushee writes, goes well beyond the typical process of adults growing up and charting their own life course, as humans have always done to some extent: "What we are seeing is not just rebellion against parents or normal ebb and flow. We are witnessing *conscientious objection.* Ex-evangelicals are leaving based on what they believe to be specific offenses against them personally, or against their family and friends, and specific experiences of trauma that have left lasting damage . . ." Those experiences, he says, include a host of ills within the evangelical community: clergy sex abuse, bigotry against LGTBQ+ people, hypocritical leaders, and more.[12]

Gushee describes being approached by many "promising but troubled (ex-)evangelicals" at an American Academy of Religion conference in 2018: "They hailed from the best evangelical schools. They were pursuing or had finished doctoral programs in religion and theology. And, to a person, they knew that there was something deeply broken about white US evangelicalism. . . . Since then, I have looked around a bit more and seen the signs of distress everywhere. One might even call it a movement."[13]

For Stalvey, and for me, connecting with other exvangelicals has been a relief and an important part of our journeys. With it has come a realization that "there are other people in the pews or in the audience or in the congregation that have this tension," Stalvey said. "Hearing friends of mine and people that I'm close to affirm and say to me . . . 'You don't need to figure it out. It's fine for you to just be and let it sit.' It's so crazy how restful it is to hear that."

Stalvey told me she is learning to let things "unravel" a little bit and create something new—a metaphor that makes a lot of sense to me.

"It's really hard, but it's also kind of freeing to say, 'Wait, I have agency. I have the right to explore this in any way I want to, to define it however I want to,'" she said. "It still feels rebellious, even as an adult, because you've been taught to fear that."

Peace has come not from praying harder, but from letting go of the idea that she has to save anyone.

# 2

# A "PARALLEL UNIVERSE"

The "black and white, sacred or secular" universe that Stephanie Stalvey described, and which formed so much of our evangelical childhoods, required careful construction and curation.

My parents were married in 1976, which *Newsweek* deemed the "year of the evangelical"—a time when the white conservative evangelical Christian movement was growing in numbers, prominence, and power, as members organized themselves in reaction against the rising tides of cultural change.[1] The evangelicals of my parents' generation had come of age during the height of the sexual revolution and in the shadow of the Vietnam War. But now, as they entered adulthood and married life, many were searching for guidance about how to navigate the world and raise their young families.

In the aftermath of seismic cultural shifts, many Americans, including young adults like my parents, "were ready to hear a new message, a message that cloaked itself in a very simple morality, one that appropriated the language of Christian values," historian Randall Balmer argues in *The Making of Evangelicalism*. It was also a moment when decades of work by evangelicals to build up a robust subcultural infrastructure, in the form of educational and media institutions, was beginning to bear fruit in political power and cultural influence.[2]

My parents embraced this ascendant evangelicalism, casting aside the free love ethos of their youth. Out was the drug culture and anti-war protests; in were praise choruses, sung with the aid of a guitar in each other's living rooms, while their children played cops and robbers in the backyard.

I was born in February 1981, in the earliest days of Ronald Reagan's first presidential term. He'd taken power with the help of white evangelical voters and their leaders, in what historian Kristin Kobes Du Mez describes in her 2020 book *Jesus and John Wayne* as an "election widely hailed as the moment the Christian Right came into its own."[3]

The families like mine that formed the backbone of the Christian right found themselves surrounded by a sea of conservative Christian leaders and institutions eager to provide guidance for every aspect of their lives, in the name of Jesus. While their secular counterparts were tuning in to Phil Donahue or Johnny Carson, a growing cadre of Christian broadcasters, writers, and publishers were serving up an alternative vision of life, and a safe cocoon in which to bring up the next generation of white American Christians, including my siblings and me.

This belief system took the fundamentalism of an earlier era, with its traditional gender roles and literalistic interpretation of the Bible, and repackaged it with a more accessible, modern gloss. This was more than merely a religion, or even a path to eternal salvation; the evangelicalism of my childhood offered a relationship with God and with a young, energetic community, led by confident, telegenic preachers who promised guidance and offered a vision for both families and a nation dedicated to carrying out what they saw as the will of God.

By the 1980s, when I came along, conservative Christian television and radio had become booming businesses. Televangelists entertained audiences and preached about following Jesus, promising blessings from God if their viewers would open their hearts—and their checkbooks—to their ministries. This teaching, called the prosperity gospel, saw wealth as a sign of God's favor, attainable through positive thinking and, often, by giving what little money people did have to religious leaders as an act of faith.[4] For these white evangelicals, unlike many of their forebears, the pursuit of Christian holiness no longer required separation from the earthly trappings of the political process, nor the avoidance of material wealth.

Never mind the warnings from Jesus against idolizing wealth, when he told his disciples, "It is easier for a camel to go through the eye of a needle than for someone who is rich to enter the kingdom of God."[5] For the televangelists of this era, I suppose, money could buy you a needle large enough to drive a whole caravan through. Indeed, as Balmer writes, this "spiritualized Reaganism flourished as never before in the 1980s."[6]

While some members of the evangelical community embraced the televangelists and the so-called name-it-and-claim-it or Word of Faith theology pushed by preachers such as Kenneth Copeland, my parents had reasons to reject this brand of evangelicalism. Our church, Full Faith Church of Love, embraced charismatic Christianity, a movement popular among many evangelicals, which promised the direct intervention of God in the lives of Jesus's followers. God's work in our lives, they believed, was manifested through what were known as "spiritual gifts": laying hands on sick people to pray for healing, or speaking in tongues in a "spiritual language" that we were assured God could understand, even if the speaker could not.

Word of Faith theology melded neatly with the charismatic emphasis on the active presence of God in Christians' individual lives and emphasized the power of faith to achieve financial success, health, and happiness if you believed enough. If you did *not* get what you wanted, the thinking went, you needed *more faith.*

But for my parents, those ideas had yielded deep disappointment and pain, never shaking their faith in Jesus but producing a healthy skepticism of this type of theology. By the mid-1980s, both had lost their mothers to cancer in quick succession. I was too young to remember either of my grandmothers very well, but I do recall my parents repeatedly reassuring me that both were with Jesus. My dad told me that he'd asked his mother, who'd been raised Catholic, if she knew Jesus as her Savior, and that on her deathbed she'd said, emphatically, "The Lord is my Savior," enough to put his mind at ease. My mother's mother was Lutheran, and despite my mom's concerns about the fervency of some mainline Protestants' faith, she said she was certain her parents had truly believed.

Even so, no amount of passionate, faith-filled prayer could delay my grandmothers' deaths. My mother told me that she had prayed for divine intervention, and that some of our fellow church members had encouraged her to believe in God for a miracle. But watching her mother die suddenly, only a few weeks after a lung cancer diagnosis, convinced her that sometimes it's simply God's will "to bring someone home," for reasons that we can't understand.

Whatever the televangelists might have promised, this was a fallen world, and we had to trust that even the pain was all part of God's plan, that he loved us, and that we would see our loved ones in Heaven again someday if we believed.

So we took the televangelists with a grain of salt. Many would ultimately embroil themselves in scandal or worse. Jimmy Swaggart, a gospel singer and Pentecostal evangelist, was brought down by a series of prostitution scandals, becoming for many Americans a living symbol of religious hypocrisy and greed after he delivered an infamous 1988 speech in which he perspired and cried and confessed, "I have sinned!"[7] Jim Bakker, famous for the luxurious lifestyle he shared with his wife, was accused of rape by a church secretary and later convicted and imprisoned on fraud charges related to fundraising activities by their ministry, the PTL Club (an acronym for "Praise the Lord" or "People That Love").[8] In 1987, Bakker's ministry was ultimately taken over by Jerry Falwell, Sr., who founded the massive Christian college now known as Liberty University in Virginia, and cofounded the Moral Majority, which mobilized evangelical voters for conservative political causes beginning in the late 1970s. His son Jerry Falwell, Jr., would go on to become one of Trump's most important evangelical allies and a prominent, and eventually disgraced, evangelical leader in his own right after reports surfaced of an affair between his wife, Becki, and a much younger pool attendant the couple met while vacationing in Florida.[9] The young man, Giancarlo Granda, has alleged that he and Becki carried on a multiyear affair that included having sex while Jerry watched; the Falwells have denied that Jerry was involved.[10]

If the televangelists sometimes left something to be desired, there were plenty of other conservative Christian public figures shaping evangelical thought and life during that era. Along with millions of other evangelical families, my parents wholeheartedly embraced the teachings of James Dobson, whose Focus on the Family ministry functioned as what's often been described as a de facto evangelical Vatican, issuing its pronouncements not as encyclicals or papal bulls, but through influential magazines, books, and radio shows. Dobson's organization, founded in California in the late 1970s as a ministry focused on offering parenting advice, provided entertainment and guidance for evangelical families through every stage of life, billed as alternatives to the influence of secular media.

As a preschooler, I would sit on the living-room floor of our house, soaking in the warm sunlight streaming through the picture window, and listen to Dobson interviewing his radio guests about their life stories. I remember a particularly poignant episode about a little girl who suffered severe burns in a fire, and how God had provided comfort and strength to her family during that time. Dobson's voice radiated warmth and interest in the people whose stories he shared, and his radio show provided ambient entertainment as my mother and I spent quiet afternoons at home.

Dobson soon branched out into politics, launching the Family Research Council in the early 1980s, which grew into a powerful evangelical think tank that has worked to promote abortion restrictions and anti-LGBTQ+ policies nationwide and around the world.[11] A wicker basket that sat by our kitchen telephone was filled with stacks of Focus on the Family's monthly magazine, and *Citizen,* a publication focused on politics and news from Washington, DC.

For the kids, there was a radio drama called *Adventures in Odyssey,* with characters who were entertaining, but also wholesome and prayerful, and a magazine called *Clubhouse,* a pared-down Christian answer to *Highlights for Children,* full of games and recipes and interspersed with mentions of Jesus. Later, I'd subscribe to *Brio,* marketed as a wholesome alternative to *Seventeen* or *YM* for girls, with articles offering advice on dressing modestly and dating cautiously, so as to stay pure until marriage. One summer, we even visited the Focus on the Family headquarters in Colorado Springs on our family vacation, stopping off long enough to tour the radio studios and scoot down the giant slide in the children's play area.

Dobson was such a constant presence, my parents told me later, that as a toddler I would bounce through the house quoting the most recognizable line from his radio show over and over in a singsong voice, "I'm Dr. Dobson! I'm Dr. Dobson!"

At that age, I didn't yet recognize that this man with the cheerful voice was the same man who'd provided my mother, and many other young evangelical parents, the term "the strong-willed child." Dobson's book by that name, published a few years before I was born, built on his earlier work *Dare to Discipline*. Dobson's parenting philosophy called for "shaping the will" by spanking children as young as fifteen months—some still in diapers according to his description—with a "neutral object" like a "small switch or belt," but not the hand, which should be seen by the child only as an "object of love rather than an instrument of punishment."[12]

I'd heard my mother use that phrase in describing me to her friends. "Sarah's strong-willed," and I wasn't quite sure what it meant, but I felt a hot sense of shame spread over my body when I heard it. I tried to be good. I was desperately afraid of the consequences for misbehaving, and my teachers would later describe me as a "delight to have in class," with the occasional exception of some excessive chatter. But for Dobson, and for my parents, part of being a good Christian mother and father required controlling a child's will and bringing it in line to "train up a child" in the way she should go, as the Bible instructs.

Another part of my training came through Christian television designed specially for kids. *Superbook,* from Pat Robertson's Christian Broadcasting Network, took us on colorful adventures through the stories of the Bible, from Adam and Eve to Jesus and his disciples. The Christian TV station in Kansas City, Channel 50, carried *Superbook* as well as *The 700 Club,* along with some local programming for women that my mother would watch.

Our media diet was limited and selective. Books given to us at the holidays by my grandfather were sidelined in favor of creationist children's books, like *Dinosaurs: Those Terrible Lizards,* which described dinosaurs as directly created by God, alongside colorful illustrations.[13] On the radio, it was mostly the two Christian stations, except for NPR on road trips or sometimes the ride to and from church (I have a memory of my dad jokingly calling it "National Liberal Radio" and "National Perverted Radio"—though he doesn't remember calling it that. But either way, I knew it was a bit suspect;

even so, we'd catch the headlines there sometimes). On TV, it was network news in the evenings and children's programming on PBS or the Saturday morning cartoons lineup. My parents preferred that we watch the classics from a bygone era, like *Tom and Jerry* or *Rocky and Bullwinkle*. Some cartoons were forbidden altogether. Rumor had it that *The Smurfs*—those weird blue characters so popular in the 1980s—were actually demons, so I was trained from an early age to turn off the TV or quickly change the channel. (I'm not sure where this rumor originated, but apparently this was a belief shared by some Jehovah's Witnesses, a group we viewed as a cult.[14])

Even public television sometimes had to be filtered. *Sesame Street* and *Mister Rogers' Neighborhood* were allowed, under the supervision of watchful eyes. In one episode of *Mister Rogers,* the puppet Daniel Tiger is asking the human character Lady Aberlin about the origins of things like flowers and rainbows and snow. Lady Aberlin tells Daniel Tiger unequivocally that she believes God made all of those things: the mountains and the sun and the stars. But there was a problem, at least from my mother's perspective. In one concluding stanza, Lady Aberlin sings, in an early nod to gender neutrality, *"God made the sea and She made the land . . . made the people, He made it all."*[15]

It went by quickly, but not without the notice of my mother. She allowed me to keep watching but wanted to make sure I knew that the use of the female pronoun for God was unbiblical. "The Bible makes it clear that God is male," she said. "We do not worship a he/she God." These perceived violations of "biblical truth" underscored the need for evangelicals to create their own institutions and publications, and to carefully monitor the secular influences shaping their children's thinking.

By the late 1980s, when I was still in elementary school, nearly one in four Americans identified as white evangelical Christians, approaching levels that matched the once-dominant religious movements of mainline Protestantism and Catholicism.[16] Those numbers would bounce around slightly before returning to that peak around the mid-2000s, and then begin a steady decline that's continued throughout my adult life.[17]

And yet, we perceived ourselves as a maligned minority, as the "remnant" of faithful believers spoken of throughout the Bible. Around the country, Christian schools like mine, many initially opened by white churches in the 1960s and '70s in a revolt against school integration, and later, the Christian homeschooling movement, sheltered white Christian students from the outside world and reinforced a nostalgic vision of an America once dominated by (mostly white) Christians.*

By pulling out of public schools, evangelical parents could ensure that their children spent hours each week studying the Bible and absorbing a vision of American exceptionalism infused with divine blessing. They could graduate from high school without ever taking a course on evolution or sex ed and, like me, move seamlessly to a four-year Christian college with the same philosophy, where opposite-sex romantic relationships were closely monitored and same-sex relationships were cause for expulsion.

In the opening pages of one Christian high school history textbook originally published by Bob Jones University in 1988,† the writers

---

* It's important to note that these Pew figures include evangelical Protestants of all races; Black evangelicals as a group report very different voting patterns and political affiliations as compared to their white counterparts, according to Pew and other pollsters.

† I got my hands on a 2010 edition of the book, which I'm fairly certain is a later copy of one I had as a Christian school student. Regardless, it's indicative of the kind of thinking embedded in many of the texts I, and other young evangelicals of my generation, were studying in private Christian schools and homeschools.

warn against the growing secularization of the country: "Secularism is the belief that religion has no place in government. . . . As you read about American history, watch for the slow move away from religion as a central part of society. The America we now live in is far different from the America that once was."[18]

The text speaks repeatedly of the horrors of slavery and praises civil rights leaders like Martin Luther King, Jr., and Rosa Parks, but mentions lynching only once, in passing, and redlining not at all. It acknowledges the Trail of Tears and other brutal acts of violence against Native Americans. But it nonetheless paints a picture of America as a place blessed by God: "We should look for ways in which it seems He has used our nation to spread the gospel and bring His blessings to the rest of the world," the introduction reads. It then goes on to urge young Christian students to do good by working to "help end abortion," among other good deeds, like raising a Christian family one day.[19]

All of it—the textbooks, the radio programs, the magazines, the television shows—pointed toward a vision of a "Christian nation" filled with successful Christian families, led by godly patriarchs married to devout women tending to the next generation of young evangelicals, who would in turn permeate the culture and obtain political power in the service of those goals.

As Kristin Kobes Du Mez writes, this "evangelical popular culture" has been developed over the past fifty years or so through a massive industry of self-reinforcing Christian media and organizations. Of the late 1970s, she says, "The evangelical consumer marketplace was by then a force to be reckoned with, but this expansive media network functioned less as a traditional soul-saving enterprise and more as a means by which evangelicals created and maintained their own identity. . . . Christian publishing, radio, and television taught evangelicals how to raise children, how to have sex, and whom to fear." The "shared cultural identity" that had been created and sustained by that marketplace, she argues, quickly became a critical tool for evangelical political mobilization.[20]

Or, as D. L. Mayfield, a writer born into an evangelical family in the early eighties like me, put it on what was then still called Twitter, "Being born into white evangelicalism as marketers were figuring out how to package and sell Christian nationalism and reformed theology to people was really bad timing, I guess."[21]

That mobilization arguably reached its zenith in the last several years with the election of Donald Trump, who was swept to victory in 2016 with the support of 81 percent of white evangelicals and who made good on his campaign promise to appoint US Supreme Court justices who would vote to overturn the 1973 *Roe v. Wade* decision, which legalized abortion nationwide.

And yet, for all of the successes of the religious right, white American Christianity has been experiencing a precipitous decline, dropping from 65 percent in 1996 to 42 percent in 2022, according to the Public Religion Research Institute's Census of American Religion.[22] White *evangelicalism* in particular appears to be undergoing seismic shifts. The religious group that during my lifetime has supplied the Republican Party's most important single voting bloc, making up close to one-third of GOP voters, and which supported Trump in 2016 and again in 2020 in massive numbers,[23] is getting older and whiter at a time when the nation as a whole is becoming increasingly diverse.

"Since 2006, white evangelical Protestants have experienced the most precipitous drop in affiliation," the Public Religion Research Institute reported, "shrinking from 23% of Americans in 2006 to 14% in 2020."[24] That figure has held fairly steady in recent years, according to updated data from the Public Religion Research Institute. Meanwhile, white Christians, including white evangelicals, are growing older, as growing numbers of Americans—particularly younger people—are disaffiliating from formal religion altogether.[25] A Pew Research Center survey from December 2021 found a similar trend, with people who described themselves as evangelical or "born-again" slipping from 30 percent to 24 percent of the population since 2007.[26]

Even so, there is not a single story about what is happening in American evangelicalism; at minimum, this is a time of change, of shifting crosscurrents. Even as white Christianity declines, the number of Christians of color appears largely stable in the United States, with Hispanic and Latino Christianity on the rise.[27] In a 2021 piece in *The Atlantic*, writer Meaghan Winter described Latinos as "The Fastest-Growing Group of American Evangelicals," arguing they could have the power to dramatically alter the nation's religious and political landscapes in coming years.[28] And this is all happening in the context of a larger, general shift away from religion among Americans as a whole.[29]

In recent years, Pew data also has noted an opposing current: some white conservatives newly identifying as "evangelical" because of their support for Trump, even as others leave in part because of his influence.[30] A 2021 Pew survey found "solid evidence that White Americans who viewed Trump favorably and did *not* identify as evangelicals in 2016 were much more likely than White Trump skeptics to *begin identifying* as born-again or evangelical Protestants by 2020."

In *The Great Dechurching*, a 2023 analysis of some 40 million Americans who've left Christian churches of all stripes over the past 25 years, the authors argue that some former evangelicals are actually moving to the right after leaving the church. They cite research that found that more than a quarter of "dechurched" evangelicals expressed support for the idea that America is a "Christian nation."[31]

Furthermore, according to sociologist Robert P. Jones, the president and founder of the Public Religion Research Institute and author of *The End of White Christian America* and other books on these trends, the decline of white Christianity and particularly white evangelicalism has not immediately resulted in a corresponding decline in evangelical power. Jones notes that white evangelicals have historically voted at above-average rates compared to many other groups,[32] and they've overwhelmingly directed their political power toward Republican candidates and causes.

"The reason why they've stayed so influential is because they are so lopsidedly aligned with one political party," Jones told me.[33] "When you've got a two-party system, and they make up a third of one of the two political parties, that still gives you a lot of influence, even if your absolute numbers are dropping."

The future of evangelicalism as a movement is difficult to predict, but all of the data points to a time of rapid change, with the country's increasingly diverse demographics challenging the long-standing dominance of white Christianity, and many younger evangelicals rethinking their faith or leaving the tradition because of concerns about racism, homophobia, and xenophobia.

Samuel Perry, a sociologist at the University of Oklahoma who was raised in a conservative Christian church and describes himself as still "loosely" evangelical,[34] told me that he and many other researchers expected the Trump presidency to be the death knell for the movement. But he was surprised to see that opposition to Trump in some quarters has been counterbalanced by a doubling down among many conservatives.

"We were all predicting it after Trump in 2016. We were all like, 'That's it. Evangelicalism is done, people are going to leave right and left,' and we all expected there to be this huge abandonment of the evangelical category as people kind of ran for the hills," Perry said.

Perry argues that in a society that is both increasingly polarized and nonreligious, evangelicalism is morphing into an "ethno-religious" category, defined far more by race and ideology than theology. He describes younger exvangelicals who vocally disaffiliate from the movement as a "natural expression" of coming of age in a world with growing support for LGBTQ+ rights and concern about systemic racism, and white conservatives embracing the evangelical identity as a sign of the nation's increasing polarization along ideological lines.

It's a long-term trend that preceded Trump by at least a decade, he said, and it's one that has escalated in the aftermath of his administration, influencing both churches and the culture around them.

"Americans more and more are choosing their religious identification and categories by their political views," Perry said. "So Americans who would have previously otherwise called themselves Christians, and believed Christian things, and don't want to reject Jesus, but they want to reject all of the negative things that are associated with that, are now calling themselves nothing. And I think more and more, they feel pushed out of Christian spaces."

For many of the exvangelicals I've met, those Christian spaces feel less and less like home, and Jesus seems harder to find in them. And for some, following Jesus, or at least the truth as they see it, means stepping out of those spaces—out of that "parallel universe"—and onto a new and unfamiliar path.

# 3

# AN EXODUS

For many exvangelicals, finding a new path means stepping out of churches, communities, families, and, sometimes, high-profile ministries and politically powerful organizations.

For Promise Enlow Councill,[1] who grew up as a missionary kid and a pastor's daughter, evangelicalism was the family business. As a child, her parents started a church in their Atlanta basement that grew over time into a large congregation, opening up speaking gigs and book deals for her dad, Johnny Enlow. He started traveling internationally, and eventually moved the family to California to serve as a self-described "prophet" to Hollywood.

Enlow Councill was in her early twenties when she moved with her parents to Los Angeles and began meeting people whose very existence seemed to challenge her vision of the world.

"I had friends and neighbors for the first time in my life who were gay or Buddhist or just different," she said.

For a while, Enlow Councill said, she felt like she and her family were "progressing" together. She remembers her dad expressing support for the Black Lives Matter movement, and her mom calling her in a celebratory mood on the day in 2015 when the US Supreme Court ruled to legalize same-sex marriage nationwide.

"And then," she said, "the Trump thing happened."

At first, the family watched together, curiously, as the 2016 campaign unfolded. She'd invite her parents over to watch debates.

"We're getting popcorn, we're going to talk about this, because we were all interested," Enlow Councill said. "And then everything kind of took a hard right turn."

Fast-forward a few years, and Johnny Enlow, like many prominent evangelical leaders, would become a vocal Trump supporter. Enlow persisted and even doubled down in that support after the insurrection of January 6, 2021, when extremist Trump supporters motivated by his lies about the 2020 election stormed the US Capitol. In June 2021, Enlow told ElijahStreams, a Christian prophecy channel on YouTube, that God would bless pastors and other "people who didn't back off Trump."[2]

Meanwhile, Enlow Councill is among a growing number of younger former evangelicals who've been using Facebook, TikTok, and other social media platforms to speak out about her reasons for breaking with white evangelicalism. Like Enlow Councill, many have ties to evangelical pastors and leaders or once played roles in the evangelical subculture that includes Christian ministries and nonprofits, colleges, publishing, entertainment, and a massive political machine. For Enlow Councill, Trump's election, and her community's sustained support for him, was the major catalyst for that break.

"And as I started questioning some of those surface hypocrisies, I couldn't stop there. I had to question further," Enlow Councill said. "I thought, this affects my entire faith; this is not just about this election or this one politician that they're worshiping. This is about a deep-rooted thing that is surfacing in a bigger way."

*  *  *

I first heard the term "exvangelical" while working on a story for NPR in 2016 about the dilemma Trump posed for many white evangelical women. It was right before the election, soon after the now-infamous *Access Hollywood* video that had surfaced in which he was recorded bragging about "grabbing" women "by the pussy." When that scandal broke, I was taking a day off to hike and rest after a reporting trip in Nevada, and was napping in my hotel room when my editor called. I spent the next several hours calling sources, particularly conservative Christian leaders, trying to assess the fallout and talking with editors about how *exactly* to describe this event on the radio. Could we say the word "pussy" on NPR? If not, how could we convey what was happening here? (The verdict: we could, within reason, with a language warning.) This was not a discussion I'd ever had in a journalism class.

A few weeks later, as the dust settled and evangelical leaders continued to rally around him in the days before the election, Christian singer-songwriter Nichole Nordeman told NPR in an interview, "I find it sickening that these men can face their congregations and their families and their college campuses and feel OK with trusting Donald Trump with their voice and their vote and their country—and still somehow explain it away through the lens of the teachings of Christ. It boggles my mind." Nordeman said she'd been hearing the term *exvangelical* "thrown around quite a bit—just the sense that we are trying to find new language to define us as followers of Christ, because this old term has felt unbelievably compromised by this election and by some of the old guard in evangelical leadership."[3]

In the years that followed, I'd heard a similar disillusionment from several women raised in the evangelical world—feelings of shock and anger that the same leaders who ordered us to remain sexually pure until marriage and who condemned Bill Clinton's moral failings in the 1990s would not only tolerate but embrace and promote Trump.

For Promise Enlow Councill, it was impossible to ignore the difference between how her community responded to Trump's transgressions and her own. She'd been raised in evangelical purity culture, married at eighteen with little knowledge of herself or serious relationships, into what she describes as a "toxic relationship." She divorced a year later, something she said simply wasn't done in her family.

"That was a big deal; everyone at my parents' church was freaking out about it," Enlow Councill said. Suddenly, she felt out of place at church, shunned.

So it was hard to watch, several years later, she told me, as that same community embraced Trump, despite his own litany of transgressions, including not only divorces but alleged affairs; racist and misogynistic attacks on his opponents; mocking a disabled reporter; even his assertion that he could "stand in the middle of Fifth Avenue and shoot somebody" and not lose supporters. Enlow Councill found all of it distasteful, inconsistent with the values she'd been taught, and disorienting.

"I would ask people around me, 'How is that not outrageous to you? Even as a Christian, how can you not see that and think, *Oh, Jesus would probably not be cool with that*? And they all defended it, and were so hypocritical," she said. "The things that I had held against me were so small; I was surprised about the judgments that I received, or my gay friends received, or my Buddhist friends received, and then this guy who has not an ounce of integrity or character to be found was being called God's Chosen One. And then that made me start questioning everything."

That questioning led her to rethink not only her political beliefs but also her evangelical beliefs about the Bible, sexuality, and Hell.

*   *   *

For many exvangelicals, the Trump phenomenon has seemed like a bright light suddenly flicked on in a dark house, exposing every crack in the foundation, every leak, every bit of detritus. Enlow Councill said the January 6 insurrection, where extremist Trump supporters carried crosses and signs bearing the name of Jesus alongside a gallows set up on the Capitol lawn, validated the growing sense of disenchantment she and others had been experiencing for several years.

"I think it empowered a lot of us to go on the record of where we stand and to kind of point to something and say, 'Look at this. This is the perfect illustration of why we cannot associate with this world anymore,'" she said.

In an article for *Religion Dispatches* a few weeks after the attack on the Capitol, writer Deirdre Sugiuchi, who was born into an evangelical family in the mid-1970s that was heavily influenced by the nationalistic Christian Reconstructionist movement, said seeing it unfold "all feels like echoes of my past." Sugiuchi described her horror at watching white evangelicals and Republican leaders continue to support Trump, and wondering where it all could lead.

"Given my upbringing, I worry that neither the white evangelical church nor the public at large understands the danger that Christian nationalism poses to democracy," Sugiuchi wrote.[4]

For many, the sense of disillusionment was much bigger than one politician.

"It really came to a head in my mind with the collusion, with Trump and these white nationalist leanings, and people very judgmentally standing up against things that in my opinion were very needed, like the BLM movement," singer Kevin Max told me.[5]

For 1990s evangelical youth group kids such as myself, Max is best known for his time in the super-popular Christian rap group DC Talk. In church vans, as we rode to summer camp, we'd sing along with songs like "Jesus Freak"—lyrics we all knew by heart—celebrating the way our faith made us stand out: different, but special.

Max said he's become increasingly disturbed about what he describes as a dismissal of science, hatred of LGBTQ+ people, and refusal to address systemic racism, concerns he said he has felt for years, until reaching a breaking point recently. Max is among a growing number of high-profile Christians to publicly use the term "exvangelical" to describe his religious identity. He told me he's "still following after Jesus" and believes in God but has felt compelled to distance himself from evangelicalism in recent years.

"I find myself relating more to [being exvangelical] than I do the American evangelical church," Max said. "That system to me is broken, and has been broken, and needs to be healed from the inside."

Meanwhile, in a sign of how the internet is subverting existing evangelical power structures and giving rise to exvangelical voices, Abraham Piper, the adult son of John Piper—the influential pastor, writer, and founder of the prominent evangelical ministry Desiring God—has rapidly developed a following as a TikTok personality known for his biting critiques of his father's faith. As described in a *New York Times* profile[6] in 2021, the younger Piper rose to prominence "nearly overnight," amassing more than one million followers in a matter of months, often posting under the #exvangelical hashtag. His followers tune in for the younger Piper's takedowns of the evangelical views of Hell, women's roles in the church, and the expectation of tithing, or giving a share of one's income to the church: "I just now noticed how fucking bizarre it is that God is our Father, and we're supposed to . . . *pay him*?" Piper asks in one video. In another TikTok video, Piper calmly works on an oil painting, holding a tub of yellow paint in one hand while taking on the oft-repeated argument from conservative Christians that religion is necessary for morality. He remembers hearing a guy at church years ago saying, "That if it weren't for God, he'd be a murderer, or worse." Piper says it's a strange claim, but he's heard it more than once. "And here's what I want to agree with those goofballs about. It's a good thing they believe in God!" He laughs out loud. "Like, if your faith is why you're not a malicious maniac—fucking go for it!"

Leaving behind or reimagining religious traditions is nothing new; in every generation there have been reformers and heretics. And white evangelicalism is not alone in its struggle to hold on to the next generation. But today's exvangelicals are leaving a uniquely large and influential American religious movement at a transformational time for both the country and the evangelical movement.

They're doing so in a moment when it's never been easier to find one another. Since she's begun speaking out online, Enlow Councill has heard from strangers around the world who've said she has validated their experiences. Others, including friends and family, have reached out privately to tell her that they are "on the same journey," but afraid of the blowback they believe they'd receive from saying so out loud.

"It's like a secret society, but a lot of them can't talk about it openly the way I can," she said. "Some of them have told me, 'I'd lose childcare; my parents wouldn't watch my kids for me anymore if they knew this.' Or, 'I work for a church and my income comes from that.' It is important that I keep speaking out, because not everyone can."

Derek Webb, another veteran of the Christian contemporary music scene who has publicly discussed his departure from evangelicalism in recent years, told me it's helpful to have an emerging language to talk about what it means to "deconstruct" from evangelicalism and fundamentalism, and leave behind what for many is not only a religion but a subculture, an entire way of seeing the world.[7]

"It's really important to be understood, especially if you're coming out of a situation where you're probably, on the way out, being made to feel like you're crazy, and you are literally jumping out of Jesus's hand, and you're escaping God's will somehow, and you're thwarting God's plans in your life, and you're totally upsetting the natural order of the universe or something by not going to church and leaving this category," Webb said. "And so at that time you're going to feel very isolated, you're going to feel very alone, you're going to feel really misunderstood."

Webb said the loss of community support is one of the hardest parts of the transition out of evangelicalism.

"You're seeing people fleeing out of churches in droves," Webb said. "I'm glad that there is a place for all the orphans that are coming out of churches, or being pushed out of churches, there's somewhere for them to land. Because a decade ago, there wouldn't have been."

# 4

# UNRAVELING

The beginning of my own "unraveling" is difficult to pinpoint, but my shift away from my evangelical community had nothing to do with the rise of Donald Trump. People sometimes ask about the moment it all started for me, but the truth is there were many moments, many tiny threads being pulled one by one, rather than a single cataclysmic breach.

From my first days in the preschool classrooms in the basement of Blue Ridge Bible Church, I was tightly cocooned within conservative Christian institutions, within a world specifically built to prevent that kind of unraveling. A church—or during my college years, a seminary—was never more than a few steps away.

Except for one semester. I was on the cusp of seventeen, and, to my amazement, my parents agreed to let me spend half a school year away from home, working as a US Senate page in Washington, DC. I wasn't allowed to go on dates or go to R-rated movies, but going to Washington fit into a larger mission I was preparing to be a part of: building up God's kingdom here on Earth and, in particular, restoring the greatness of this "Christian nation" that God had blessed but which had gone so terribly awry over the past few decades through the embrace of feminism and the sexual revolution via the political process.

I'd heard about the program almost by accident, while interning in suburban St. Louis the summer before, in 1997, at the offices of Phyllis Schlafly's Eagle Forum, an organization she founded in the early 1970s to promote conservative political goals and traditional roles for women.

Schlafly, who ran for Congress and authored books on politics and national defense while championing traditional gender roles and later spearheading a nationwide movement opposing the Equal Rights Amendment, was a hero to my mother. She avidly subscribed to Schlafly's blue-and-white newsletters and responded by writing letters to lawmakers with her concerns about issues such as abortion or women in the military. My mother used to proudly describe sitting at her typewriter in early 1981, heavily pregnant with me, composing letters in opposition to requiring women to register with the selective service.

The fall following my internship, after completing several weeks of unremarkable volunteer work at Eagle Forum's headquarters, cataloging the video library filled with documentaries about conservative religious figures alongside her ideological foes, like Margaret Sanger, organizing documents in the cramped but tidy collection of filing cabinets in the basement, I'd been invited to an annual dinner hosted by Eagle Forum. There, after the meal, a group of students clustered around homeschooling-rights activist Michael Farris, who urged us to continue fighting for righteousness in the public sphere. "Two thousand years ago," he exhorted us, alluding to Christ and his disciples, "it only took a dozen men to change the world."

In that spirit, I went to Washington, ready to learn to be a good soldier for the Lord. It had been only a few years since, under the leadership of Newt Gingrich, the Republicans had retaken control of Congress for the first time since 1955. Despite Bill Clinton's re-election in 1996, and the fury of James Dobson and other evangelical leaders at the selection of Bob Dole as the Republican Party's middle-of-the-road standard-bearer, politically engaged white evangelicals were fully in the trenches of the culture war.

It was January 1998, and the Monica Lewinsky scandal was unfolding, confirming all of our community's suspicions about Bill Clinton's character. There were jokes—right in the spirit of my dad's hero, Rush Limbaugh, who entertained us with his constant jabs at President Clinton—between my parents and their friends about me staying far away from the White House.

But there was little reason to worry: I, and all the other pages who worked on Capitol Hill, would be protected around the clock by the watchful eyes of Capitol Police. The federal government had long ago learned its lesson about the pitfalls of unleashing teenagers in its custody on the nation's capital. We had to sign in and out each time we left the building and abide by strict curfews and rules against alcohol or drug use. Several of my classmates, including a roommate— a relative of a prominent Republican senator who later ran for president—learned this the hard way. After arriving to our room after curfew one night and vomiting into a plastic bowl while sitting atop her bunk bed, she was relieved of duty, along with her collaborators.

The page school and the dormitory where we lived were housed inside a stately brick building called Webster Hall, across from Stanton Park, one of DC's many famous green spaces. We were told that the building had once been a funeral home, and the common room, with its high ceilings and tall windows, had hosted funerals and wakes. But we, being teenagers, used it for group study sessions, or to watch *Dirty Dancing* on weekends or hold our (slightly less dirty) end-of-semester dance. Dancing, and that film, were frowned upon at home, but I was far from Kansas City, and the chance for a brief taste of normal secular teenager activities was seductive.

Downstairs, in the finished basement, was our school: a principal's office, a computer lab, and four small classrooms with a teacher for every essential subject—math, science, English, and social studies. These spaces, where we also did our laundry on the weekends, practiced trigonometry in the mornings, and devoured pastries before walking over to the Senate to work each day, had once held a crematorium, they told us; but usually, we were too busy being tired, anxious, overly ambitious seventeen-year-olds to think much about it.

The rest of the two-story building was divided into bedrooms, where we slept on tall bunks lofted above our desks, four students to a room, college dorm–style. We got up around 5:30 A.M., allowing for at least a couple of hours of class before the Senate gaveled in. It was new for me not to begin the school day with prayer and Bible reading, and it was the first time I'd heard a science teacher casually reference evolution, not as a lie from Satan to be carefully explained away but as an obvious and innocuous reality.

Though I sometimes felt out of place in the classroom, I loved the excitement and novelty of being in the Senate, seeing the work of government up close—straining from the back of the House Chamber to watch President Clinton's State of the Union address, learning the signals for when a senator wanted a cup of water or an easel to display a pie chart designed to buttress a policy argument. I loved listening to the senators debate their legislative proposals—even though we sometimes nodded off right there on the Senate floor, exhausted from our early morning calls—and watching the votes unfold in real time.

I even laughed off the awkwardness of helping Senator Strom Thurmond, the infamous lecher, up the steps to the Senate rostrum to gavel in each morning. As the senior member of the majority party, he was, by tradition, the president pro tempore of the Senate, and that was his daily duty. Even at age ninety-five, Thurmond's lascivious reputation preceded him. As female teenage pages, we were warned about him, almost as a joke, at the beginning of the term. But from what I observed, his old habits appeared intact, whether or not his other faculties were, entirely. Almost every time he saw me, he'd ask my name, lean in close, and whisper in my ear in his raspy-voiced, South Carolina drawl, "Yuh sech a pretty guhrl! And yuh have sech pretty haaaair!"

Working the Senate floor or running messages through the maze of tunnels that connected the three Senate office buildings, I felt at home. It was in dorms, on the weekends, when I felt most out of place.

The other students were my age, but the glimpses I caught of their lives back home looked nothing like mine. One roommate, about a month after arriving in DC, shouted from the bathroom, "Thank goodness, I got my period!" Another, one of Thurmond's many pages who regularly rotated through the program every month or two, arrived from South Carolina and mentioned she'd gone to church on a recent Sunday. That seemed like a good start. Then, she mentioned being so hungover that morning that she'd almost vomited on the priest as she walked up to receive Communion. Having only ever consumed a few sips of alcohol during a toast at my aunt's wedding and taught to see Communion as one of the holiest and most special moments in a church service, I tried to contain my shock and horror, but I have no doubt it was written all over my face.

In those moments, I couldn't help but feel a little superior at never having done anything that would cause me anxiety about missing a period or vomiting on a clergyman. But I also felt like I'd never . . . done *any*thing. I tried to be friendly, but I often felt like I didn't really know how to talk to these people. I missed home.

I didn't fit. And they knew it, too. One evening, feeling lonely and out of place, I did what I'd been taught to do: opened up my Bible and searched for something that spoke to me. The one I'd brought to DC was a neon hardcover Youthwalk Bible, a special edition mass-produced for evangelical teenagers, with funky font and articles in the margins about applying the Scriptures to teenage American life, with titles like "The Futility of Anxiety," citing a passage from Matthew where Jesus admonishes his followers against worry. My Bible, given to me by my parents on my thirteenth birthday, was now covered in highlighter and scrawled with margin notes, my efforts to understand and feel a connection to God.

As I flipped through the pages at my desk, I heard behind me the same girl who'd been afraid of what a missed period might portend begin singing, *"The B-I-B-L-E, yes that's the book for me . . ."* She and another roommate giggled in my direction. I shrugged and tried to act like I didn't care.

I sometimes imagined what it would be like to be one of the other girls. One of my roommates had hinted about wanting to sleep with the guy who cut her hair. The thought of already knowing what it felt like to be that close to a man was fascinating, forbidden.

In the dark, as I curled up in my bunk, my mind drifted. I thought about another intern, a boy from Utah, tall and kind of handsome, almost annoyingly innocent with a familiar, reassuringly religious vibe, always smiling, open and friendly. I assumed he was a virgin, too. I never really spoke to him, but I fantasized about him, about the empty room down the hall, set aside as an infirmary for sick pages. What if we slipped in there together and explored? Somehow, it felt less lonely, and a little less guilty, to imagine it that way, even though I knew I would never, in a million years, take the slightest step in that direction.

\* \* \*

There were other moments that semester when my carefully constructed view of the world pushed hard against the one in DC that I found myself in. One of my favorite classmates was Sina, who managed to be popular with everyone but also kind, even to the less-than-cool kids like yours truly. Sina had an easy laugh, a warm smile, and a radiant gentleness. As we passed long hours on the steps of the rostrum in between Senate business, he told me that his parents had been born in Iran, where they worked as an airline executive and a physician before fleeing during the revolution. They'd come to America and had to start their lives over from scratch, retraining and recertifying in the United States to do the work they'd done for years back home.

We talked about the fact that my name, Sarah, is cross-cultural, and exists in some form in so many languages, cultures, and religions. Sina had a family member with the same name. He knew that I was a devout Christian, and I knew that he was a Muslim.

A better evangelical than I might have tried, at some point, to "win him for Christ." Though I would have said then, if you'd asked me, that I believed Jesus was the only way to Heaven, bringing myself to insist that another person adopt my beliefs and change their own was a step too far. On the rare occasions I had tried—at the skating rink when I was a little girl, or "street-witnessing" to strangers in downtown Kansas City with youth groups as a teenager—my heart raced and my stomach hurt. It was like my body was telling me that I was violating something sacred.

So when Sina asked me about my faith, as we sat, just the two of us, on the blue-carpeted steps in our navy suits, it could have been a perfect opening. And yet, his question caught me off guard in its simplicity and directness: "Do you believe that because I'm Muslim, I'm going to Hell?"

Suddenly, everything that felt wrong about the belief system I'd been told to promote crystallized in my mind.

I looked at Sina and thought about how much I liked him and respected him, and how grateful I was for his kindness. I thought about what every major authority figure in my life had told me, again and again: that Jesus says, in John 14:6, "I am the way, the truth, and the life; no one comes to the Father except through me." The answer, from what I'd been taught, should have been as simple and clear as the question. But I couldn't bring myself to say it, because for the first time I really had to look squarely at the fact that I wasn't sure I believed it. I couldn't look at my friend and say, "I believe my God will send you to Hell because you don't believe as I do." He'd called my bluff.

I could only muster, "I don't know. I think it's between you and God."

I worried, had I failed? Had I wasted an opportunity to save a soul? And yet, somewhere deep inside, my answer felt right.

A few years after that conversation with Sina, during my second or third year of college, I was confronted with essentially the same question about the eternal destiny of people of other faiths in a different and even more dramatic way.

My communications professor, Carmen Mendoza, or "Dr. M," as some of us called her, was one of a handful of professors I could confide in as I began to feel increasingly adrift on my evangelical campus. Born into a large family in Bolivia that sometimes struggled to make ends meet, she'd come to the United States as a teenager at the invitation of evangelical missionaries, who'd promised opportunities to this bright young girl that were not available to her at home. Dr. M had attended an evangelical college in Kentucky and navigated her way through language and cultural barriers to become a communications professor at my college. I was intrigued by her; she didn't fit the typical mold, particularly for an evangelical woman, and she radiated a curiosity and empathy that I found inspiring.

Felicia Brenner was in her seventies when Dr. M invited her to speak to our class about the suffering her Polish Jewish family had endured during the Holocaust decades earlier.[1] Brenner's obituary in the *Chicago Tribune* in 2008 said she decided to start speaking publicly about her experiences in 1977, when a neo-Nazi group made plans to march on her adopted hometown of Skokie, Illinois.[2]

Many of us in Dr. M's class were moved by Brenner's story of the horror her family endured after the Nazis marched into their hometown in central Poland, forcing them into a ghetto. Near the end of the war, they were taken to Auschwitz, where her parents would die in the gas chambers.[3] Out of a family of six brothers and sisters, only Brenner would survive the war, according to another obituary.[4]

Those talks to student groups like mine took their toll, but Brenner gave them anyway, her daughter told the *Tribune*: "My mother was often in great distress and was depressed for days after she gave those presentations . . . but she felt it was much more important that her suffering had meaning."[5] Brenner had come to our school five times, Dr. M told me later,[6] and each time, she was unable to eat because of the stress of delving back into those memories.

And yet, Dr. M confided in me one day after class, some of her evangelical students seemed fixated on the fact that Brenner was Jewish and, therefore, according to our theology, not saved. Why invite her to speak to us at all, a student in one of the classes had asked later, if Jews were all going to Hell anyway?

Dr. M has long since moved on from teaching at my alma mater. But we're still in touch, and I wrote to her recently to ask for her reflections on that incident, which had thrown the ugliness of evangelical theology into such stark relief.

"I'm breathless now as I recall the moment in class," she wrote back, telling me that for her, too, it had served as a "crystallizing moment."

Dr. M watched in horror as other students chimed in to agree, "as though he had hit a raw thing they wanted to get at, a deep dark thing they really thought beneath the veneer of kindness and compassion. I felt helpless in the face of their deeply seeded smugness."

Saying too much could risk your job at a college like mine, but Dr. M. had to say something.

"I only said, 'If Mrs. Brenner, our guest, were with you in your hour of trial, she would lay down her life for each one here in this room.'"

Brenner spent the last three decades of her life telling her story about the Holocaust and raising alarms about the dangers of antisemitism. In a grainy oral history video recorded in 1985, an interviewer asks her how she reflected on her experiences after many years. She's bitter, she says, not only at the Nazis but at the rest of the world who'd abandoned the Jewish people.

And she points to the Christians who've enabled and participated in those evils.

"We gave them the Ten Commandments. We gave them their Jesus. What do they want from us?" Brenner asks. "[They say], 'You killed Jesus,' which is wrong; we did not. But they crucify us and crucify us and crucify us, over and over again."[7]

As Dr. M told me this story about my peers, I could feel that something had permanently shifted inside me. I had felt the same horror she was expressing, and I knew that I did not believe what these students believed. I sensed that there was no stopping the unraveling now.

Dr. M told me her time in those evangelical classrooms included many similar moments: "I wondered, if Christianity doesn't produce better moral beings, what good is it?"

If these were the threads I was grasping to hold together, I was ready to let them go.

# 5

# "WERE YOU THERE?"

Fundamental to every aspect of my Christian school curriculum was a belief in the authority of the Bible in all matters; even our understanding of basic scientific facts must be subordinated to this vision of Scripture.

And it all began with the creation story. To compromise our understanding of the literal truth of the Bible in any way, we were told, could threaten everything. If there was no direct creation in the Garden of Eden, and no literal Adam, did that mean there was no sin? And if not, then why did Jesus come to save us? We *knew* we were sinners and he'd come to save us, so there must have been an Adam and there must have been a garden.

With that in mind, one night, when I was still in elementary school, my parents drove the family to church for a special evening of instruction about the truths in Genesis. After the lights dimmed, we sat in the darkness of the cavernous sanctuary, the only glow emanating from a giant overhead projector screen at the front of the room. On it flashed images of rocks, plants, and animals, even dinosaurs.

At the front of the room, the speaker repeated a single refrain: "WERE. YOU. THERE?"

Were you there, he asked, when the world was made? When God said, "Let there be light!" and there was? Were you there when God filled the seas with fish or the skies with birds? When he reached into the Earth and formed it into man and made the woman, Eve, from Adam's rib? Were you there for any of it?

We were not, of course, and neither, he noted, were the evolutionary biologists who claimed to know how it all began. In their arrogance, they'd concocted for themselves a story that enabled their refusal to submit to God's authority, to construct for themselves a world where they had the final say over their lives, and where they were free to pursue their sinful lusts and selfish desires. This scheme, the idea of evolution, had taken in so many people, eager to find a way to deny God. What other motive could there be for refusing to acknowledge the creator of this beautiful world, for dismissing the story God had written down in Genesis?

It was all very dire, but it was also *thrilling*. The evening felt special, different from Sunday mornings, when I, along with the other elementary school–aged children, would stay with the adults for the singing portion—what we called the "worship service"—before slipping out the side doors and walking down the hall to children's church. While our parents sang half a dozen hymns and praise choruses, lyrics displayed at the front of the sanctuary on the overhead projector, I'd watch from below as they closed their eyes, tilted back their heads slightly, and lifted their arms toward the sky. Some of them seemed completely absorbed, transfixed, carried away to a different place. I was always happy when it was time to leave these strange, emotional displays of a feeling I couldn't quite understand and head into a world of puppet shows and Bible stories.

But that night, I was drawn in by the images on the screen, and the stories of how God had created all of the plants and animals and everything else, probably about six thousand to ten thousand years ago if you added up all of the genealogies in the Bible and did a little educated guesswork; and how later, God had to send a flood to punish people for being so wicked, and how Noah's flood had covered the entire Earth about four thousand to five thousand years ago, leaving behind fossils all over the world.

I'd heard these stories many times already, but it was fascinating to see them presented by a narrator who seemed so wise, and who seemed to have figured out so much about the world of nonbelievers. I listened as he explained that evolution was the ridiculous theory—and only a *theory!*—that you could get something out of nothing if you only had enough time, if you waited for "MEEL-yuns and BEEL-yuns of years." He said it mockingly, in an accent that I would decades later realize was intended as a mimicry of the late scientist Carl Sagan in the TV series *Cosmos.*

But what we saw around us, and what we knew in our hearts, was confirmed by Genesis and other Scripture. As the psalmist had written, the beauty and grandeur of creation was meant to inspire us to a sense of awe, wonder, and worship of God and a recognition of our smallness in comparison:

> *When I consider your heavens,*
> *the work of your fingers,*
> *the moon and the stars,*
> *which you have set in place,*
> *what is mankind that you are mindful of them,*
> *human beings that you care for them?[1]*

Who was there, at the beginning? Only God was there and only God knew what had happened, and he had given us a record of it right there in the Bible, his "love letter" to humankind, and an account more reliable than any science book written by human beings could hope to be. Who would *want* to believe that all of this came from nothing, after a big explosion; that it would all eventually burn out and return to nonexistence; that there was no divine presence guiding anything, including, and especially, our own lives? That vision of the universe felt frightening, cold, and empty. I felt grateful to have the truth, to be part of a community of people whose hearts were open to it, willing to give up fleeting sinful pleasures for the joy of understanding that we had a creator and could live in harmony with him.

The evening's theme was an early iteration of the teachings being promoted by Young Earth creationists like Ken Ham, who now leads Answers in Genesis, probably best known for the Creation Museum in northern Kentucky, which includes a life-sized Noah's Ark. In 2014, the museum hosted a debate between Ham and celebrity scientist Bill Nye the Science Guy, which went on for more than two and a half hours.[2] Ham was among the most prominent Young Earth creationists, a movement popular among evangelicals and fundamentalists, which promoted the idea that the Genesis account of creation was literally true, and that embracing this was essential to being a true believer in Christ.

The reason that so many scientists believed in evolution, we were warned, was that they were unwilling to submit their lives to the truth of the Bible. They wanted to be their own gods and call their own shots, the thinking went, and that was why they were so eager to embrace evolutionary theory.

"I had been told as a child that scientists were actively lying, especially in evolutionary biology and paleontology," said Sarah Treadwell, who grew up in a conservative branch of Lutheranism in Wisconsin and attended private Christian schools. "It was a way to get people out of the church, and they were so devious."[3]

There was no need to study dinosaurs, Treadwell said, and NASA, she was told, was "wasting its time because they were looking for answers we already had."

Treadwell told me that when she first went off to a state university in Wisconsin, that framework began to crack a little, as she discovered to her surprise that her nonevangelical classmates and professors were normal, even nice.

"It was so shocking to me, because it was so ingrained that it was us versus them, that there are dangers, devils, lurking around every corner," she said. "It was like, 'Huh, this isn't what they told me.' And I had that same feeling when I got into science."

After a traumatic car accident in her early thirties prompted her to rethink several aspects of her life, Treadwell realized she had a burning desire to learn more about science. She went back to school, and developed a career as a science communicator known as "Space Case Sarah," focusing on astrobiology and diving deep into topics she'd never imagined while reading her Christian school textbooks.

In graduate school, Treadwell said it was eye-opening to discover how friendly the science professors and students were, and how serious they were about their work—an insight that became an important part of her deconstruction process.

"I met people who work in these fields and they were like, 'Yeah, I don't have time to really be part of some big conspiracy cover-up. I should be working on my dissertation,'" she said.

This vision of the world, where science was suspect and always checked against a particular reading of the Bible, was an outgrowth of an ideological movement that traces its roots back at least to what Richard Hofstadter, in his 1964 Pulitzer Prize–winning book *Anti-intellectualism in American Life,* described as "the revolt against modernity." In the post–Civil War period, many conservative Protestant Christians,[4] faced with competition from ideas including Darwinian evolution and movements toward liberalization within

Christianity, pushed back.[5] As Hofstadter explained, "The feeling that rationalism and modernism could no longer be answered in debate led to frantic efforts at suppression and intimidation which reached a climax in the anti-evolution crusade of the 1920s."

Indeed, William Jennings Bryan, who failed three times in his quest for the presidency before famously aiding the prosecution in the 1925 Scopes trial of a Tennessee teacher charged with teaching evolution, wrote that all of America's ills could be traced back to such teaching: "It would be better to destroy every other book ever written, and save just the first three verses of Genesis."[6]

Rather than destroying other books, the evangelical leaders of my youth wrote their own. While there have always been Christians, including some theologically conservative ones, who've accepted evolutionary science, some of the loudest voices in the public square became those of evangelicals and fundamentalists insisting that creationism must be considered as a reasonable alternative to evolution, even in public schools.[7]

By the 1980s, the anti-evolution crusade had been taken up by groups including Jerry Falwell's Moral Majority.[8] That was a fight that, by and large, evangelicals ultimately lost,[9] in spite of support from high-level Republicans, including President Ronald Reagan. But it was an effort that helped galvanize and mobilize conservative Christian voters to elevate other issues such as opposition to abortion and same-sex marriage.[10]

If the public schools could not be protected from evolutionary science, then evangelical children could be protected from public schools. The Christian private school and homeschool movements provided a haven from the influences of the godless outside world. In addition to providing Southern Christians with an alternative to integration beginning in the 1960s, private Christian academies soon sprang up all over the country, such as my own school in Kansas City, which assured parents that their children would be protected from worldly influences and ideas like evolution, and given instruction not only in reading, writing, and arithmetic but also in the ways of the Lord.[11]

Conservative Christian theology and ideology were reinforced throughout the curriculum, from science to history, in textbooks published by Bob Jones University Press and Abeka Book, a Christian publisher affiliated with Pensacola Christian College in Florida.[12] The latter, in the words of writer Katherine Stewart, "is rooted in themes that appear to fuse a biblical literalist understanding of Christian identity with right-wing ideology,"[13] a description that I would also apply to much of the Bob Jones curriculum, having grown up, like so many other Christian school students, with textbooks from both publishers.

As exvangelical writer Chrissy Stroop noted in a 2019 Twitter thread, these texts provide direct insight into the ideologies that have infused much of the private Christian school and homeschool curricula used by many evangelicals for decades.

"Exhibiting primary sources—along with our reactions as those directly affected—may be the single most effective way to give people who weren't raised evangelical/fundamentalist just a glimpse of what it's like on a visceral level, and thus to expose Christian Right extremism," Stroop wrote.[14]

In a teacher's edition of one science workbook for sixth graders, published for homeschooling families in 1995 by Bob Jones, parents are encouraged to tie each lesson back to God, and instill a vision of a creator with his hand very much at work in the world, even in horrific events. In a section on the deadly 1980 eruption of Mount St. Helens in Washington, which killed at least fifty-five people, the book instructs, "Point out to your child that since God controls the volcanoes, He has a design in the results of their eruptions. . . . Much of what man calls disaster, God sees as divine. As in the case of Mount St. Helens, God often has to destroy one thing before He can do something new."[15]

Another chapter encourages parents teaching children about the concept of scientific theories to "remind your child that what a person believes about God will affect his opinions and any theories that he might come up with or accept. Therefore, the Christian should always compare a theory with Scripture to make sure the theory does not contradict anything in God's Word."[16]

For many exvangelicals, the expectation to constantly be comparing what was learned and observed from the outside world with evangelical teachings eventually created an insurmountable cognitive dissonance. Jocelyn Howard grew up primarily in Virginia and attended a mix of public and Christian schools before graduating from Bob Jones University in 2006. Children's science shows like *Captain Planet and the Planeteers* were forbidden as what Howard's parents described as "liberal propaganda."

Instead, at Howard's Christian school, teachers instructed students in a dizzying mix of basic science interspersed with Bible verses and discussions of how to counter evolutionary theory.

It felt like "constantly playing this game of what I can and cannot believe," Howard said, "of what I'm allowed to accept as fact and what I'm not allowed to accept as fact."

Studying science was a way to learn about God through creation and as such, scientific discovery was acceptable, but only to the degree that it aligned with Scripture, as understood through an evangelical lens. There was a feeling, Howard said, that you shouldn't ask too many questions, certainly not about anything that might compromise a view of the Bible as literally true and infallible.

"If that is a cornerstone of your faith, then the minute you say that maybe the Bible isn't scientifically accurate, it all comes crumbling down," Howard said.

For many young evangelicals growing up in Christian schools and homeschools, those prior commitments to a literal view of Scripture constrained what could be studied and left students, like Rebekah Drumsta, with an incomplete understanding of basic, mainstream scientific concepts.

Drumsta grew up in a homeschooling family in Houston in the 1980s and '90s, studying textbooks from Abeka and Bob Jones.

"Science wasn't a thing, outside of creationism and apologetic arguments to defend creationism," Drumsta told me. "There were no other thoughts."[17]

As an adult, Drumsta said she's found herself having to "fake it" to mask her lack of scientific knowledge, a deficiency she's discovered at unexpected moments. She recalls visiting a science museum with a friend and noticing that her friend, and even her own daughter, were familiar with basic concepts and terminology that were foreign to her. She watched in awe as her friend breezed through a chemistry-based game that involved putting together different compounds.

"And I was like, 'You're brilliant. You're brilliant!' And she's like, 'No, I just went to high school,'" Drumsta said. "You're presented with situations like that, when you think, 'Man, I had a really, really crappy science foundation growing up.'"

For some exvangelicals, the challenges go beyond minor embarrassments. Sheila Janca grew up as an "evangelical preacher's daughter" in what she describes as an abusive home in the Midwest, in the 1960s and '70s. Any questions that bubbled up to the surface had to be quickly suppressed in favor of "blind faith." "Things were not making sense to me, and if I dared ask why, I'd have been flown across the room," she said. "So I was used to not asking questions. Skepticism was not permitted."

Janca remembers the humiliation of finally discovering, during a nursing school class, that men weren't actually missing a rib. Taking her cues from the creation story in Genesis, she'd believed that because God made Eve from Adam's rib, men had a different anatomy—until she saw a diagram of a human skeleton and tried to figure out why there wasn't one for women and another for men.

"I remember my hearing going away, because I felt such shame," Janca said. "Blood rushed to my ears when I read that in the textbook. It was that feeling of, I've been lied to, that feeling of betrayal."

For Rebekah Drumsta, a shift in her thinking about science began when she became a parent and started wrestling with what to teach her daughter. But she, too, was held back at first by her own set of fears.

"I was so scared of believing a lie," she said. "Of believing something that wasn't true, or hurting God's heart, doing something wrong, believing something bad. There's so much fear."


I was afraid, too, as I encountered my own moments when things didn't seem to make sense. In junior high, when my family visited the Smithsonian museums during my trip to Washington to compete in a Christian spelling bee, I couldn't help but notice that all of the placards described moments in history that stretched back millions of years. The timeline was mentioned casually, as though it was not at all controversial. I noticed these same kinds of references in books at the local public library, and in the *National Geographic* subscription my grandpa gave me for Christmas several years in a row.

My dad would roll his eyes when he saw these references to evolution, repeating Ken Ham's "MEEL-yuns and BEEL-yuns of years" parody of Carl Sagan. But something about it felt off. Why did everyone seem to believe the world was very old? Everyone . . . but us?

For me, that question came to a head in college, when some of my devoutly Christian professors confided in me that they were uncertain of what to make of evolutionary theory, or that they had come to peace, like many Christians before them all the way up to the Roman Catholic pope,[18] with the idea that one could accept evolutionary science and still leave room for belief in God, if not for a fully literalistic interpretation of Genesis.

I remember sitting on my bed in the darkness of my dorm room one night, talking on the phone with my father about a lecture I'd attended, with a guest speaker who had advanced degrees in both biology and theology. It was somewhat brave of the professor who invited him to allow him to speak on our Christian college campus, where science classes did not teach evolution. The guest didn't tell us what to believe, only that he, too, had once been a creationist, and that his years of studying both science and religion had led him to accept evolutionary theory. On the overhead projector, he displayed an image of a strange, snakelike creature with tiny legs.

"You might have been told there are no transitional forms," he said.

It was true. At lectures like the one at my church, and in science classes at my Christian school, we were often told this: that evolution could not be real, because there was nothing in the fossil record that suggested one species becoming another.

"That is not true," the speaker told us. "Look at this fossil right here."

I told my dad about all of this, eager to share what I'd learned. He didn't really know what to say, but he seemed concerned.

For Treadwell, the science radio show host in Illinois, studying geology and the fossil record made it abundantly clear that her old beliefs couldn't hold up under minimal scientific scrutiny. But, she said, studying science without having to force it through a literalistic filter has actually enhanced her feelings of awe and mystery about the world.

"The layers of rocks and the stories that they tell us about Earth's history are so amazing," she said.

Take the Grand Canyon, Treadwell said. Explaining it simply as a result of Noah's flood or an act of direct divine creation, as she might have in the past, seems much less interesting.

"It's such a glossing-over of a way cooler story," she said. "Sometimes I even say, if I would have maybe learned cosmology and space science as a kid, maybe I wouldn't have left [the church]."

For Jocelyn Howard, watching the 2014 update of the TV series *Cosmos* with astrophysicist Neil deGrasse Tyson—a reprise of the original from 1980 featuring Carl Sagan—was eye-opening, revealing how "mysterious and beautiful and exciting" the world could be, if you give yourself permission to truly learn about it.

"It's infuriating that it was kept from us because—why?" Howard asked. "Because of this need to be right?"

Howard thinks the rejection of science, combined with apocalyptic beliefs about the future of the world, has real consequences, not only for what evangelicals believe but for how they take care of the Earth.

"When you're taught that science is basically a fairy tale, and you're taught not to trust scientists, then why would you care if the world is burning around us?" Howard said. "It's about this heavenly battle, and it's about winning souls to Christ, and that's what's important, right? So the world around us doesn't matter, because this is all going to burn like in Revelation anyway."

In March 2022, I went home to Kansas City to see my grandfather, who was ninety-seven and had been markedly fading for months.

Hospice nurses had been called in, and he'd been moved to a hospital bed in the room where his original bed used to be. I needed to be sure that I could see him at least one more time. I stopped by my parents' house and slipped down to the basement, where items from our childhood were moved into storage, and the bookshelves were still lined with old copies of the Hardy Boys, our school yearbooks, and stacks of books about Christian parenting and conservative politics.

In one of the boxes, I found one of my old high school science papers, dated December 1997, my junior year. There were two pages about the biology of plant growth before the paper took a turn to the subject of *spiritual* growth.

"Just as plants must be grounded in good soil and have the right environmental conditions to do well, Christians need to be surrounded by people who share their faith and can 'nourish' them spiritually by encouraging them to do the right things," I wrote in this "research" paper, which, somehow, according to the grade penciled on the cover sheet, earned a score of 102 on a 100-point grading scale.[19] A couple of paragraphs later, I quoted a passage from the book of John, where Jesus compares God to a gardener who prunes away unfruitful branches.

I was taught to believe that people like me—the spiritually withered—are the unfruitful branches that Jesus warned about, who deserve to be cut off. But I've come to suspect that maybe such pruning is intended for ideas like the ones taught in our church sanctuaries and homeschool classrooms—ideas that close off inquiry and confine us to narrow ways of seeing the world. The pruning is for getting rid of dead weight that stifles the growth of healthy branches, which can spread and reach toward the sky, and whatever is beyond it.

# 6

# ALTERNATIVE FACTS

In that same box in my parents' basement where I found my old high school science paper was one I'd written for an English class, dated January 1998, weeks before I would leave for Washington, DC, for my Senate page semester. The cover page read, "What I Believe About Truth."

Inside I wrote: "The author recently had a conversation with her grandfather, a man of genius intellect, but extremely confused just the same. Although he is a Harvard graduate and a retired neurological surgeon, his intellectual abilities have not led him to the truth."[1] At not quite seventeen, I went on to hold up my grandfather, notwithstanding his professional achievements, as a cautionary tale, an example of someone unwilling to accept what all of my teachers, parents, and pastors assured me was the clear and unquestionable Truth about the purpose of life, the key to living well, and the path to salvation after death.

"There are many people in the world like this man," I continued. "Regardless of their level of intelligence or education, truth seems subjective and indefinite to them. What they do not acknowledge is that God has set the immovable standard for truth," which, I go on to say, is revealed through the Bible.

The paper was assigned as part of a series of essays where we, high school juniors, were assigned to explain and defend our worldviews. Another paper in the series was titled, "What I Believe About Man," and another, ". . . About Sin." It was, whether consciously or not on the part of my English teacher at Blue Ridge Christian School, one tiny piece of a much larger project.

In her 2013 book *Apostles of Reason,* historian Molly Worthen writes about what she describes in her subtitle as a "crisis of authority in American evangelicalism." Underneath the political and ideological project of the Christian right, Worthen argues, is a long history of intramural battles within evangelicalism about the nature of truth—over the role of science; the idea of "biblical inerrancy," the principle that the Bible is without mistakes and that every word is absolutely true; and the relationship between evangelicalism and academia and the overarching anxiety about those questions.

Worthen describes a campaign to promote a "Christian worldview" through publications, camps, and curricula focused on evangelical youth. These efforts were led by Christian right leaders such as James Dobson, the man whose voice constantly filled my home, and Focus on the Family; Gary Bauer, the former president of the Family Research Council; creationist Ken Ham; and David Barton, the conservative activist known for touting his revisionist portrait of American history that paints the Founding Fathers as Christian nationalists.[2]

These men approached this endeavor by framing their vision of a "Christian worldview" against any secular one that might challenge it—a strategy, Worthen writes, that enables them "to dismiss opposing interpretations of the evidence . . . They insist upon their own worldview as the only clear window on reality."[3]

For many of us who grew up as the targets of this worldview

education, it was comforting to believe that we had the Truth with a capital "T." That special revelation not only provided structure and guidance for how to live every aspect of our lives, but it armed us with a justification for our efforts to make sure others lived their lives in the same way. That might mean witnessing on street corners or inviting friends to youth group, walking in antiabortion marches, or volunteering to work the phone banks for the conservative Christian political candidates.

"Though the result of rejecting truth is extremely bleak," I wrote in the conclusion to my essay, "the rewards for accepting it are equally blessed." I quoted a verse from the book of Romans: "Although they claimed to be wise, they became fools. . . . They exchanged the truth about God for a lie, and worshiped and served created things rather than the Creator."[4]

The message I'd internalized was that no matter how wise, or educated, or credentialed, someone might seem to be, they could, in fact, still be fools and therefore enemies of God. And the consequences, both for this life and for eternity, were too dire to risk that. This message was repeated throughout my evangelical education, backed up with a litany of biblical citations woven together in service of the idea that one cannot, and must not, trust secular authorities, or even one's own internal sense of right and wrong. This was especially true if any of it came into conflict with the Bible and interpretations endorsed by the overwhelmingly white, heterosexual, and male religious leaders in our churches, Christian educational institutions, and evangelical ministries.

As my mother went about her domestic chores, tidying up the stacks of Christian magazines and books on the desk in the family room or folding piles of laundry on the living-room floor, she often sang a praise song based on a passage from Proverbs: "Trust in the Lord with all your heart, and lean not on your own understanding. In all your ways, acknowledge Him and He will make your paths straight. Be not wise in your own eyes; fear the Lord and turn from evil."[5] Or, when warning about the risks of being deceived by the world, she'd quote another sobering line from Proverbs: "There is a way that appears to be right, but in the end it leads to death."*

Hearing these things from the lips of not only my mother but from all of the adults I trusted, I often doubted my own mind. As I matured into a teenager, I noticed more cracks in the intellectual foundation that had been laid for me. When in my junior high history class we studied European explorers such as Vasco da Gama and Ferdinand Magellan, I began to ponder the expanse of human history, and the sheer size of the Earth. So many people, and places, and cultures God had made—and yet, to save only a tiny fraction of them?

"What about people who've never heard about Jesus?" I asked my teacher. It was hard to understand, but it was all part of God's plan, he said. God's ways are higher than ours, he added, referencing the prophet Isaiah,[6] and we can't understand the mystery of who he chooses to save or condemn. Still tormented by this question when I entered my freshman year of high school, I put it to another teacher I was close with, Miss Taylor, who would spend hours with me during my study hall sections, talking through my doubts about Christianity.

"All you need to know is that God *chose* you, Sarah," she said,

---

* This line appears in both Proverbs 14:12 and Proverbs 16:25. Rereading these passages now in context gave me a very different understanding of this idea. While I usually heard it presented as a caution against relying on one's own intuitions about right and wrong if they conflict with traditional Christian teachings, in chapter 14 in particular, the line comes amidst a litany of aphorisms that seem to me to describe the world as it is, more than offering a warning about one's personal epistemology. The next verse, for example, is, "Even in laughter the heart may ache, and rejoicing may end in grief," which I hardly take as a caution against laughter and rejoicing.

reflecting what I now recognize as a form of Calvinist theology, a system of beliefs held by some but certainly not all evangelicals, which teaches among other things that God "predestines" some people for salvation, and others for damnation. "Even if you were in a far-flung part of the world, he would have found you, and saved you."

That thought offered brief comfort—my salvation was never really in question—and yet, it seemed unfair and unjust. Why should *I* be chosen, but others lost? But, desperate to stay on the "straight and narrow path," to avoid the way of death and distancing myself from Miss Taylor and my parents and everyone I loved, I tried to push those doubts aside. I spent more hours in prayer, writing in my journals, and reading books by Christian writers including the famous British theologian C. S. Lewis, all in an effort to convince myself that this all made sense.

I often second-guessed the uneasy feelings that seemed to rise up from somewhere deep in my belly when I thought about these questions. It was as if I had been asked to perform a total system override, to ignore and silence the blaring alarms and hand over the keys to my mind to an outside authority. I would always come back to the idea that these doubts were simply "my own understanding" getting in the way. Or worse yet, it could be the Devil, who was always trying to pull human souls away from God. The Bible warns us that Satan comes like a thief, seeking "to steal and kill and destroy."[7] I knew that I should always fall back on the biblical advice to "trust in the Lord" and choose faith over doubt, or my own extremely fallible sense of reason.

"If you are on the inside of this narrative, everything makes perfect sense," Shannon Montgomery, an Atlanta-area exvangelical who has spent years studying theology, told me. "There is absolutely nothing that can come in from the outside that cannot be incorporated into this fundamentalist worldview. Everything. Because even contradictory information can be as simple as 'Well, God's ways are higher than ours and we don't have all the answers.'"

Like many of the people featured in this book, I met Montgomery in a social media group for exvangelicals. Montgomery was born in 1974, grew up in a conservative Baptist home, and has spent much of her adult life studying Christianity through an academic lens, earning several degrees from Georgia State and Emory University in religious studies and related disciplines. When I reached out to Montgomery to talk about the evangelical relationship to science and authority, Montgomery described how this dedication to the idea of every part of the Bible as absolute truth leaves many evangelical believers open to accepting whatever their religious leaders say is true, and promotes skepticism of outside experts, regardless of their credentials or experience.

"If you tell people that scientists are evil, they're going to believe that scientists are evil," Montgomery said. "And that kind of opens the door to say that all authorities are being misleading, and the paradox is, 'So you need to believe us.'"[8]

When Kellyanne Conway, advisor to the newly inaugurated President Trump, looked into the camera on NBC's *Meet the Press* in January 2017 and infamously told host Chuck Todd that the White House had provided the media with "alternative facts," it felt unsettlingly familiar.[9]

Conway was defending Sean Spicer, who, the day before during his first ever briefing as White House press secretary, had exaggerated the size of Trump's inauguration crowd, falsely claiming it was the "largest audience to ever witness an inauguration," despite overwhelming evidence to the contrary, including aerial photographs and public transit ridership data.[10]

What caught my attention wasn't merely Conway's unapologetic offer of a competing set of "facts" when the actual facts didn't suit her narrative, as alarming as that was for anyone concerned with getting at the truth. What I recognized was her rationale for doing it: angry at Todd for calling the White House press secretary on his false statements, Conway subtly threatened not to play ball with the network in the future: "Chuck, I mean, if we're going to keep referring to our press secretary in those types of terms I think that we're going to have to rethink our relationship here," she said.[11]

Conway had not only refused to face the facts; she had declared unhelpful facts to be *out of bounds.*

So much of my history came to mind. The dark sanctuary of my childhood, where I was told not to believe the godless scientists who said we'd evolved from monkeys; the skepticism toward experts with fancy degrees in favor of the guidance of pastors who claimed divine callings; our certainty that we had special access to the Truth, so much so that the whole world around us was so horribly misinformed that they were destined for eternal damnation— all of it flashed before my eyes. The commitment to upholding a specific set of ideals, at all costs, even if it required turning a blind eye to new information that might destabilize that conclusion.

I had chosen journalism as a career, in retrospect, to escape from all of that. By the time I'd graduated from college and begun working in my first newsroom at a small newspaper in the Chicago suburbs, I was exhausted from trying to get my brain to conform to the contours of the supposed Truth I'd been taught. I was beginning to feel deceived: Why did certain types of knowledge seem forbidden, and why were only *our* experts to be trusted? I craved a space to ask questions about the way the world really was, and the freedom to take in new sources of information. Journalism required that; it honored the process of seeking truth and demanded the consideration of multiple points of view without rigging the game.

And somehow, everything had come full circle. My journalism

career eventually brought me face-to-face with the world I'd left, a world that now often seems to be at the center of the political universe. As Conway spoke, I recognized these "alternative facts."

As Christopher Douglas argued in a piece for *Religion Dispatches* in February 2017, the groundwork for this approach to information had been laid over several previous decades, as earlier Christian fundamentalists, followed by many of today's evangelicals, rejected both evolutionary science and modern biblical scholarship in large numbers. "Recognizing the power of expertise's infrastructure," Douglas wrote, conservative Christians developed a "counter-infrastructure" in the form of an "alternative educational and media ecosystem of knowledge." The consequence, he said, has been skepticism and often outright rejection of secular knowledge.[12]

"This cognitive training to reject expert knowledge and to seek alternative, more amenable explanations has helped disarm the capacity for critical thinking and analysis," Douglas said.[13] In a piece for *Vox* in May of 2017, David Roberts argued compellingly that what he described as a type of "tribal epistemology," which had existed for years but largely operated under the radar in conservative media, had now made its way into the White House. In this epistemic approach, Roberts said, "Information is evaluated based not on conformity to common standards of evidence or correspondence to a common understanding of the world, but on whether it supports the tribe's values and goals and is vouchsafed by tribal leaders. 'Good for our side' and 'true' begin to blur into one."[14]

The article pointed to a 2009 quote from Rush Limbaugh, in which the conservative talk radio host decried what he claimed was pervasive corruption in "government, academia, science, and media." Limbaugh, who died in 2021 after ardently supporting Trump, had told his audience that Americans on the left and on the right live in "two universes," and that the universe of the left is "an entire lie." Prior to his death, Limbaugh was awarded the Presidential Medal of Freedom by Trump, in a move regarded by many as highly unusual for an award intended to be bestowed by the president of the United States to recognize those who have made "an especially meritorious contribution to the security or national interests of the United States, world peace, cultural, or other significant public or private endeavors."

In 1994, when I was in junior high, evangelical historian Mark Noll sounded an alarm about a pervasive anti-intellectualism he was observing in white evangelical Christianity, which he described in his book *The Scandal of the Evangelical Mind*. Noll praised what he saw as an "extraordinary range of virtues" found among American evangelicals, including charitable service and giving, and a robust congregational and community life. But he warned that "modern American evangelicals have failed notably at sustaining serious intellectual life," and had largely disengaged from mainstream universities and the arts. While evangelicals had built up a massive infrastructure of Christian colleges and seminaries, broadcasters, and parachurch organizations, they'd created "not a single research university."[15]

This lack of robust intellectual grounding had consequences for the evangelical movement, Noll argued. Citing the work of two fellow historians, Ronald Numbers and Paul Boyer, Noll observed that evangelicalism was experiencing an intensifying "fixation" with beliefs about the end-times, including a desire to interpret biblical prophecies and point to current events as signs that the apocalypse is near.

Evangelicals had become susceptible, Noll stated, to buying into a wide range of specious theories. He pointed to the early days of the 1991 Gulf War, when evangelical publishers rushed to put out books interpreting the events in the Middle East as a "direct fulfillment of biblical prophecy heralding the end of the world." Rather than a "careful analysis of Middle Eastern culture or the tangled twentieth-century history of the region," Noll wrote, these books offered "speculation about some of the most esoteric and widely debated passages of the Bible." Evangelicals enthusiastically imbibed these books, sending several of them to the top of Christian bestseller lists.[16]

Ruth Braunstein, a sociologist at the University of Connecticut and director of the Meanings of Democracy Lab, argues[17] that this network of evangelical media and educational institutions has isolated many evangelicals from deep engagement with mainstream thought. This isolation, she says, has created an "imperviousness to counter-ideas," creating a fertile breeding ground for conspiracy theories that can be nearly impossible to eradicate.

"[These institutions] can essentially provide their own version of information and a propensity to trust insiders instead of outsiders," Braunstein told me. "Once misinformation gets into that echo chamber, it's very difficult to convince people otherwise, particularly if they are trying to do the convincing or are considered outsiders."[18] As another sign of how insulated right-wing Christians can be from historical and scientific facts, particularly those that challenge narratives advanced by their leaders, a 2021 study coauthored by Braunstein and other researchers found a strong correlation between expressing Christian nationalistic views and a failure "to affirm factually correct answers" about the history of religion in the United States.[19]

To be sure, an appetite for misinformation and conspiracy-theorist thinking is far from an exclusively evangelical problem. In his 2017 book *The Death of Expertise*, writer Tom Nichols, a former professor at the US Naval War College and self-described "Never-Trump Republican," expressed a fear of what he observed broadly in American society as "a Google-fueled, Wikipedia-based, blog-sodden collapse of any division between professionals and laypeople, students and teachers, knowers and wonderers," which he characterized as a "death of the ideal of expertise." At that time, mere years before the COVID pandemic, he pointed to the rise of anti-vaccine activists such as actor Jenny McCarthy[20] and false conspiracy theories like the alarmingly resilient and racist "birther" movement, which questioned former president Barack Obama's citizenship status in spite of repeated debunkings.[21]

Nichols offers a description of the frustrating and self-perpetuating nature of conspiracy-theorist thinking, and the difficulty in combating it through logic: "Each rejoinder or contradiction only produces a more complicated theory. Conspiracy theorists manipulate all tangible evidence to fit their explanation. . . . Nothing can ever challenge the underlying belief." Their appeal, he argues, often comes from a deeply emotional, existential place in the human spirit, a desire to feel some measure of safety, comfort, and control. These ideas are attractive "to people who have a hard time making sense of a complicated world" and to those "who would choose to believe in complicated nonsense rather than accept that their own circumstances are incomprehensible, the result of issues beyond their intellectual capacity to understand, or even their own fault."[22]

There's mounting evidence that white evangelicals are particularly susceptible to conspiracy theories[23] and misinformation about a wide range of issues, including vaccine safety[24] and the validity of the 2020 election.[25] In February 2021, the *Washington Post* reported that the rapid spread of COVID-related conspiracy theories in evangelical social media spaces was causing "debate and concern" among pastors and other leaders about how to manage the problem.[26] That April, I reported for NPR on efforts by some prominent white evangelicals, including Franklin Graham, son of the famous revival preacher the Reverend Billy Graham, to persuade their fellow believers to get vaccinated, as their group reported some of the lowest vaccination rates in the country.[27] Many white evangelicals were persistently resistant, even as story after story of prominent conservative leaders who'd publicly refused the vaccine, only to become extremely ill or die of COVID, filled the headlines.[28]

In a March 2021 article for the news site *FiveThirtyEight* titled "Why QAnon Has Attracted So Many White Evangelicals," writer Kayleigh Rogers described evangelical distrust in the mainstream media, and the strong evangelical overlap with the Republican Party—a group that has a higher rate of belief in conspiracy theories like QAnon—as among the factors contributing to the misinformation swirling around many evangelical online communities.

Rogers pointed to the evangelical emphasis on taking things "on faith" as a likely cause. She quoted Ed Stetzer, director of the Billy Graham Center at Wheaton College, with this explanation: "People of faith believe there is a divine plan—that there are forces of good and forces of evil at work in the world. QAnon is a train that runs on the tracks that religion has already put in place."[29]

Doug Geiger, an exvangelical in his early forties who lives in Michigan, has seen this firsthand in his relationship with a relative whose belief system in recent years began to metastasize from a charismatic form of evangelicalism—characterized by an intense focus on concerns about demonic activity and an emphasis on apocalyptic beliefs—to an obsession with conspiracy theories. He said he watched with concern as the religious beliefs she used to make sense of the world became "fused" with Trumpian politics and misinformation.

"QAnon was tailor-made and genetically modified to be the perfect thing to sweep up someone like her, who in the eighties was worried about demons in the toy box," Geiger said.

People are drawn to conspiracy theories that align with their larger understanding of the world, said sociologist Ruth Braunstein. "QAnon is about a battle between forces of good and forces of evil," she said. "The forces of evil happen to be the enemies that evangelicals identify already in the world, of secular liberals, in many cases, 'sexual degenerates,' and so it fits this broader worldview." Similarly, she said fears about vaccines tie in neatly with preexisting distrust of scientific authorities.

Geiger grew up attending a variety of conservative churches and an evangelical school deeply enmeshed in the Christian right movement of the eighties and nineties; he remembers evangelical political activists coming to visit and speak at school events. As a young adult, he began gradually "deconstructing" his faith over many years. The first cracks appeared in his midtwenties, when a trusted pastor and mentor was exposed for his involvement in multiple sex scandals, shaking Geiger's confidence. He traces the ultimate breaking point to the 2016 election, when he became disillusioned with what he saw as hypocrisy on the part of his fellow evangelicals.

Around the same time, Geiger was watching his close relative become involved in Tea Party politics, before eventually sinking into a web of misinformation, moving from watching Fox News to obscure YouTube videos.

"She seemed to be simmering during the Obama administration, and it absolutely turned to a roaring boil with Trump," he said. "It was kind of the intersection of the weird political stuff, and then her fixation with end-times and spiritual warfare and QAnon."

Geiger, whom I met through an online support group for people struggling with loved ones who are caught in a swirl of misinformation, said his family has "completely blown up" in recent years over these issues. Discussions about QAnon began to permeate conversations. He became concerned about his kids being exposed to those ideas, but he said his relative refused to stop talking about it. Eventually, they stopped communicating completely.[30]

Misinformation is also dividing evangelical churches and

communities. In February 2021, several of my NPR colleagues told the story of a northern Virginia pastor, Jared Stacy, who left his pulpit after struggling to fight back against election conspiracy theories and other misinformation circulating through his congregation. He described an erosion of a common understanding of reality among church members, which was breeding divisions within the church, and even within families and marriages.

Stacy was disturbed at how it all reflected on his faith.

"If Christians in America are serious about helping people see Jesus and what he's about and what he claims, then the label 'evangelical' is a distraction because it bears, unfortunately, the weight of a violence,'" he said in the NPR interview. "I would not use that term because of its association with January 6."[31]

Beyond the political and social upheaval exacerbated by the erosion of a shared consensus over basic facts, there are other consequences. While it did not break down the data by religious affiliation, an NPR analysis in December 2021 found that counties that voted heavily for Trump experienced COVID death rates nearly three times higher than those that voted heavily for Joe Biden[32]—a grim illustration of the dangers of making decisions based on a set of "alternative facts."

# 7

# WHOSE "CHARACTER" MATTERS?

Long before the majority of white evangelicals would rally around Donald Trump and forgive his unfortunate behavior, their forebears were rallying in opposition to Bill Clinton and excoriating him for his. In September 1998, before picking me up from school one afternoon, my mom had spent the day digesting the *Starr Report*. The *Kansas City Star* had joined several other major newspapers across the country to print portions of Independent Counsel Ken Starr's report—the culmination of his yearslong probe, which had started as an inquiry into some of the Clintons' financial dealings in Arkansas and morphed into a detailed examination of former president Clinton's now-notorious affair with the White House intern Monica Lewinsky. Starr had spent months looking into allegations that Clinton committed perjury in a separate civil case involving a sexual harassment claim against him by Paula Jones, a former Arkansas state employee.

That summer, I'd returned to Kansas City to begin my senior year of high school after spending the first half of the year in

Washington as a Republican Senate page. The sordid allegations about Clinton and Lewinsky had been in the air for months. So I was intrigued when, sometime during that semester, a staffer approached me in the Republican cloakroom—the area where senators in that era reconnoitered and made phone calls and took messages, and where pages filled up water glasses to take to senators on the floor. He handed me a copy of the heavy Senate rule book, with careful instructions: turn to a specific section, photocopy it, and take it down the tiled corridor to Majority Leader Trent Lott's office.

I did as instructed. "RULES FOR IMPEACHMENT TRI-ALS," the section heading read in capital letters at the top of each page. I asked what this was all about. "Don't ask questions," the staffer told me. "Copy it and take it to Lott's office right away."

I walked the papers down to the leader's office, where I was greeted by two flawless young women, at least one of whom was a recent graduate of Ole Miss, who were always smiling and hovering around the front door. They directed me back to a room where Lott and several other top Senate Republicans sat around a wide boardroom table. I handed off the papers and didn't ask any more questions.

And now, months later, Ken Starr had concluded that there were several grounds for impeachment against Clinton, including lying under oath by denying having had sexual relations with Lewinsky. Much of the ensuing controversy hinged on the definition of "sexual relations," and whether or not oral sex should count.[1]

My mother had read all of the lurid particulars. As the oldest, I sat "shotgun" in the front passenger seat of our blue minivan while my siblings crawled in the back. Mom told me she'd read the report and had a question for me.

"Do you know what oral sex is?" she asked, lowering her voice slightly to avoid the little ears in the back.

It felt like a trap. In my seventeen-year-old mind, I assumed my innocent mom didn't know what this term meant and was asking *me,* the teenager who would surely be more informed, to explain. In retrospect, I now believe my mom was testing me, trying to determine how much I actually knew.

Sheltered as I'd been, I knew what that meant, but only in the most purely academic sense. I had only, a week or two earlier, been on my first date. We didn't even hold hands, so I had yet to come anywhere close to a sexual encounter of any type, however narrowly the president might define such things.

I answered the question, gingerly.

"I think . . . I think it's just what it sounds like, Mom?"

She paused, hands at ten o'clock and two o'clock, eyes straight ahead on the road as my siblings chattered in the back.

"Well, I think," she said, contemplating her words. "I think, if you have Jesus, you don't need oral sex!"

I don't remember how I responded, but I've been telling that story for decades when people ask me to describe my childhood.


The news of the Lewinsky affair elicited much consternation in my world.

Days before the release of the *Starr Report,* Dr. James Dobson wrote a letter taking to task those who argued that Clinton's affair with Lewinsky was merely a private matter. "That disregard for morality is profoundly disturbing to me," Dobson wrote. "The rules by which behavior is governed appear to have been rewritten specifically for Mr. Clinton." To his credit, Dobson highlighted the power imbalance inherent in the president of the United States having an affair with a young subordinate: "He was the most powerful man in the world and she was a starry-eyed intern. That situation would not have been tolerated in any other setting—*ever.*"[2]

But the problem, Dobson argued, went further back to the tacit acceptance of Clinton's long history of alleged sexual impropriety, dating to his first campaign for president and beyond.

"As it turns out, character DOES matter," Dobson wrote. "You can't run a family, let alone a country, without it. How foolish to believe that a person who lacks honesty and moral integrity is qualified to lead a nation and the world! Nevertheless, our people continue to say that the President is doing a good job even if they don't respect him personally. Those two positions are fundamentally incompatible."[3]

Dobson then quoted from the book of James: "Can both fresh water and salt water flow from the same spring?" The answer, Dobson concluded, was a resounding *no*.[4]

In an op-ed in the *Wall Street Journal* in August 1998 titled "Clinton's Sins Aren't Private," the Reverend Franklin Graham argued that public officials must be judged by their private actions. He rejected "the notion that what a person does in private has little bearing on his public actions or job performance, even if he is the president of the United States." Graham responded to Clinton's defenders who argued that he should be viewed like "King David of the Bible, one of history's great leaders, as an example as they call on us to forgive and forget the president's moral failings. Since God pardoned David's adulterous act with Bathsheba, the reasoning goes, we should similarly forgive Mr. Clinton," Graham wrote. But, he went on to say, David's story didn't end with "forgiveness" but rather with "huge consequences for David," including the death of his own child. He called on Clinton to publicly repent as a step toward national healing.[5]

In a TV ad running in the critical early-caucus state of Iowa around the time of the *Starr Report*'s release, Gary Bauer, then president of the Family Research Council[6] and an aspiring Republican presidential candidate, went a step further, explicitly calling on Clinton to resign. Bauer bemoaned the Clinton scandal's impact on America's children, arguing that his behavior had "taught our children that lying is okay, that fidelity is old-fashioned and that character doesn't count."[7]

The concerns about Clinton's moral character had long predated the Lewinsky scandal. The Reverend Jerry Falwell, the evangelist and founder of the Moral Majority, had been ahead of the pack. As early as 1994, he was marketing a videotape which, for a "donation" of forty-three dollars, would walk you through a litany of unproven accusations against Clinton that had been floating around the right-wing mediasphere, including an array of alleged sexual misdeeds. Long before the advent of Facebook or Twitter/X, Falwell distributed the tape by mail from Liberty University, the mammoth Christian college he'd founded in Lynchburg, Virginia. Writing for the *Los Angeles Times* in May 1994, Robert L. Jackson called the effort "the most visible venture to date by conservative critics circulating damaging anti-Clinton material."

Two decades before Trump would point to my colleagues and me in the press pen at the back of his campaign rallies, calling us "liars" and "sick people" to cheers from his crowds of delighted supporters,[8] Falwell admitted to CNN that he didn't know if the allegations were true, but that he was releasing the tape because "the national media should have been doing (it) and has been hypocritically quiet."[9]

I dutifully internalized all of this. In the pages of a purple spiral-bound notebook I used as a journal for a class assignment during my senior year of high school, I described spending the weekend laid up watching television with ice packs pressed up to my mouth after having my wisdom teeth removed. The *Starr Report* had been published days before, and the news would have been all over *Meet the Press* and the other Sunday-morning political talk shows my dad and I taped and watched together after church.

"Speaking of TV, I'm so disgusted with the President," I wrote in an entry on September 14, 1998. "He's such a despicable person . . . Mr. Clinton should do everyone a favor and resign."

As I reread those words now, I see some foreshadowing of my eventual departure from this world. I said nothing about Clinton's sexual or moral behavior, only the perjury allegations.

"If he gets away with this, it will be like saying that power makes lying acceptable," I wrote. "The President should be held to a standard that is at minumum," I said, underlining and misspelling the word *minimum*, "as high as the standard for everyone else."[10]

Even as a seventeen-year-old virgin wearing a purity ring on my left hand as a sign of my commitment to chastity and future marital fidelity, I didn't seem overly concerned about Clinton's extramarital activities. I suspect that on some level, I must have sensed, even then, that the hand-wringing from the institutional leaders my community followed was at least slightly hyperbolic and a distraction from more pressing national concerns.

Against that backdrop, the white evangelical embrace of the twice-divorced, proudly womanizing Donald Trump less than two decades later—often by the very same leaders who'd decried Clinton's actions—was confounding for some evangelicals.

Writing for *The Atlantic* in August 2016, writer Jonathan Merritt, a Southern Baptist Theological Seminary graduate, called out what he saw as hypocrisy and a betrayal of the movement's ostensible ideals.

Since the dawn of the Moral Majority, Merritt wrote, evangelical leaders "have claimed it is about character. They have claimed it is about values. They have claimed it is about biblical principles. . . . But evidence indicates that evangelical political engagement is really about cultural influence, social dominance, and power."[11]

For Stephanie Stalvey, the artist who depicts her "deconstruction" journey out of evangelicalism through drawings she shares on Instagram, it was a clarifying moment that revealed something she hadn't expected to find beneath the surface of the belief system that had shaped her. At every turn, every new revelation, she kept expecting evangelicals to break with the Republican nominee.

"I kept thinking, 'This is it, he just ruined his chance with the evangelicals,'" she said. "You can't talk about fucking people and grabbing people's pussy. And I thought, 'This is done.'"

But it was never done. She watched, dismayed, as her friends, fellow churchgoers, and family members rationalized each incident.

"Then I realized, this isn't what we said it was about," Stalvey said. "That brought into crystal-clear focus that a lot of this evangelical culture has been about political power since the beginning. And I didn't even realize that."[12]

In *Red State Christians,* her 2019 taxonomy of conservative Protestants and Catholics who supported Trump, Angela Denker suggests that some of the predominantly white evangelical women who voted for him had been conditioned to do so by their culture, which emphasized submissiveness, the dangerous lure of female sexuality, and the importance of being sexually available to their husbands. "The wives and mothers who were the children of purity culture in the late 1990s and early 2000s were among the Red State Christians who delivered Donald Trump to the White House," Denker writes. "For women reared in a world where their sexuality was to be hidden and 'available' to men, 'grab her by the pussy' was, of course, nothing out of the ordinary."[13]

But for some exvangelicals like Amy Snidow, the incongruity was disorienting. Snidow lives in central Texas, where she works in the real estate industry and posts about her exvangelical journey on several social media accounts.

"All these evangelicals said, 'This is our guy,' and I'm like, 'How?'" Snidow said.

Now in her early forties and divorced, Snidow spent much of her twenties as a pastor's wife in a conservative denomination. After her marriage ended, she felt out of place as a divorced single mother in evangelical churches, which often structure social activities around stages of life: young singles, married couples with kids, empty nesters. Snidow eventually stopped attending church, and began studying the Bible and praying on her own. She ultimately left around 2014, coincidentally, she said, "right before people started praising Trump from pulpits."

Freshly tending her wounds from her church experience, Snidow said she watched it all from a distance, feeling dismay and confusion as her community embraced him.

"Watching this corrupt—per the church, morally corrupt—individual be praised by people who would not even let a man who divorced a woman be the leader of a church or a deacon, or pick up the tithing plates . . . how are they justifying this?" she said.[14]

They justified it by pointing pragmatically to what Trump could do for them. In my own reporting during the 2016 campaign, I encountered many conservative Christian voters who said they wished Trump wouldn't tweet quite so much, or would soften his language and tone. But fundamentally, they told me, they believed he'd advance their agenda—and what's more, they knew that Democratic nominee Hillary Clinton would not.

In a 2018 interview with *Politico* regarding allegations that Trump had had an affair with the porn star Stormy Daniels, Tony Perkins—Gary Bauer's eventual successor at the Family Research Council—defended Trump. Perkins said evangelicals were willing to give him a "mulligan," or a do-over, because he was delivering on their policy goals like opposition to abortion "more than any other president in my lifetime."[15] Around that time, the Reverend Franklin Graham delineated a distinction between Trump's personal transgressions and his public role. "We certainly don't hold him up as the pastor of this nation and he is not," Graham told MSNBC.[16]

Speaking on televangelist Pat Robertson's Christian Broadcasting Network in May 2019, James Dobson offered not begrudging acceptance but superlative praise for Trump, saying, "I couldn't be more pleased with him." Dobson went further, describing him as "much more of a gentleman than anybody knows he is. . . . I really do love and appreciate that man," and said he wished people would "get off his back."

Dobson added, "He's not a perfect man, but I'm not either."[17]

It reminded me of a conversation I'd had with Jerry Falwell, Jr., son of Liberty University's late founder, in the early days of the Trump administration. Trump was giving the commencement address to the Class of 2017 at Liberty. That day in May, as Falwell and I sat in a conference room after the graduation ceremony, I asked him the question that many people who knew about my family's religious background had asked me as I covered the 2016 campaign: Why would evangelicals accept and even promote such a man?

Falwell told me it was fundamentally about Trump's support for the evangelical agenda, and that made it possible to set aside his personal character.

"Because the ones that you think are so perfect and sinless, it's just you don't know about it," Falwell told me. "They're all just as bad. We all are, and that's the bottom line."[18]

That moment stuck with me, and came to mind again in August 2020, when Falwell, Jr., was forced to resign from leadership of Liberty after mildly racy vacation photos surfaced, along with allegations that he and his wife, Becki, had engaged in sexual escapades in violation of the university's honor code. The Falwells claimed that Becki had engaged in an extramarital affair in the past, but that the couple had reconciled.[19] In a *Vanity Fair* profile in 2022, Falwell said he was not "a religious person"—at least, not like his father was.[20]

But in 2016, while still at the helm of the institution his father founded, Falwell, Jr., became one of the first prominent white evangelicals to endorse Trump in the Republican primary, comparing him favorably to none other than King David in an interview with the Liberty student newspaper, the *Liberty Champion*.

"God called King David a man after God's own heart even though he was an adulterer and a murderer," Falwell told the *Champion*. "You have to choose the leader that would make the best king or president and not necessarily someone who would be a good pastor. We're not voting for pastor-in-chief. It means sometimes we have to choose a person who has the qualities to lead and who can protect our country and bring us back to economic vitality, and it might not be the person we call when we need somebody to give us spiritual counsel."[21]

Many prominent evangelicals would soon join him in his endorsement and in his efforts to defend Trump throughout his campaign and presidency. Others also would explain Trump's misbehavior by drawing parallels to flawed biblical figures. Creationist Ken Ham compared Trump to King Cyrus, who is described in the Old Testament book of Isaiah as an unwitting instrument of divine purposes for the Jewish people.[22] As Ham put it in a 2017 piece by the Religion News Service, "[God] raises up kings and destroys kingdoms. He even calls a pagan king, Cyrus, his anointed, or his servant to do the things that he wants him to do."[23]

Evangelicals were beginning to advance that argument in support of Trump at least as early as June 2016, when Trump met with around a thousand mostly white conservative Christian leaders at a New York City hotel, a meeting convened in an effort to shore up support for the presumptive nominee among this key Republican voting bloc. As NPR's lead reporter covering the Trump campaign,

I was one of a handful of those allowed by organizers to be inside the giant hotel ballroom. As pastors and ministry leaders sat around tables, Trump promised to nominate conservative judges who would advance evangelical goals like religious freedom and restrictions on abortion. At that event, Franklin Graham ticked through a list of imperfect biblical figures—Moses, St. Peter, and yes, King David—making the case that, like them, God could use Donald Trump. "There is none of us that are perfect," Graham said. "There's only one, and that's the Lord Jesus Christ, but he's not running for president of the United States."[24]

But Trump's appeal with many white evangelicals often went far beyond a reluctant devil's bargain. In the *Washington Post* in November 2019, Eugene Scott documented how widespread white evangelical support for Trump had transformed into something more, comparisons to Christ himself.

As Scott noted, in the lead-up to what would turn out to be the first of two impeachment votes Trump would ultimately face, Republican representative Barry Loudermilk of Georgia compared Trump's impeachment hearing to the trial of Jesus Christ that led to his crucifixion: "When Jesus was falsely accused of treason, Pontius Pilate gave Jesus the opportunity to face his accusers," Loudermilk said. "During that sham trial, Pontius Pilate afforded more rights to Jesus than the Democrats have afforded this president in this process."[25]

It was all too much for some evangelicals, especially women like Beth Moore, a high-profile speaker and writer whose status as a female evangelical leader sometimes provoked criticism from her theologically conservative coreligionists.[26] Moore was among a handful of prominent evangelical women who publicly criticized Trump after the *Access Hollywood* scandal.[27] Moore finally reached her breaking point with the Southern Baptist Convention (SBC) in early 2021, leaving after several tumultuous years that included public sparring between Moore and prominent Southern Baptists over the role of women in the church, clergy sexual abuse, and evangelical support for Trump.[28]

Upon announcing her decision to leave the SBC, Moore told the Religion News Service, "At the end of the day, there comes a time when you have to say 'this is not who I am,'" she said.[29]

Disillusionment with the way white evangelical churches responded to Trump and his treatment of women drove others out of their churches more quietly, or widened their growing distance from their churches.

"How we got from 'grab 'em by the'—I don't know if I can say that word, but you know what I mean—to images of him being [almost another] Jesus. I don't understand it," Amy Snidow said. "It's one thing to say, 'Okay, so he's the closest we can get to protecting our interests in the nation.' But I will never understand how these people have elevated the man to savior."

Snidow said she's come to see Trump as an avatar for all the ideas and feelings that many of his white evangelical supporters had secretly harbored, but mostly held inside.

"He said everything that they couldn't say," Snidow told me. "He was what every white man aspired to be, and what a lot of white women are conditioned to want a spouse to be, outside of the womanizing piece: wealthy and powerful and a provider. I think that those things justified it."

There was something else about Trump's rhetoric. The way he talked about women, people of color, immigrants, and other people on the margins reminded her of some of the ugly whispers she'd heard growing up in the church.

"I grew up witnessing it," Snidow said.

Living in Texas, Snidow said some in her religious community were drawn to Trump's rhetoric about immigration.

"They were like, 'Well, he's saying the truth—all the people who are crossing the border illegally *are* drug dealers, murderers, and rapists,'" Snidow said. "These are the things that they wanted to hear affirmed, and there he was on this national stage, in the most powerful position in the world, saying exactly what they say around their truck bed when they're done fishing on a Saturday afternoon."

Snidow felt similar frustrations in the summer of 2020, in response to the murder of George Floyd, the Black man killed by a white police officer in Minneapolis who knelt on Floyd's neck for nine minutes as he lay in the street. She was distressed by what she saw as many white evangelicals' indifference toward the deaths of Black Americans at the hands of law enforcement.

"I kind of sunk into a sad place," Snidow told me.

In that place, she began to more deeply deconstruct her faith. She reread the Bible, searched for answers, and sought out progressive Christian writers like former pastor Rob Bell, theologian Peter Enns, and historian Kristin Kobes Du Mez, who each offered critiques of evangelical theology and practice. She began to chafe at what she saw as a fusion of her faith and anti-gay bigotry, partisan Republican politics, and Christian nationalism.

"I needed to understand how they're taking what I truly thought at one point was the most loving point of view of how to do life and how are they making it like *this*?" Snidow said. "I don't know what label I would put on myself. Because when you tell people in America that you're a Christian, the knee-jerk reaction is all these things that I'm not."

Snidow no longer identifies as a Christian, at least not officially, she said. For now, at least, the term is too tightly wound up with ideologies she wants no part of.

# 8

# "LEAVE LOUD"

If the Trump years and the death of George Floyd were a breaking point for some white evangelicals, for many Black Christians in evangelical spaces, they represented yet another chapter in a long history characterized, at best, by lip service to addressing racial injustice.

A generation before Floyd was murdered, footage of another high-profile case of police brutality against a Black man sparked a public backlash and demands for reform. The beating of Rodney King in Los Angeles launched days of racial uprisings in 1992, after four officers were acquitted of assault.[1] It also prompted a response from some white evangelical churches, which, conscious of the long-standing segregation of their pews, embarked on "racial reconciliation" initiatives in the years that followed.

By this time, more than thirty years had passed since the Reverend Martin Luther King, Jr., famously lamented the racial separateness of the American Christian church.

"Eleven o'clock on Sunday morning is one of the most segregated hours . . . in Christian America," King said in a 1960 interview on NBC's *Meet the Press*. "Any church that stands against integration and that has a segregated body, is standing against the spirit and the teachings of Jesus Christ. . . . But this is something the Church will have to do itself."[2]

The church has tried at various points in its history. As historian Jane Hong wrote in a *Washington Post* article marking thirty years since the Los Angeles uprisings, the events appeared to mark a possible turning point: "While calls for Black and White Christians to forge meaningful relationships and connect across bitter racial divides were not new, they became mainstream as never before." Churches held interracial gatherings and pledged to work harder to form relationships across racial and ethnic lines.[3] Promise Keepers—the giant gathering of evangelical men much maligned for its retrograde views on gender roles—made racial reconciliation a major focus of its mission.[4]

But to many Black evangelicals and other people of color, these efforts have seemed to produce superficial, rather than structural, changes. At the time of the Los Angeles uprisings, religion scholar Anthea Butler was living in the area and attending a large evangelical church. In her 2021 book, *White Evangelical Racism,* Butler describes her church's efforts to bring together a multiracial group of theologically conservative Christians. At one event, Butler sat next to the pastor's mother, a woman she'd met multiple times. "Welcome to Church on the Way," the woman told Butler, looking at her like a stranger. In that moment, Butler writes, she felt that as a Black woman in this predominantly white evangelical space, she would always be viewed as an outsider: "I knew no matter how much I had worked or served or prayed with people, I was simply a Black person visiting the Church on the Way."[5]

A few years after the uprisings, in 1995, the Southern Baptist Convention ratified a resolution formally apologizing for its racist past and pledging to work toward building an inclusive, multiracial denomination. The document came 150 years after the denomination had been founded by slave owners and their sympathizers because of a split among Baptists over the issue of slavery.[6]

Butler calls the acknowledgment "commendable," but argues it fell short in several ways, including by failing to "deal with the roots of racism that run deep within both the religious and political positions of the denomination." Even as white evangelicals took steps to bring Black and brown Christians into their churches and other institutions in greater numbers, Butler says, "in the political realm white evangelicals supported candidates and positions that were unremittingly conservative and designed to keep African Americans and other ethnic groups out of positions of power."[7]

I was eleven years old at the time of what I knew as "the LA riots." I vaguely remember images of Los Angeles appearing on the TV news and chatter on the radio about Rodney King, but not much more. What was happening halfway across the country seemed to have little relevance to my life.

My friends and family rarely talked about race. But I remember one incident of overt racism, from around that same time. My fifth-grade teacher was taking "prayer requests," an opportunity for students to share their worries and joys with the group, and ask for God's intervention and blessing. One of my classmates, a girl whose home I'd visited many times for sleepovers and birthday parties, raised her hand.

"Pray for my neighborhood," she asked. "It's going downhill. And my dad says, 'If the Blacks move *in*—we're moving *out*!'"

There was awkward silence. The teacher looked uncomfortable, quickly moving on to the next student.

I knew this was wrong, but I said nothing. To speak out of turn was frowned upon, and to openly criticize an adult, unthinkable.

When we did occasionally talk about race in my own home, my

parents had a simple message, rooted in their understanding of humanity and creation: God loved everyone, regardless of their skin color, they said. We were all made in God's image, and we should love everyone, too.

During a conversation one day in my early elementary school years, probably prompted by a coffee table book we had about the trial of the conspirators convicted of assassinating President Lincoln, my mother told me about the Civil War and the horrors of slavery. She described the untold damage to Black families, the tearing apart of husbands and wives and children that would be felt for generations.

"That's the one thing Democrats have right," she said. "They believe in civil rights."

For my parents, who believed that marriage and family were among the most sacred gifts from God, to destroy those bonds was among the greatest evils perpetrated by slavery. Racism was wrong. Slavery was a terrible evil. Those things were pretty clear.

Still, from our vantage point, most of that ugly history seemed to be long in the past. And for all of the explicit messages about God's love for all of his children, we existed in mostly separate spaces from Black and brown people. My hometown of Kansas City is more than one-quarter Black, the birthplace of Negro leagues baseball,[8] with a rich Black history that helped shape the city's legendary jazz and food scenes.[9] But I knew only a handful of people who were not white, none very well. While my parents praised many of the advances toward racial justice of the civil rights movement, they also decried the "forced busing" policies promoted by some liberal community leaders, and what they saw as inadequate public schools, and sent me instead to my private Christian school, where, intentionally or not, I was surrounded almost entirely by white faces of both students and teachers.

The textbooks that I stuffed in my backpack each afternoon

were published primarily by presses based at Pensacola Christian College and Bob Jones University, white Southern evangelical institutions. The curriculum reflected a vision of America filled with Christian families led by strong, godly patriarchs, and settled by Europeans who were uniquely blessed by God and called to establish a great Christian nation.

One typical social studies book from that era for first graders, Heritage Studies for Christian Schools, paints a rosy, uncomplicated picture of a nation founded by Christians who were carrying out God's plans. It glosses over the impact on Native Americans, saying only that "the Indians helped the Pilgrims" and that "the Pilgrims thanked God for His care." Christopher Columbus is depicted in one sketch arriving on the shores of the New World with a team of sailors carrying crosses in their rowboats, as Native Americans look on. "Christopher means Christ-bearer," the caption reads, "God wants us to be Christ-bearers." The pages devoted to the Civil War, which it describes as the "War Between the States," make no mention of slavery, saying only that "the states were divided."[10]

The book, published in 1979 by Bob Jones University Press, based in Greenville, South Carolina, warned that "many families of our nation have forgotten God, their Creator." It urged young readers to "promise to be loyal" to America by pledging allegiance to the flag, adding, "We should promise God that we will be good Christian citizens."[11]

There were images of white children standing in a Christian school classroom, much like my own, reciting their morning pledges to the Christian flag. Like the children in the picture, in my classroom there were *two* flags: the American flag, and the Christian one—which was also red, white, and blue, its large white background overlaid with a small blue rectangle in the upper left corner and a red Latin cross on top.

Each morning, we would stand up, hands over hearts, and pledge our loyalty to both flags, and to "the Bible, God's Holy Word."

"I pledge allegiance to the Christian flag, and to the Savior for whose kingdom it stands," we recited, "One Savior, crucified, risen, and coming again with life and liberty for all who believe."

No one mentioned in those days that Bob Jones University had only begun admitting Black students in 1971, nor that as I sat in my classrooms in the 1980s and 1990s, studying its history and social studies curricula, BJU still prohibited interracial dating and marriage on campus. The university defended that policy in explicitly theological terms, even losing its tax-exempt status after battling with the Internal Revenue Service over the rule for more than a decade.[12] As *Christianity Today* reported, administrators claimed that "God created people differently for a reason." The school finally dropped the interracial dating ban in 2000, a year after I graduated from high school.[13]

I was also unaware that, whatever the intentions of my parents or teachers, Christian schools like mine had been founded in the midst of a larger movement that traced its history back to what became known as "segregation academies." In the aftermath of the Supreme Court's landmark *Brown v. Board of Education* decision in 1954, which required public schools to integrate, many white churches opened private Christian schools that were tax-exempt and often functionally, if not explicitly, segregated.[14] The whiteness of my classroom was like water to a fish; it surrounded me, but I never thought much about it and never imagined any other kind of existence.

For Tyler Burns, growing up in a similar educational environment as a young Black boy in the 1990s, such obliviousness was not possible. Burns, whom I first met on Twitter, grew up in Pensacola, Florida, where he still lives and pastors a church. He's also president of the Witness, a collective that publishes essays and podcasts centered around Black Christian thought.

On Sunday mornings, Burns felt at home in the Black-led multiethnic church his father had helped found. But on school days, he attended a predominantly white Christian academy run by Pensacola Christian College, publisher of Abeka Book,[15] another popular source of Christian school and homeschool curriculum.

"I spent thirteen years in the academy reading Abeka's books," Burns told me,[16] "reading very little about my history, and very little about Black contributions. I started to believe in my heart that Black people in Black churches were the problem."

Burns compared the emotional, energetic worship of his Black Pentecostal tradition to the more stoic style favored by the predominantly white Christians at his school, and began to question himself and his community. Some of the white evangelicals he knew even derided Black Pentecostal expressiveness as a likely symptom of mental illness.

"I thought we were too loud; I thought we weren't intellectual enough," Burns said. "I thought that we didn't care enough about theology, none of which was really the truth."

As he went on to begin college at Pensacola Christian, Burns said it became clear that much of what he was learning was being filtered through a white Christian lens. In one history class, he remembers a professor suggesting that maybe slavery really wasn't so bad.

"[He said] it was a pretty good gig for them; they got free housing and all their meals were taken care of," Burns said.

Burns caught the eye of the only other Black student in the classroom. "We looked at each other like, 'Did he just say that?' I started to wake up to the reality that maybe they didn't have a good view of who we are, and who I am, and what we can contribute."

What Burns heard in his Christian college classroom was in alignment with the history lessons that textbook companies like Abeka were shipping to Christian schools and homeschooling parents across the country and around the world. In a 1998 printing of an Abeka history book for fourth graders, the text devotes extensive discussion to the perspective of Southern slaveholders:

"As they sold more crops, Southern planters bought more land in order to plant more cotton and tobacco," one passage reads. "Who could take care of such large fields? The Southern planter could never *hire* enough people to get his work done. Some people in the South believed that *buying* slaves was the answer. However, only one out of every ten Southerners owned slaves."

The next paragraph described slavery in sanguine terms: "Southern weather was warm and the slaves stayed healthy."[17]

The book's treatment of Native Americans and the role of colonization is equally dishonest. Christopher Columbus—whose list of atrocities includes slavery, kidnapping, and handing over an indigenous woman to a crew member to be beaten and raped[18]—is praised for his "bravery" and described as "a great man because he showed others the way to do something that was supposedly impossible. . . . Columbus' daring deeds started a chain of events that would lead to a new country with freedom for all," the book claims.[19]

The suffering and abuse of Native Americans at the hands of European explorers and colonists is never mentioned, but the book spends a few pages celebrating the missionaries who worked to convert them to Christianity, while dismissing tribal cultures and beliefs: "Because they did not have the Bible, telling them about the one true God, they often offered prayers and sacrifices to the 'god of the sky,' the 'god of the forest,' the 'god of the river,' and many other false gods. Then, white men came from Europe bringing the Bible with them."[20]

In what can only be described as paradigmatic "white Saviorism," the section concludes by stating, "Influenced by the Bible, Indians, like other Americans, would later have the opportunity to enjoy freedom and liberty and play their role in building the country," never addressing the taking of land and the forced migration that befell many indigenous people after the arrival of Europeans.[21]

While disregarding America's original sins, the book is riddled with Christian nationalist themes. In the introduction, titled "One Nation Under God," the author tells her elementary-school readers that "God has blessed America because of the principles (truths) for which America stands" and that in the pages to come, they would "learn how the truths of the Bible made America the greatest nation on the face of the earth."[22]

As I leaf through these old textbooks today, I'm stunned and ashamed at what I naively and uncritically accepted as a young student decades ago. White Christian nationalism was as invisible in that environment, and seemingly as natural, as the air we breathed.

As pollster Robert P. Jones, who grew up in Southern Baptist churches in Texas and Mississippi in the 1970s and 1980s, writes in *White Too Long*, his 2020 book critiquing the deeply embedded racism and nationalism of white American Christianity, it was all too easy to grow up immersed in that world without ever pondering its responsibility for racial oppression.

"Understanding how this could be," Jones writes, "that I and so many of my fellow white Christians were never challenged to face Christianity's deep entanglement with white supremacy—will help explain why we still have such limited capacities to hear black calls for equality."[23]

More than three decades have passed since the Los Angeles uprisings. In the intervening years, as Tara Isabella Burton wrote for *Vox* in 2018, many American churches had begun to make strides toward increasing the diversity of their congregations.[24] "Changes were particularly pronounced in evangelical churches," Burton wrote, "which have historically been racially segregated, and seems to have been spurred, at least in part, by the proliferation of evangelical megachurches."[25] However, she said, the 2016 election, and white evangelicals' alignment with Trump, threatened to diminish or erase any progress made in recent decades.

Those events marked an inflection point for Jemar Tisby, a writer and historian of race and religion. Tisby describes himself as "a poster child of a Black person's experience in the evangelical racial reconciliation movement." Growing up in the Chicago area, Tisby became a Christian in the 1990s through the influence of a white evangelical youth group in the city's northern suburbs, after a "dorky white guy" in his freshman health class befriended him and invited him to church. Tisby was all in, eventually attending Reformed Theological Seminary, an evangelical institution in Jackson, Mississippi. As a Black man in a mostly white conservative Christian world, there were moments of discomfort and tension along the way, Tisby said, like when he found out some classmates were calling him a "liberal" behind his back for wanting to discuss racial issues.

Tisby had been watching Trump's rise warily over the many months before he clinched the Republican nomination, hoping that Republicans would choose someone else from the pool of more than a dozen prominent candidates who were facing off in the 2016 primary.

"It was like watching a train wreck where, over time, more and more professed white Christians were saying, 'Okay, maybe this guy. Maybe Trump, maybe he's the one,'" Tisby said.

Trump had announced his campaign on June 16, 2015, sending an unmistakable message about what his candidacy would represent with his claim that Mexico was sending criminals and "rapists" across the US border. He would later claim that Mexican immigrants were "taking our jobs" and "killing us," at least economically.[26]

Lest there be any doubt about the racism still infecting the country, or the deadly impact of those racist ideas, one day later, the white supremacist Dylann Roof would walk into a historic Black church in Charleston, South Carolina, join a Bible study group for about forty-five minutes, and take out a gun, murdering nine members of the congregation, including the pastor. He, too, would invoke the specter of declining white cultural power, and the rape of white women, claiming, according to an account from a witness who survived, "You rape our women, and you're taking over our country."[27] Though not an evangelical, Roof had apparently drawn inspiration from his white Christian identity, writing in his journal that "Christianity doesn't have to be this weak cowardly religion. There is plenty of evidence to indicate that Christianity can be a warrior's religion."[28]

Soon afterward, I would be hired by NPR to cover the Republican presidential primary. But on that day, I was still in Savannah, Georgia, reporting for a local NPR affiliate. I drove through the night, up the Georgia coast, across the South Carolina line. When I arrived in Charleston early in the morning, the city was quiet and dark, except for the flashing blue lights of police cars. The shooter was still on the loose. As I approached the area around Mother Emanuel AME Church, I noticed a small group of Black residents forming a circle in the warm summer air, taking each other's hands, and saying a prayer. Since they heard of the attack, they told me, they'd been gathering hourly to pray and reeling from yet another act of racist violence targeting their community.[29]

The next year, as Tisby feared, Republican voters chose Trump as their nominee, and then, with the overwhelming support of white evangelicals, he won the November election. Tisby was living in the Mississippi Delta region at the time, in the early stages of a doctoral program at the University of Mississippi, and attending a church that had made some "gestures at racial reconciliation."

He and his friend Tyler Burns were also hosting a podcast focused on Black Christianity distributed by the Witness. The day after the 2016 election, their producer asked Tisby how he was feeling.

"I specifically said, 'I don't feel safe going to my white evangelical church this Sunday,'" he said. "'Because it's clear that this church I have been going to, they clearly don't understand my reality if they are celebrating the election of Trump.'"

The overwhelming white evangelical support for Trump weighed heavily on Tisby and Burns, and many others. In 2018, the *New York Times* reported on what it described as a "quiet exodus" of Black Christians out of white evangelical churches.[30] Some had joined those congregations as a result of racial reconciliation efforts, but now, many were feeling a profound sense of alienation as they watched their communities embrace Trump and at least tolerate his racist rhetoric. Believing it was important for Black Christians not to leave white evangelicalism quietly, but to let their reasons be known, they coined the social media hashtag #LeaveLoud, asking Black evangelicals to vote with their feet and share their departures publicly. They began collecting stories in the form of podcasts and essays, and curating them on the Witness website.[31]

The racial and political divisions within evangelicalism appear to have deepened in recent years. An analysis in 2021 by the Pew Research Center concluded that Trump had strengthened his support among white evangelicals during his time in office, and that the movement was increasingly identified with him in the minds of many Americans.

"Between 2016 and 2020, White Americans with warm views toward Trump were far more likely than those with less favorable views of the former president to begin identifying as born-again/evangelical Protestants, perhaps reflecting the strong association between

Trump's political movement and the evangelical religious label," the survey found.[32] And a 2022 survey by Pew found that white evangelicals were far more likely than their Black Protestant counterparts to hold views associated with Christian nationalism, despite often holding similar theological beliefs.[33]

Tisby sees a tipping point for evangelicalism, as many conservative white churches intensify their alignment with Republican politics.

"What I see happening now and continuing to happen is a sorting in the church of people like me who are Black or people of color, leaving these churches and these spaces and trying to find new spaces or form new ones," Tisby told me.[34] "It's a real rupture. Issues that were always there are being surfaced, and people are declaring their allegiances in a more overt way."

Those tensions were on full display in the reaction from Grove City College, an evangelical institution in Pennsylvania, to a chapel sermon Tisby had given in 2020 focused on race.[35] In the months after the police killing of George Floyd in Minneapolis, Tisby preached about the complicity of the American church in racial injustice, prompting complaints from some parents and former students.[36] In a petition the next year, they denounced Tisby for promoting what they described as critical race theory and demanded that the school's diversity council be disbanded.[37] Grove City's board of trustees ultimately released a report, finding that "most of those in GCC leadership with whom we spoke . . . allow that, in hindsight, inviting Mr. Tisby to speak in chapel was a mistake."[38]

In a lengthy open letter responding in detail to the board's report, Tisby noted, "It is, perhaps, instructive that you use the word 'conservative' 19 times in the report, but the word 'Christian' is used only 10 times." In his conclusion, Tisby writes, "If you take a stand for racial justice and reject this report, I cannot promise you more money or more students. I cannot say that you will not suffer setbacks and lose standing with certain people. I can promise that as you pursue justice you will get more of Jesus."[39]

Meanwhile, the Leave Loud campaign, along with other high-profile departures from white evangelicalism, was catching the attention of some evangelical institutional leaders, who raised alarms about the "woke" ideology they said the movement exemplified.[40] A March 2021 piece published by Breakpoint, a project of the Colson Center for Christian Worldview (founded by the late Chuck Colson, the former Nixon aide who served seven months in federal prison for his role in the Watergate scandal), warned against "leaving over silly disputes." The effort, the authors argued, "is part of an I'm-leaving-church-and-please-watch-me-leave movement. Being noisy about joining the 'exvangelicalism' movement is not only a popular thing to do, it's a way to be popular."[41]

But Black Christians like Burns and Tisby, who'd spent many years of their lives working and worshiping with white evangelicals, insist their departures are a call to repentance and reform, not a rebellion.

"'Leave Loud' is not a defiant movement; it's a movement of love," Burns said. "We love the church enough to be honest about what we're experiencing. But if they refuse to repent, then you should leave those spaces and find spaces that are healthy for you."

Many Black Christians who "Leave Loud" from white evangelicalism would not call themselves exvangelicals, Tisby said. Like "evangelical," "exvangelical" is a term that often carries political and even racial connotations that don't describe Tisby, whatever theological similarities may exist between himself and his white counterparts.

"There's a sense in which we were never evangelical because of race, so the hashtag and movement is a very white one," Tisby said.

"I think there are a lot of people who call themselves 'exvangelicals' who have also erased the Black church. Because what they're essentially saying is, the only way to be Christian is the way white evangelicals have been Christians, and I don't want any part of that, without ever deeply considering Black Christians."

People in Tisby's circles tend to talk about "decolonizing" Christianity, he told me, rather than deconstructing it, or "sorting out what is white and what is Christian."

Burns has a similar caution for white exvangelicals. As they deconstruct their faith, he said, they should engage with the perspectives of Black Christian thinkers. He's observed many white exvangelicals turning for guidance to progressive theologians, who are primarily white men.

"It's kind of replacing one problem for another, the problem of whiteness at the center," he said. "Maybe we need a little bit more openness to be honest about are we actually giving Black churches and Black leaders and people of color who are leaders a chance?"

For many white Americans, the death of George Floyd, documented in all of its cruel and excruciating detail by a Black teenage girl with her cell phone camera and viewed by countless Americans during some of the most despondent early months of the coronavirus pandemic, forced a new recognition of the realities of being Black in the United States.[42]

Multiracial groups of protesters took to the streets in cities across the country, demanding renewed attention to police accountability and racial equity. Some white evangelicals were among them. Anthea Butler wrote that she "watched with trepidation and a sliver of hope as evangelicals marched on a Sunday in Washington, D.C., in support of Black Lives Matter"[43] in the days after Floyd's death.[44]

Even Franklin Graham issued a statement that suggested an

evolving understanding of the issue. In a Facebook post several years earlier responding to the police killing of Michael Brown, a Black teenager in Ferguson, Missouri, Graham had claimed that "most police shootings can be avoided. It comes down to respect for authority and obedience," prompting criticism from progressive evangelical leaders.[45]

But in May 2020, confronted with the horrific images of Floyd's death, Graham said the footage of then officer Derek Chauvin kneeling on Floyd's neck had left Graham "sick to my stomach" and called Chauvin's actions "inexcusable." (He went on to emphasize that "this is not the story of every police department.")[46] Later that year, Graham called for bail to be denied to Chauvin. While expressing opposition to "defunding" police departments, Graham wrote on his Facebook page in October 2020 that the $1 million bond set by a judge was too low, and that Chauvin "obviously shouldn't be walking free."

Malcolm Foley, a pastor of a multiethnic congregation in Waco, Texas, said George Floyd's murder was an event that forced some white Christians to pay closer attention.

"It was the first time that a lot of people witnessed a lynching," Foley said. "People are starting to recognize the stakes of their alignment. People are understanding now that the stakes are really life and death."

In this environment, the boundaries of those alignments are also becoming starker. In late 2021, Foley's congregation voted to leave the Presbyterian Church in America, a mostly white, conservative denomination that subscribes to evangelical theology. The departure came after clashes with denominational officials around issues including some of Foley's sermons about Floyd's death and the insurrection staged by extremist Trump supporters at the US Capitol on January 6, 2021.

The month after Floyd was killed, the influential evangelical magazine *Christianity Today* began a twenty-part series reflecting on racial issues in the church.[47] It concluded with an essay by Cheryl J. Sanders, a pastor and Howard University professor of Christian ethics. She exhorted evangelicals to finally confront structural racism in their midst.

"It is time for the white church to renounce unequivocally the horrific legacy of racial resentment represented by gun-toting Christian nationalists and cross-burning Christian terrorists," Sanders wrote. "Repent, lament, and put on a new garment, the white linen of justice."[48]

Promises to change are not new. They've emerged again and again from white Christian leaders, in the aftermath of deadly violence against Black people, often at the hands of white Christians.[49]

But the urgency and unrelenting nature of the problem is painfully clear. In May 2022, the weekend before Tyler Burns and I were scheduled to speak by phone about the Leave Loud movement, another white supremacist carried out yet another murderous attack on Black people. Fearful of diversity and motivated by racist conspiracy theories, the young white man shot up a grocery store in Buffalo, New York, killing ten Black people. In his manifesto, the shooter discussed his belief in replacement theory—a racist and antisemitic conspiracy theory that imagines a coordinated effort to replace white people with people of color. While he wrote that he did not consider himself a Christian, the shooter described himself as believing in and trying to practice "many Christian values."[50]

Burns believes evangelicalism as a movement has failed to offer effective guidance to young people who become enamored with racist ideas they're encountering online, and too often from pastors who preach about "taking back the country" for Christ.

"The white evangelical church has basically punted on race and justice," Burns said. "Until white evangelicals as a whole come up with a coherent strategy to weed out racist and white supremacist and white nationalist ideals, not only from its churches but from its theology, I don't know what substantive change we're actually going to see."

That will require white evangelicals to rethink everything from their church power structures to their theology, Burns said, creating more space for Black people to lead and shape the direction and priorities of their churches.

Short of that, Burns thinks the best thing Black Christians can do is simply to leave white evangelical churches and organizations and cultivate their own spaces for spiritual development. But he holds out hope for the redemption of his white sisters and brothers.

"My hope has always been that white evangelicalism as a movement will repent and commit itself to deconstructing and reconstructing itself," Burns said. "And then participate in the repair of communities it's harmed."

Like the pastor that he is, Burns summons the most important imagery of his faith to call for a spiritual and moral rebirth for much of white Christianity.

"For there to be a resurrection, something has to die," Burns said.

He tries to hold out hope that white evangelicalism itself could be born again.

# 9

# WHOM DOES JESUS LOVE?

Closer to home, one of my own classmates was trying to make sense of what the evangelical world had to say about *his* identity. Daniel Doss and I met at around five years old when our parents enrolled us in the Christian school where we learned to read and write together, before eventually moving a few strides across campus to the adjoining junior high and high school. In those days, Daniel was a wonderfully quirky kid obsessed with magic tricks and trivia about roller coasters, and a masterful pianist who often accompanied our choirs.

He was also quiet and shy, and when we reconnected recently he told me he was surprised that I remembered those details about him.

"I always felt like a bit of an outsider," Daniel said.[1] "I generally thought that I kept to myself a lot, and that I was a very private person, and that grew into me not sharing a lot about myself in high school."

But for years, he told me, he couldn't put his finger on what it was that made him feel different. It dawned on him suddenly, in his early teens, in what he describes as "almost a light bulb moment." He was at a family function, eating a meal, when something clicked into place in his mind—a thought that seemed so horrible, he stopped eating.

"The thought of me being gay actually made me sick to my stomach," Daniel said. "It just came onto me, this sudden overwhelming pins-and-needles feeling. Because I knew what that meant to my family, to my church, to the circle that I grew up in."

Overcome with nausea, he had to leave the table and go lie down.

Across town, at roughly the same time, I was having my own epiphany.

I'd often babysit my three younger siblings while my parents went out for a date night or a fundraiser for my school. They enjoyed the low-cost childcare, and I enjoyed the freedom of a night without supervision. I could watch whatever I wanted on TV and eat the fruit snacks and oatmeal cookies intended for our school lunches. After everyone else was in bed, I usually spent those evenings watching fairly tame stuff—news shows such as ABC's *20/20* with Barbara Walters, or the network's TGIF lineup of Friday-night sitcoms: *Family Matters, Boy Meets World,* and even *Step by Step,* which my parents mildly disapproved of because of its focus on a blended family formed by the marriage of a couple that included a divorcé.

One evening, as the TV droned in the background after I'd shouted at my younger siblings to "GO to BED!" for the last time, the phone rang. It was Grandpa, calling the house unexpectedly. Holding the beige handset for the landline phone on our kitchen wall, I told him my parents weren't home. He quickly said goodbye.

Moments later, the phone rang again.

"I'm sorry I was abrupt," Grandpa said, haltingly.

I didn't understand. It wasn't as if we normally spent time talking on the phone. Besides major holidays, I really only saw him on a handful of special occasions when he'd take me to the opera or the ballet or a museum exhibit. When I was younger and sick in bed with asthma, he'd come over with a small present once or twice, art supplies or a game to entertain me. But I had no expectation of a long heart-to-heart over the phone that night.

"When you're sixteen, I'll be able to spend time with you," he said.

"What do you mean?" I asked. "We spend time with you."

His voice sounded odd.

"Your parents don't want me to see much of you until you're older."

He apologized for not being around more, and said goodbye again.

I stood for a moment, looking at the phone. None of this made sense. I wanted to ask my parents about it immediately. But this was the early 1990s, and I could only reach my dad on his pager. When he called back, I told him what had happened and asked what it meant. He said he would explain when they got home.

I waited, anxiously. Something important, but ambiguous, felt imminent.

Later that night, my parents sat me down on their bed. They told me they were sorry about what they had to tell me.

"Your grandfather is a homosexual," my dad said simply.

I wasn't sure what I was supposed to say, or how I was supposed to feel.

As I reflected on this revelation, suddenly a lot of things made sense: the strained relationship with my family; the "friend" who'd lived with Grandpa for years now and sometimes showed up at family events; his large circle of friends in Kansas City's arts scene. It all felt very strange and unexpected and obvious.

My parents told me that they'd wanted to protect my siblings and me. They didn't want to "normalize" all of that during our formative years, and they wanted to make sure we understood what was right and wrong. We should primarily spend time with Grandpa on their turf, they'd decided. He could sometimes take us places like the theater but only alone, not with his partner. That's what Grandpa had been referring to in that strange phone call.

"Please don't talk to your siblings about this," my parents stressed. "We didn't want you to know this, and we don't want them to know until they're ready."

I promised to keep it a secret.

A few years later, after a family event, one of my younger sisters began asking me questions about Grandpa's "roommate." She even asked, point-blank, if I thought he might be gay.

I found myself caught irreconcilably between two commandments: "Honor Thy Father and Thy Mother" and "Thou Shalt Not Lie." The former seemed the least likely to disturb the family peace, so I broke the latter.

"I don't know," I said. "Maybe you should ask Mom and Dad."

Everything I knew about gay people had been filtered through the evangelical community's literal interpretation of the Bible, and the teaching that homosexuality was an "abomination" that violated God's natural order for creation. God had made Adam and Eve for each other, and such relationships were a perversion of that and a rebellion against God's design.

This was repeated in sermons or Bible studies on the subject, by pastors and teachers who would quote from passages including Romans 1, where Paul warns about what he describes as "shameful lusts":

"Even their women exchanged natural sexual relations for unnatural ones. In the same way the men also abandoned natural relations with women and were inflamed with lust for one another. Men committed shameful acts with other men, and received in themselves the due penalty for their error."[2]

Within the constraints of our worldview at the time, it was hard not to read that passage and conclude that God was very angry at my grandfather. At the same time, as I watched the debate over same-sex marriage intensify during my teenage years, I sometimes struggled to understand why the conservative people I knew who often spoke of their distrust of government control were so concerned about preventing gay people from getting married. It felt like a private matter, and it was hard to see who would be harmed.

I felt guilty for questioning that; after all, if we knew with certainty the Truth about what God intended, and we had an opportunity to build our nation's laws around God's Truth, shouldn't we?

For my classmate Daniel, the growing realization that he was gay, and the understanding of what that would mean to his family and community, was a secret he carried alone. He had no one to talk to about it, and very little information.

In the room in his parents' house where Daniel spent most of his time, there was a giant bookcase, filled with books from his father's Bible college days.

"That's the room my piano was in, that's the room where I'd practice magic," he said.

One day, a title caught his eye: *The Unhappy Gays.*

Daniel slipped it off the shelf, looking around to make sure no one in the family saw what he was reading. He flipped through the pages. The author painted a dark picture of life as a gay man—one of loneliness, shallow and temporary sexual entanglements, social rejection by the straight world, broken family relationships, and an early death.

"It's the only thing that I had around me that even broached the subject of these feelings that I had," Daniel said. "And to understand that not only is it a sin but if I were to continue as a gay man, my life would be ended early—it's brutal. It's absolutely horrible."

The book had been published before the AIDS crisis, in 1978, by Tim LaHaye, a prominent and prolific evangelical writer best known today as the coauthor of the apocalyptic *Left Behind* novels, which spun off into a movie in 2000 starring the actor Kirk Cameron. LaHaye died in 2016, after a long career that also included cofounding the Council for National Policy, a secretive conservative group whose members over the years have included Wayne LaPierre of the National Rifle Association, Focus on the Family founder Dr. James Dobson, and another cofounder, Paul Weyrich, who also helped start the Heritage Foundation—an influential, Washington, DC–based, conservative think tank.[3]

As the title suggests, the book is riddled from cover to cover with sweeping generalizations, bizarre conspiracy theories about a supposed "international network of homosexuals [that] has been working its way into governments for years,"[4] and dire predictions about the influence of homosexuality on individuals and American culture at large. LaHaye traffics in dangerous tropes, claiming that gay people engage in the "recruitment of children and young people into homosexuality"[5] and many other slurs not worth repeating.

He dismisses the idea that LGBTQ+ people could also be Christians, warning against anyone who claims to be a believer but "persistently clings to this perverted lifestyle" and claiming that "all such cases with which I am familiar eventually came to an untimely and tragic end."[6] Non-Christian gays and lesbians aren't spared, either; in earlier pages, LaHaye warns that they are likely to either "spend the last two decades of life alone and empty" after a series of "transitory" relationships or "experience illness as they grow older and probably have a shorter life span."[7]

In 2013, as my grandfather was approaching his nineties, I asked him to sit down with me for an interview about his life. While his partner of more than twenty-five years drifted in and out of the room, Grandpa and I sat on his airy, screened-in porch at a small table.

I didn't know how many more years we'd have with him, and there were many things I'd wanted to ask him about but never knew how to broach. I knew Grandpa loved me, but I found him intimidating—intensely accomplished and intensely aware of that fact, with the often formal demeanor of a Greatest Generation New Englander. Grandpa had high expectations and could be difficult to please. I still hadn't forgotten the time he came to my voice recital in high school, sat politely through the performance, and afterward asked pointedly, "Have you learned about diaphragmatic breathing?"

But he was the only grandparent I'd known for most of my life, and we'd been little more than acquaintances for many of those years. By this point, in my early thirties, I'd years ago come to accept who my grandpa was, as well as his unique journey. But I wanted to know more about him and our family—to fill in some of the gaps from my childhood and all the years of enforced emotional distance.

So for a moment, I stepped into the role that made me feel most comfortable getting personal and asking probing questions: a reporter, microphone in hand. I set my small digital recorder on the table between us.

We talked about his childhood in Massachusetts, his military service, his medical studies at Harvard during World War II, his marriage to my grandmother, and her death from breast cancer in 1984. By all accounts, they had a close and supportive relationship and deeply loved each other—but knowing what I now knew, I couldn't help but wonder if something had been missing, for either of them.

"Do you think your relationship with her was different because you were gay?" I asked cautiously, after about forty minutes of mostly biographical questions.

"I don't know," Grandpa said. He seemed to be searching for the right words.

I jumped in. "I've always gotten the impression that you guys were really good friends."

"We were," he said. "Best friends."

They raised three children together, including my father, during a marriage that lasted more than three decades. But another truth had been submerged all that time. I asked Grandpa how he understood himself as a young man, born in 1924, a couple of years after Harvard—his eventual alma mater—had engaged in a now-infamous attempt to purge its campus of gay men.[8] A time when gay relationships were treated as a crime.

"You could be put in jail," he said. "There was a lot of oppression."

Much like Daniel decades later, my grandpa grew up in a world where his sexuality—if he'd even been able to articulate it—would have been seen as unacceptable.

"I didn't have a name for it. You weren't allowed to in those days," he said. "I knew I wasn't quite the same."

Grandpa said he'd "tried to be" attracted to girls, and went on at least one date in high school. But mostly, he channeled his energies into his studies.

"I probably wouldn't have gotten into Harvard if I'd dated much," he said with a laugh. "You transform things in your mind into work, and other activities. And you deny it."

Daniel told me he feels that keeping his sexuality a secret for so long, and being cut off from such an important part of his inner self during important developmental stages, set him back at least a decade in the process of becoming a fully formed adult.

"I wasn't able to explore until I got outside of the bubble," he said. "That set me back, for personal development and understanding how the world works. None of that was taught in high school—we were guarded against the world all the time."

After graduation, he threw himself into his musical studies, attending a local community college in Kansas City and then the conservatory at a state university, learning composition, conducting, and musical theory. He got a job in a restaurant, and for the first time in his life, found himself surrounded, and accepted, by people who had not been raised in the evangelical world. After years of being told to be on guard against outside "worldly" influences, it felt like a revelation and a relief.

"We were told how 'the world' is an evil place, and you have to stay out of it," Daniel said. "I found the opposite to be true. I found that 'the world' was a much more loving place, and much more comfortable to be a part of than a strict religious bubble."

Although he wouldn't work up the courage to begin a relationship with a man for several more years, Daniel was quietly developing a growing understanding of who he was, even as he continued to work as a pianist at his family's church. He was building a career as a professional freelance musician, and he was grateful for the steady work.

But one Sunday, in the mid-2000s, as the debate over marriage equality was raging across the country, the pastor began to preach a sermon that made Daniel feel deeply out of place from behind the piano.

"God intended marriage to be between a man and a woman!" the pastor declared.

Daniel thought about the gay people who'd become his friends over the past several years. He thought about how their lives would be affected by the outcome of this debate.

"Not only did the pastor say those words but the way that the other members of the congregation responded, I think that was more upsetting to me than hearing it from the pastor," he said.

As he looked around the sanctuary, his fellow church members were nodding enthusiastically and calling out, "Amen!"

He felt alone.

"I remember wanting to stand up and walk out of the church and never look back," he said. "And in a lot of ways I did."

Daniel didn't want to embarrass or hurt his parents and siblings. They're still close, and often spend time together, although they never speak about his sexuality or his romantic life, he told me.

So for the moment, Daniel stayed put. But he'd been having doubts about his religious beliefs for a while, and after that service, he decided he'd finally had enough.

"I resigned from my position as church pianist," he said. "And I never looked back."

For young LGBTQ+ people growing up in evangelical homes, coming out to their families is often as unthinkable as it was to my grandfather growing up in the 1930s. I have many friends who've come out as adults, but to announce such a secret to your parents or pastor would have carried dire consequences for many young evangelicals still living under their parents' roofs.

The 2021 documentary *Pray Away,* whose release I covered for NPR, describes the fallout from the "ex-gay" movement and conversion therapy, a discredited and harmful treatment promoted with the promise that LGBTQ+ people could—and must—change if they wanted to be right with God and in fellowship with their communities. The documentarian Kristine Stolakis told me she was inspired to make the film by the tragic story of her uncle, who'd been subjected to conversion therapy after coming out as trans and who suffered the aftereffects of that experience throughout his life.

"I really expected to be furious at people who had led this movement," Stolakis said. "But the overwhelming feeling that I had was sadness, actually. I think it was because of most of the people's good intentions. I don't think this is a movement of a few bad apples. It's a movement that's born out of a larger culture of homophobia and transphobia that still persists in the majority of Christian churches today."[9]

That made me think about my own parents, and parents like Daniel's. How do you weigh someone's "good intentions" against the pain their actions cause? And when is it okay to be furious?

For my friend, the writer Jeff Chu, being gay meant leaving evangelical churches, but not leaving the church altogether. Chu's 2013 book, *Does Jesus Really Love Me?*,[10] chronicled his search for a deeper understanding of what it could mean to be both gay and a Christian.

For Jeff, that journey has included trying to balance loving his parents, conservative Southern Baptists who disapprove of his marriage to his husband, with a career that's been largely centered around his ongoing relationship with Christianity. A close friend of the late Rachel Held Evans, who died suddenly in 2019 at age thirty-seven, Jeff has been among a cohort of younger progressive former evangelicals who write and speak about their continued quest to follow the teachings of Jesus while discarding much of the baggage of white evangelicalism.

But there's not always a linear path for discarding that baggage, and many exvangelicals retain close ties to people they love, who now see them as suspect, sinful, a cause for "fervent prayer"[11] and great concern. Jeff's parents are still conservative Southern Baptists. Like Daniel, he feels out of place and unwelcome in their church.

"It's very tough for me to show up and hear the sermons and participate in the worship service that doesn't recognize a big part of my humanity," he said.

They get by through a series of uncomfortable compromises. When he was accepted to Princeton's seminary, Jeff said his father made it clear that he "did not and still does not believe that a theologically sound seminary would accept me as a student." But when Jeff graduated, his parents came—on the condition that they would not have to interact with his husband, Tristan.

"So here I am, walking down the aisle at my graduation from seminary, and my parents are on one side of the chapel, and my husband is on the other," he said. "I think the most Christ-like person in that picture was Tristan. Because he said, 'Go be with your parents. I'll be here when you're finished.'"

I asked Jeff why he and his husband put up with it and why he still wants to maintain a relationship with his parents, despite their behavior. Ironically, perhaps, he said it's part of his understanding of how to live as a Christian.

"I am never going to cut them off," he said. "They can choose to cut me off if they believe that their faith calls them to. But I'm going to show up with as whole of a heart as I can bring, and love them as best I know how."

Make no mistake—alongside that love, there is anger.

"I am not an evangelical in large part because there's no room in most of American evangelicalism for queer people," he said. "I'm angry about that. I'm angry and sad for the kids that are still in evangelical churches who are being told they can't be themselves. But I'm not bitter towards those evangelicals who have deep convictions and are trying to do the best they know how."

Those evangelicals—who believe their only viable theological option is to view homosexuality as incompatible with their Christian faith—are a group David Gushee has been trying to reach for years. He dedicated his book *Changing Our Mind,* first published in 2014, to "LGBTQ Christians who still love a church that has not loved them."[12]

As a Christian ethics professor at Mercer University in Georgia, and a former Southern Baptist, Gushee said he was seeing students dealing with rejection from their families and churches because of their sexuality or gender identity. In the book, he makes theological and academic arguments for the inclusion of LGBTQ+ Christians.

"I'm enough of a student of history to know that Christianity has been articulated and practiced in a nearly infinite variety of ways," Gushee told me, "and that some of them are healthier than others."[13]

Gushee delves into the ancient Greek to analyze biblical texts; discusses the ways Christians who've appealed to biblical authority in the past have nonetheless often failed to confront great moral evils, including slavery and Nazism; and argues that the time has come for change in evangelical churches.

As a professor teaching undergraduate and seminary students for more than a dozen years, Gushee also sees young people leaving evangelicalism out of concern for their LGBTQ+ friends who are deeply hurt after they're forced out of ministries or excluded in other ways. According to a Public Religion Research Institute survey from 2016, nearly one in three adults who'd disaffiliated with the faith of their childhood cited their religion's treatment of gay and lesbian people as a significant reason for their departure.[14]

"The losses to evangelicalism are definitely not just the LGBTQ kids themselves," Gushee said. "It's everybody who feels sufficient loyalty and solidarity, that 'if you did it to them, you did it to me; I'm out of here.' I admire that kind of empathy."

Gushee points to some famous words of Jesus: "[A] good tree bears good fruit, but a bad tree bears bad fruit." He sees the pain and division surrounding the issue as a sign that the evangelical church needs to reexamine itself.[15]

"This teaching bears constant bad fruit," Gushee said. "It constantly hurts people. It divides up families. It creates alienation."

For many gay Christians, forming a "chosen family" helps to

fill in the gaps left by biological family members. Matthias Roberts, who hosts the podcast *Queerology* about the intersections of faith and queer sexuality, grew up evangelical and also has struggled to find acceptance from his deeply religious parents.[16] In 2020, Roberts said in an interview with public radio station KNKX that his parents had threatened to cut off their relationship because of his sexual orientation. Roberts said that experience is "incredibly common" for LGBTQ+ people, pushing many to form alternative support networks.

"A lot of people have had their families completely disown them, especially people in faith communities," he said. "So queer people have to find other ways to get that emotional fulfillment that families are supposed to be bringing."

For Roberts, his "chosen family" has taken the shape of practicing yoga at a studio run by the spouse of an Episcopal priest, who "quickly became parental figures" to him.[17] For others, like my friends Jeff and Daniel, it's meant maintaining a complicated connection to the families that they love, however tenuous that connection may sometimes seem, while also cultivating meaningful relationships outside their families.

Eventually, my support for my grandfather's "lifestyle" became an ongoing source of tension between my parents and me. One Christmas years ago, in a tearful conversation in the family room of the home where I'd spent much of my childhood, I worked up the courage to tell them how I really felt—that I supported gay rights, and that I regretted being kept away from my grandfather all those years. My mother told me I was condoning "apostasy," a nice theological way of saying you're probably going to Hell, and the conversation devolved from there.

Several years ago, she emailed me a Facebook post from a Christian writer celebrating the news that a lesbian coming-out scene had been pulled from a *Jurassic Park* movie.[18] The post advised parents to protect their children from the "homosexual lifestyle." After years of fraught and fruitless conversations, I often bite my tongue or ignore these kinds of messages. But this time, I decided I couldn't let it go—I needed to say something. I composed a response, trying to put it into words that I hoped would resonate with her:

> *Mom,*
>
> *I have to tell you we are not on the same page about LGBT issues (I'd kind of assumed you realized that already to be honest). I understand your theological position very well, and I've never wanted to offend you with mine. But after a lot of thought and prayer about this I long ago came to a different set of convictions. I didn't do that because I wanted to hurt you, but because my conscience required it. I'm close to many gay and lesbian people, some of whom I believe are sincere Christians and who've been hurt by the church but have held on to Jesus anyway. I love and admire them and would just ask you to respect that we have different ideas here.*
>
> *I love you and you're my mom regardless of our differences.*
>
> *Sarah*

She responded, in part:

> *Yes, Sarah, I'm aware of our differences, and I want to agreeably disagree. I just think it would be good for you to read opinions that do not support your own, that challenge your rationale.*
>
> *Teachableness has never been your strong point. I challenge*

*you to read the Bible through from Genesis to Revelation every
other year or yearly.*

*The biggest difference in what we believe is how we
define and live out our "love" for homosexuals. Love does not
affirm or support behaviors or attitudes or agendas that are
detrimental to the well-being of an individual or society. The
greatest issue is their eternal souls.[19]*

It was a long message, with references to Romans 1 and other
Scriptures. Like millions of other evangelicals, she believes that
God designed the world in a particular way—that a family, led by a
man married to a woman, is the ideal for human thriving, and that
anything short of that is less than God's best for humanity, and
worthy of God's judgment.

"It's important to give your homosexual friends both friendship
and truth," my mom wrote. "To do anything less, to confuse right
and wrong, is to cause them to stumble. Friends encourage what is
good."

We told each other we loved each other, and she offered not to
send me any more messages about the subject.

Admittedly, there was a time when I, too, would have said I was
praying for God to change my grandpa, that I believed he was living
a sinful lifestyle. For me, and other exvangelicals who've held such
beliefs for a time, there's often a sense of shame and regret, as we
come to terms with the harm we participated in or perpetuated.

For Chrissy Stroop, a writer who helped popularize the exvangelical hashtag and has led efforts on social media to call out abuse
in Christian schools and churches, that awareness carries a particularly complex set of feelings. She recalls struggling, as a young

evangelical in high school and college, with the feeling that she must "insist that being gay is a sin."[20]

Now in her early forties, Chrissy came out as a trans woman in 2019. She leans toward atheism, and she's no longer concerned with trying to harmonize her faith with her queer identity.

"I look back and I cringe thinking about some of the conversations I had with certain LGBT folks," Chrissy told me. "I was still desperately trying to hold on to [my beliefs] because my whole childhood and identity were wrapped up in there. . . . I feel really bad about certain things that I said in the past and hope that I didn't do too much harm to too many people."

I'm grateful that my own change of heart came before it was too late to know my grandfather. By my early twenties, as I'd learned about the Bible and church history as I studied them in college, it was becoming more difficult to defend biblical literalism. And I began to realize: I didn't want to. Like Daniel, I had many doubts. And like Chrissy, I was tired of trying to hold on to beliefs that felt harmful.

Ultimately, for me, it came down to love: love for my grandfather, and for the LGBTQ+ friends and colleagues I'd begun to meet as I discovered the world outside of what Daniel calls the "bubble."

Years later, in my late thirties, Grandpa would return that love and acceptance. After I'd finally worked up the courage to tell my parents that my Christian college sweetheart and I had decided to end our marriage, a handwritten letter arrived in the mail. Grandpa knew that this news had not gone over well, and that I was struggling.

"Be sure of our support," he scrawled in his familiar script, getting shakier in his midnineties. "You are mature and smart people. I'm sure you gave this long and careful thought. I am in strong support of you whatever you decide is in your best interest."

He closed the letter: "Stay strong and forgive the unsteady handwriting."

A couple of months later, Grandpa emailed to check in and again express his support. His text was uncharacteristically dotted with several errors, but the message was clear. He said he regretted that he hadn't been able to be more involved in shaping the early years of my life, but that even so I'd "done well," and that he was proud of me.

"Keep it up and follow your own basic best instincts," Grandpa wrote. "I am always here for you."

I can still quote many of the Bible verses—in both the Old and New Testaments—that evangelical Christians have used to argue that being gay is a sin and a perversion, and that marriage is only for heterosexuals. I've wondered if liberal Christians have done themselves a disservice by seeming to gloss over these inconvenient passages at times and over the fact that Christian marriage has traditionally been understood as the union of a man and woman.

There is much to say about the limitations of a tradition that, for example, once treated women as property[21]—and the ways the institution already has evolved over time. There's also a conversation to be had about the variety of cultural understandings of human sexuality, and the ways that the writers of the Bible were limited by their cultural contexts; or the range of ways that Christians over the centuries—and Jews, who gave us half of our Bible after all—have thought about the meaning and purpose of Scripture. I could talk about the evolution of my own view of the Bible, or the views of thoughtful theologians like Gushee who've articulated an affirming and inclusive Christian view of homosexuality.

Moreover, I could talk about the many passages—from blithe references to slavery and genocide, to admonitions against women braiding their hair or wearing gold jewelry—that those who claim to take the Bible literally, and see it as an inerrant and absolute guide for life, also gloss over. Not to mention the passages that some choose to focus on instead.

But those are well-worn conversations for anyone who's spent time in proximity to the evangelical world. Many of us who've left have had these conversations many times. We've prayed and cried until the backs of our eyes were heavy and hot, pleading with God for clarity and family members for understanding. These conversations often feel like tilling rocky ground: everyone walks away bleeding a little, and in the end, there's still no fertile soil to be found.

# 10

# A VIRTUOUS WOMAN

If you *were* attracted to members of the opposite sex, there was still plenty to worry about, and plenty of sin to avoid. Particularly if you were a girl.

My Christian school's dress code for boys was straightforward: slacks and collared shirts, clean-cut hair. For girls, there were more rules: dresses or skirts only—no pants of any kind; no cleavage; straps must be at least one inch thick; hemline at or below the knee. If there was any question about skirt length, a teacher would ask the girl to kneel on the ground and prove that her skirt could touch the floor.

Hearing about this ritual, one of my friends from church with slightly more permissive—or at least slightly less well-off—parents who sent her to public school, asked me, aghast, "Do they make you kneel all the time to pray?"

"Of course not," I said, defensive. We weren't *that* extreme.

I was never asked to kneel. But later there were rumors, when some of us alumni reconnected in a Facebook group about ten years after graduation, about at least one teenage girl being sent to the principal's office for repeated dress code violations. As someone told the story, her skirt fell short and her punishment was to receive "swats," as they were called, from one of the wooden paddles that were kept around the school. The story may have been apocryphal, the product of someone's fantasy. Or, it may have been the product of someone's fantasy—and also true. Corporal punishment was certainly a part of the culture of the school and our larger conservative Christian community used to enforce all sorts of rules, and there's no reason to think the dress code wasn't one of them.

Modest dress was seen as an expression of, and way of preserving, purity of mind and thought. Girls were told to save our bodies for our husbands and reminded in countless ways that as young women, we had a special responsibility not to lead men into temptation. That responsibility began as soon as we became sexually attractive to boys and men.

In *Why Wait?*, the 1987 precursor to what eventually became a much larger genre of evangelical books promoting abstinence until marriage, the prominent evangelical writer Josh McDowell and coauthor Dick Day had complained that "the dress of many girls and women screams of sensuality. . . . Most teenage girls, including Christians, think nothing of wearing the latest provocative fashions." As a remedy, parents were to "educate their daughters to understand the effect their dress can have on men."[1]

A decade later, in *I Kissed Dating Goodbye,* a book that would sell more than a million copies and quickly become the most emblematic text of the evangelical purity movement, writer Joshua Harris had similar advice for young women: "Your job is to keep your brothers from being led astray." Though Harris claims he does not "want to dictate" to girls and women how they should dress, and acknowledges that men have a responsibility to control themselves, he adds, "You can help by refusing to wear clothing designed to attract attention to your body." Harris, himself in his early twenties at the time of the book's writing and publication, goes on to praise a friend who had made a practice of asking her father to "evaluate every outfit she buys" for modesty. "There have been many times her dad has asked her to return items," he writes. "But she doesn't complain, even in the summer, when it seems impossible to find a modest pair of shorts!"[2]

Our responsibility to protect men from lusting after our bodies included everyone—even, as we found out, our high school teachers.

Instead of homeroom in high school, we started our days in devotion groups. These small groups, of about a dozen students or so, were divided by gender and assigned to one teacher, who led us in morning prayers and often read from the Bible to set the tone for our days. Many mornings, while the teacher took prayer requests from the students, we used this time to discreetly complete last-minute homework assignments or put on our makeup (my mom allowed it as long as the eye makeup wasn't too heavy or the lipstick too bright).

Girls in my group would pray for things like a sibling down with the flu, a relative fighting cancer, a father looking for work, or an "unsaved" friend who had yet to give their life to Christ. Sometimes, a girl would raise her hand to tell the group she had an "unspoken" request—something too personal to share specifically. It was a way of reaching out, of letting everyone know you were going through something, without revealing all of the details. Sometimes one person would have several unspoken requests, or on a good day, an "unspoken praise." I had plenty: fights with my parents, probably; unrequited crushes on boys, certainly. It allowed us to connect and find support from each other and, we hoped, from God, before the bell rang and we rushed off to begin the instructional day.

My group leader, who was also my choir director, was a no-nonsense woman, with wiry gray hair and thin-rimmed glasses. While raising a daughter, she was leading the junior high choir, junior high band, high school choir, high school band, handbell choir, orchestra, and several vocal ensembles that met before the school day even began. She was seemingly always at the school, organizing performances for countless events throughout the year. The responsibility seemed to radiate from her body, in her stiff posture and stern expression. Her wardrobe consisted of a nearly identical array of calf-length, A-line skirts with tucked-in, buttoned-up blouses and sensible shoes.

But one morning, she dispensed with the exchange of prayers and praises, telling us she had something important to discuss. We sat on the music room risers in a half circle around her. Facing us, she took her seat at the front of the room.

She began to unbutton the top of her blouse.

"How do you think this looks?" she asked us.

She leaned over, revealing a bit of cleavage.

"How about this?"

No one said anything.

She hoisted up her skirt, right above the knee. I could see a white slip and white flesh. A soft, uneasy giggle moved through the room, and I felt a little queasy. None of us wanted to see this.

"Some of the male teachers have noticed that they are seeing an increasing number of dress code violations," she told us. "They asked us to speak to you about it."

My mind ran through a catalog of my male teachers. Was it the newlywed, who must have been in his twenties, mathematically, but seemed two decades older, with his khaki pants and somber demeanor? Or the lanky gentleman who made eye contact for a little too long at the female students, who leaned in a little too closely to check our work, who the older girls whispered about? Or could it be the one who seemed to avoid eye contact with the girls but easily joked around with all the boys sitting in the front of the classroom?

Once, that teacher told a joke about Adam feeling lonely in the Garden of Eden. God offered to make Adam a woman, someone who would be a wonderful, ideal companion—beautiful and sweet, supportive, a helpmeet focused on his needs and desires. But there was a catch, God told Adam: she would cost him "an arm and a leg." The punch line involved Adam bargaining God down to a more realistic version of this creature called a *woman*: "What can I get for a rib?"

Later, I found out that my friends and classmates in the other devotion groups for girls had received the same warning about the male teachers' concerns, and the same performance from the female teachers. The dress code would be more rigorously enforced going forward.

My teacher's performance at my Christian high school in Kansas City wasn't the only time I'd be called upon to witness a cautionary slutty fashion show. At my evangelical college in the Chicago suburbs, freshman orientation involved separate sessions for men and women, including one ambiguously and hilariously titled, "Keepin' It Real," in the freshman orientation brochure.

We all laughed, but the subject matter was serious: young men were told to avoid not only sex but also pornography and masturbation, which could inflame lust and send them on the path of deeper sexual sin. Young women were counseled about how to avoid tempting the young men—once again, through a fashion show, this time put on by the resident assistants.

As freshman girls, we sat on the floor of the student center while a parade of upperclasswomen strutted along an imaginary catwalk, displaying slinky dresses and low-cut necklines, shimmying and pantomiming hair flips. They seemed to be having a lot of fun, but the message was clear: *This isn't cute, not really, not on this campus.* A couple of years later, during my own turn as an RA, I took part in the ritual again, this time wearing my tightest turquoise spandex top, which I normally wore under another layer, with a black skirt, hiked up a bit for extra effect. The younger girls whooped and hollered as we dutifully passed on the message to them.

By the time Emily Petrini was coming of age, a full decade after me, these ideas were deeply entrenched in the evangelical subculture and being efficiently propagated through Christian publishing and media. Petrini was born in 1991 in Kentucky while her father was completing a degree at an evangelical seminary. She grew up in North Carolina, in a nondenominational church, reading many of the books of the modern evangelical canon—from authors such as the twentieth-century British theologian C. S. Lewis to Joshua Harris—and also subscribed to *Brio* magazine, like I had.

"I read everything, especially surrounding dating and Christianity, men and women in relationships," Petrini said. "I soaked up every single last little bit of it, and wanted to know everything."

She, too, remembers the modesty talks directed at teenage girls. When she was in middle school, Petrini's church youth group brought in a female speaker—a slight, petite woman, probably no more than a hundred pounds—to talk to the girls about dressing appropriately. Much like my experience, there were *very* specific guidelines.

"She's sitting there telling all these girls, 'If you're wearing a shirt and you push down on it in between your boobs and it bounces back, then it's way too tight," Petrini said.

The girls—especially those with curvier figures and larger breasts—looked around at each other in disbelief.

"I remember a girl next to me who had a very different body than me was like, 'I don't think I can not do that with a shirt,'" Petrini said.

Having a female body came with heavy responsibility and fear.

"It was presented to me as: if I wear too short of shorts, I was going to force someone into sexual sin," she said. "It was always,

'Think about the men who have to see you, and how hard it would be to be them.'"

The message was clear: be modest, be pure, and wait for a godly man to pursue you. I don't remember much, if any, serious attention to women's desires. There was no warning to *us* not to watch porn or masturbate, though there were occasional whispers about such things in the dorms.

A girl on my floor freshman year confessed to me that she'd "struggled" with masturbation in high school, and her parents had taken her to a youth pastor at their church to talk about her "problem." She asked me if I had ever struggled in this way. I wasn't sure how to answer that. I'd rarely heard the word "masturbation," and even at eighteen, I wasn't entirely confident about how to define it. I had a vague idea it involved some kind of sex toy, and I certainly wouldn't do something like that!

I remember the first time I'd heard the word: oddly, in retrospect, from my mother, in the kitchen, around age twelve or thirteen. I don't know why it came up, but somehow, maybe from something we heard on the kitchen radio, we were talking about the word, "masticate," or *chew.*

"It sounds a lot like another word, doesn't it?" my mom asked.

"What word?"

"*Masturbate,*" she said in a low voice, looking around to make sure none of my siblings were listening from an adjacent room.

I don't know why she brought it up. Maybe she was testing my knowledge. If so, there was no knowledge to test. I looked at her blankly.

"You don't know about that?" my mom said. "It's what teenage boys do to themselves sometimes because girls dress inappropriately."

Somehow, I made a tentative connection. The awakening of desire, the need for release. Maybe I actually *did* know something about that.

I thought about how I'd naturally, intuitively, explored my body ever since I was a little girl, lying in bed at night. As I'd gotten older, sometimes feelings would come over me when I thought about people I found attractive. It was a feeling that seemed to demand some kind of action.

Apparently I wasn't alone. There was even a word for this!

As a young teen, I had started to become aware of a new and persistent physical need that I was beginning to understand had some kind of connection to sex. I knew that what I was longing for was sinful, and that the satisfaction I was craving was far, far away—at least any form of satisfaction that would be pleasing to God. One night, lying in the dark, I did the math. I was thirteen. Sex was only for marriage, and marriage was probably a decade away. Aching with desire, but wary of committing the sin of lust, I tried to imagine my wedding night, the moment that God would finally sanction and bless my sexuality. What would my future husband think if he knew I was doing this?

And wasn't this just a sin that boys struggled with? If a *girl* touched herself, did it even count? Did it matter that I'd, instinctively, explored these sensations years before I knew words like "orgasm" and "ejaculate"? Was it still impure, even when I didn't know what it was all about?

I wasn't sure how to answer my floormate's question. I was ashamed to tell the truth, that of course I'd "struggled" in this way. I rationalized to myself that I wasn't 100 percent sure what those words meant; no one had ever explicitly told me that female masturbation was a thing.

"No, I haven't done that," I said. "But I don't judge you for it."

\* \* \*

Marriage was the only path to resolution of this tension, and the courting began with urgency as soon as each new class arrived at Trinity International University in suburban Chicago. Couples quickly paired off, meeting at night in the lounge in the lobby of the girls' dorm to study and cuddle. Being alone in a dorm room with a member of the opposite sex was forbidden by campus rules, but the lounge offered a public place to be together until late at night, a place where they were less likely to give in to temptation. Those of us who were still single learned to avert our eyes as we hustled through, each love seat filled with a pawing, longing couple.

Engagements represented a crowning achievement for young women. As religion scholar Donna Freitas writes in *Sex and the Soul,* her study of religion and sexuality on college campuses, by senior year at many evangelical colleges, "the clock is ticking." She mentions hearing one phrase from these students again and again: "Ring by spring or your money back."[3]

I first heard that line while touring my eventual college campus as a prospective student when the tour guide, a student herself, mentioned it in what almost seemed like part of the marketing campaign. The not-so-subtle promise to eager students and their protective Christian parents was, choose *us* and you, or your child, will find a Christian mate to carry on both the faith and the family.

Accordingly, engagements at my college were celebrated for women with an elaborate, secretive ceremony. Several times each month, sometimes each week, we'd find small notes stuck to our bathroom mirrors: "Candlelighting, Johnson Hall Lounge, tonight."

At the appointed time, dozens of girls gathered in a circle. "On behalf of the bride-to-be, I welcome you to this candlelighting," said an RA, flicking off the overhead lights. She held up a candle, with a ribbon tied to the bottom, and at the other end of the ribbon, a diamond ring. She lit the candle, hit "play" on a boom box, and, to a mix of romantic pop songs and worship music, we carefully passed the candle around the circle. One by one, each woman touched and admired the ring, before passing it on to the next woman.

After the first round, a hush fell. The RA took the candle, paused, and began to pass it a second time. At some point, as the ring made its second round, a girl would suddenly blow out the candle, prompting immediate squeals and screams from the rest of the circle. The bride-to-be would tell her story: how she met her groom, how he proposed, usually something like a night at the Cheesecake Factory on Navy Pier, followed by a trail of rose petals leading to the proposal spot.

For all the excitement about marriage, there was little explicit talk of sexual desire, my unusually honest hallmate notwithstanding. Girls with looming wedding dates would nervously talk about getting in shape for the wedding night, or making an appointment with the gynecologist to get on the pill. One evening in the dorms, several of us were talking about one young woman's impending engagement, and I said in a cheeky way that I couldn't wait to get married, and by that I meant, to have sex.

My classmates looked at me in stunned silence, and the girl who was about to get engaged wrinkled her forehead and asked, "Sarah, have you looked at *porn*?"

I had never looked at porn, and I didn't need to. My body was sending me clear enough messages, all on its own.

The point of all of this was to arrive at your wedding day a virgin, ready for a heterosexual marriage to a godly Christian husband. This, our evangelical parents believed, protected us as we moved toward adulthood and gave us the best chance for happiness and fulfillment, in accordance with God's design for human flourishing: a strong marriage that would carry us through our lives and provide us with love, safety, and family.

When purity culture was at its worst, it left many young women feeling distant from our bodies, and ashamed of our natural sexual desires. But at its best, it could offer a vision of a woman's body as something more than an object for men to use. In a culture where women lacked power, it also provided a framework for women to insist on more than a transient physical connection with men.

In a box of old letters I keep in my basement, I recently found a handwritten note from my mother, written on flowery stationery, from October 1998. It was the fall semester of my senior year of high school, and I'd just been through my first minor romantic heartbreak.

Our classmate, with whom I'd sensed a flirtatious chemistry in our AP English class, had called my parents' house one evening to invite me to a performance at Kansas City's outdoor Theatre in the Park. Officially, I wasn't allowed to date yet—my parents still wanted me to practice courtship and wait until I was eighteen—but they allowed me to go. My birthday was a few months away, and this seemed innocent enough: a nice guy, with good grades, asking me to go see a musical. I remember feeling incredibly nervous in my floral sundress as he drove me home from our first date—a very wholesome trip to the show, followed by French fries at a suburban restaurant—struggling to make conversation. We went out one more time and then he stopped calling. I was still holding out hope until, a few weeks later, I discovered he'd started dating a cheerleader and heard through the grapevine that he was telling his friends, "She wanted to have all these deep conversations and honestly all I wanted was some tongue."

My mother somehow got this story out of me. I wasn't used to talking to her about boys—the subject felt so forbidden—but after I spent the better part of a Saturday in bed crying, she must have demanded to know what was going on. So she wrote me a letter. On the outside of the envelope, she wrote:

*Sarah, I never know for sure how you will react, so I'm a little concerned that because of the sensitive nature of the subject discussed within that you'll react angrily or resentfully. If you have grievances with me over this, please cool down and then talk to me. I am trying.[4]*

I have no memory of how I reacted, but what she had written inside in her flawless cursive reminds me that our evangelical parents were indeed trying—trying to protect us, trying to guide us toward relationships that would have meaning and permanence:

*I'm so thankful that you were not reduced to being the spoil ("some tongue," as he so aptly put it) that he was in pursuit of. . . . He should spend his time in pursuit of something else, perhaps a commodity or pastime which consumption of is expendable and plentifully cheap. You, Sarah, are a rare, special, and unique, one-of-a-kind creation of God. Recognize your worth, preserve yourself and your intrinsic gifts for His purposes, His choices. He has much better for you.[5]*

The prize we were promised for patiently waiting for "God's best" was, eventually, the dream of a chaste romance with a godly Christian man—a man on the path to being a capable patriarch and provider. He would take you to Bible studies and Christian concerts, and, usually after six to twelve months, ask for your father's permission to propose. The courtship would culminate with an engagement ring in time for college graduation, to pair with the purity rings most of us wore, given to us by our fathers.

Having seen older girls wearing them, I wanted one, and around the time I turned twelve, my dad had happily agreed to take me to a jewelry store at the mall. I chose a heart-shaped fire opal set in a yellow gold band. The stone was gorgeous, sparkling with glints of pink and green against the white, a symbol of my purity.

In truth, whether they understood it or not, my parents wouldn't have needed to worry too much about guarding my virtue. It wasn't exactly in high demand. I'd gone to school with essentially the same small group of children for most of my life, and the boys felt more like siblings than potential romantic partners. I was bookish—more comfortable around teachers than my peers—with acne and weight that fluctuated between curvy and a little chubby, at least by 1990s standards. Several families in my church had come under the influence of Bill Gothard, the now-disgraced former leader of the Institute for Basic Life Principles who has been accused of sexual harassment and abuse by several women whose families were involved in his organization. As depicted in the 2023 Amazon Prime documentary series *Shiny Happy People,* Gothard traveled the country promoting a highly patriarchal family structure, telling young people to pursue "courtship" instead of dating, and to choose a spouse based on their fathers' guidance, without engaging in physical intimacy. I had no idea how to flirt, a behavior that was actively discouraged by those who believed that dating should be approached with seriousness, and with the intention of moving toward marriage. It was a lot of pressure.

By 1999, when I started college, the evangelical movement was in the full flowering of the True Love Waits campaign, where, en masse, teenagers signed pledges to save sex for marriage. It was two years after Joshua Harris had published *I Kissed Dating Goodbye,* which offered a glossier, more youthful take on courtship and purity culture. The girls in my dorm and I had all read *Passion and Purity,* the early purity-movement classic written in 1984 by the missionary Elisabeth Elliot, chronicling her own courtship with her late husband.

As Donna Freitas writes in *Sex and the Soul,* for many young women in evangelical circles, there's an ambivalence surrounding the exaltation of virginity. She describes one anxious single woman named Jessica, whose feelings were in line with those of other evangelical women she'd interviewed: "She fears that no men are interested in her, regardless of how cautiously she has guarded her 'prize.' . . . She worries that her success at purity is not simply due to the fact that she is an especially good, Godly girl but instead because nobody wants her."[6]

For men raised in purity culture, there is tremendous pressure to be strong, masculine, and, I now see in retrospect, preternaturally mature, ready to take on the lifelong financial, spiritual, and emotional responsibility of marriage and family at a young age. There is no space for fooling around, only the serious and intentional pursuit of a godly marriage.

This vision of powerful, patriarchal masculinity was perhaps most popularly laid out for evangelical readers in the book *Wild at Heart,* written by John Eldredge and published in 2001, while I was in college. The book decries what it sees as the feminization of modern men in both the church and corporate America, and asserts that "in the heart of every man is a desperate desire for a battle to fight, an adventure to live, and a beauty to rescue."[7] Men are to be "warriors"—a word used dozens of times throughout the book—and strong leaders of their wives and families.

They're also to avoid any sexual gratification until they are ready to be that leader, within a marriage. Eldredge advises young men to repent not only of sexual intercourse outside of marriage but also oral sex, pornography, masturbation, and sexual fantasies.[8]

In its most extreme manifestation, this culture around male sexuality can contribute to unhealthy and even dangerous ideas about women. As Katelyn Beaty noted in an op-ed for the *Washington Post* after a young man shot and killed eight people, most of them Asian American women at three spas in the Atlanta area in March 2021, the murders had both racial and religious under-tones.[9] According to news reports, the man told authorities that he killed the women because he saw them as "a temptation for him that he wanted to eliminate."[10]

Beaty observed that the shooter had been raised Southern Baptist—a culture replete with admonitions to women to dress modestly and to avoid provoking men's lust. She called on Christian leaders to think twice about the ways purity culture might fuel misogyny.

"Now more than ever," she wrote, "Christian communities must reexamine attitudes and actions that blame women for men's sexual problems. They must help men take responsibility for their own temptations. They must protect rather than blame victims of crime, violence and abuse."[11]

Purity culture often portrays male sexuality as something dark and uncontrollable, said Matt, who grew up in a homeschooling evangelical family in the mid-1990s, and asked to go only by his first name because of the sensitivity of the subject matter. Growing up on an acreage in Colorado and attending a small church without much of a youth group, Matt was largely isolated from other young people. Sex was rarely discussed, and he mostly relied on Google and Wikipedia to learn the basics.

Matt, who now lives in Oregon and describes himself as religiously agnostic, said the messages he did receive from his family and church focused on sex as a "dangerous force that must be contained at all times."

"You're teaching people to pathologize and to feel struggle in something that's normal," he said.

As a teenager still developing physically and sexually, Matt said those messages felt confusing and disturbing. Missing from the conversation, he said, was any meaningful discussion of consent.

"[The thinking is] you don't need consent because you're only going to ever have sex with your good Christian spouse," Matt said. "It leads to people who don't know what consent is; they're most worried about harming God, because you're taught that sexual sin is first and foremost against God, not against other people."

When we spoke, Matt was in his late twenties. He told me he's been trying to date, but he's struggled. He's felt at times that he would never be able to clear all of the hurdles that evangelicalism seemed to place in front of him before he would be deemed worthy of a loving relationship.

"There was this idea that the man is to be the leader in the relationship," he said, "which means no dating until you're established, you have a set job, you've got a place to live, they can support an additional person. It was just like, 'Okay, message received.' I will never date. I will never be good enough."[12]

By my junior year of college, I was becoming impatient. I'd slimmed down and gained some confidence, but still had never been kissed. Casual kissing was frowned upon, and I hadn't met Mr. Right, but my emotional and physical desire for men was becoming harder to ignore. I went on a few dates with a cute transfer from Liberty University but that didn't really go anywhere. He wanted to be a youth pastor; I didn't really want to be a pastor's wife. And he was still getting over another girl back at Liberty.

Later, I flirted with a friend from choir. There'd always been a little spark there, but I was never sure what I wanted. And, in that world, agreeing to date a good friend was tantamount to getting engaged. One night, when he came to visit me in the newspaper office while I was working, I was inches away from letting him kiss me before I changed my mind. A furtive make-out session in the *Trinity Digest* office might lead to a ring, I reasoned, and I wasn't ready to sign on that particular dotted line.

I still held out hope that, like some of the most pious girls I knew—the thin, bubbly, unassumingly pretty, elementary-education majors who seemed to have been created for the glossy pages of the Trinity prospective student brochures—my first kiss would be with my husband, maybe even on the day of our engagement. But a husband didn't seem to be materializing, and my lust and curiosity were quickly exceeding my patience. Not to mention that it was a little embarrassing to be approaching my twenty-first birthday with virgin lips.

I met a guy I'll call John around that time, the second semester of my junior year. I noticed him immediately in my literature class: tall, with shiny, dark hair and a muscular build. He was different from the aspiring youth minister types: twenty-eight years old, a full-grown man. He'd come back to get a degree after a few years of playing semiprofessional soccer, I learned.

We had very little in common: I wasn't a sports fan, and he showed no sign of being particularly religious. But I felt a heat when he sat near me in class, and I hungrily thought about him later, alone in my dorm room.

Within a few weeks, he was picking me up for a first date to watch football at his off-campus apartment. It didn't seem like a very romantic date idea, but I let that go. As we walked up the stairs to his second-floor flat, I was nervous, on guard, full of fantasies and terrified that I might follow through on one of them. His one-bedroom apartment was a den of potential iniquities: hard lemonade in his refrigerator, technically forbidden under the code of conduct even for students living off campus, not to mention his bed. He opened his bedroom door and gestured toward it as he gave me a brief tour. "This is where the magic happens," he announced. Taken aback, I told myself I wouldn't come back again.

But later, on his couch, as the Bears played on TV, John leaned in. In a moment, we were kissing. I'd imagined this moment as some kind of magical epiphany, but it was more interesting than erotic. His tongue felt thicker than I'd imagined, and he tasted like the salty chips we'd been eating. His hands went for my breasts and I pushed them away. I don't remember particularly enjoying the kissing, or not enjoying it, either; my entire focus was on slowing him down, pacing him, keeping his hands from wandering too far too fast.

As I was lying on my side, watching the TV, I felt him smack my rear end.

"Did that hurt?" he asked. It felt surprisingly—and confusingly—exciting.

"Not enough," I responded, emboldened. He did it again. I decided that maybe I *could* come back, once or twice.

And I did come back, each time feeling the tension between my desires and my fears. We wound up in his bed once: still fully clothed, he reached between my legs. I let him touch me there for several seconds, fascinated and guilty, before pushing him away and hopping up. It was *my* responsibility to draw the line and hold the line, one that John never fully crossed but repeatedly tried to renegotiate.

One night as he drove me home from his apartment back to my dorm, Linkin Park blared over the radio: *"I tried so hard and got so far/But in the end it doesn't even matter."*

John gestured toward the car speaker. "You're trying so hard," he said. "But maybe it doesn't matter."

I told him it mattered to me. I wanted to be a virgin when I got married.

"I know," he said. "I want you to keep your promise."

And then, he had a suggestion: we could try oral, or even anal sex, instead?

"You'd still be a virgin," he said hopefully.

I was shaken by that suggestion—so many steps beyond my experience or understanding of sex, so far from the romantic fantasies I'd entertained. I felt degraded by the very idea, and somehow responsible for letting him think I'd do that. I never should have let him push me as far as he had, I told myself. This was all my fault for fooling around with someone I knew I had no intention of marrying.

I ended it. And I married the next man I dated: a Southern Baptist preacher's son, sweet and smart and a little nerdy like me—and even more pure.

He'd grown up homeschooled, in small-town Georgia and then rural Ohio, in a family even more deeply influenced by Bill Gothard and his courtship teachings than mine. And although he was three years older, had even less dating experience than I did. Three weeks after we started seeing each other, I hinted that maybe it would be nice if we held hands, or even kissed.

I felt shy and guilty for asking. He didn't know about John, at least not the details. I didn't know what he would think of me if he knew I'd compromised my purity in that way. I felt shame that I'd fooled around so recently, after waiting for so long, when the man that God had for me appeared to be right here in front of me. If only I'd been more patient, we could have shared our first kiss together.

We kissed that summer, and most of our courtship was overwhelmingly chaste. I wanted to prove that I was wholesome, and worthy of marrying a pastor's son who'd saved even his first kiss for me.

He took great pains to make sure he preserved my reputation and my purity. One night that first summer we were dating, while I was subletting an apartment in downtown Chicago, a long car ride from his place in the suburbs, we stayed up too late. I told him to sleep on my sofa. I'd be in another room, and he'd be safer that way. He refused. *What would my father say if he knew?*, I wondered.

In the strangest act of chivalry, he'd taken a blanket and pillow and stretched out his tall frame in the hallway outside my apartment door. I thought this was a bad idea, but what kind of wanton woman would I be if I insisted that he sleep in my apartment? Within a couple of hours, I woke up to my landlord, Bruno, shouting in his heavy Polish accent, "What are you doing? You cannot do this!"

He spent the rest of that night, and every other late night that summer, on my sofa, and we never even came close to having sex. It became almost unthinkable, and when I went away to England in the fall to study abroad, I struggled to imagine what it would be like to touch each other the way John and I had touched each other. But those thoughts were quickly chased away by shame. Here was a good man, and I was indulging—or trying to indulge—in impure thoughts that would steal from the joy of our future marriage. I couldn't let myself picture it. But I figured that on our wedding night, everything would come together.

For most of our marriage, I had a recurring dream. The setting changed each time: sometimes we were at his parents' house, sometimes in my childhood bedroom, sometimes a place I didn't recognize. But the circumstances were always the same: we were alone, wanting to touch each other, but there were people moving around outside our door. Never sure if the door was locked, we'd move from room to room with a growing sense of frustrated desire, with no opportunity to act on it without embarrassment and shame. And suddenly, without consummation, the dream would end.

## 11

# NAKED AND ASHAMED

On the other side of the shame and anxiety around sex was the promise of deep intimacy and sexual fulfillment within marriage. Alongside purity culture, evangelicalism developed a notably *positive* message regarding sex within marriage. Once you'd crossed that threshold with your bride, the thinking seemed to go, you were free to get busy—with God, metaphorically, cheering you on.

Within a few years of kissing dating goodbye, Joshua Harris said hello to marriage. In his 2000 sequel, *Boy Meets Girl,* he describes meeting and courting his wife, Shannon, a young woman he had worked with for several months at their church office before he began to see her as a romantic option. Harris acknowledges it wasn't "love at first sight" and that Shannon was initially "not the kind of person I envisioned marrying." And yet, Harris says, God slowly began "changing his heart"—a metamorphosis that culminated with a conversation over two glasses of Sprite at a bagel shop, where he told her he wanted to spend some time "courting" her in an effort to discover whether marriage was in God's plan for the two of them.[1]

While that beginning sounds, to me, about as romantic as many business meetings I've attended, Harris goes on to describe a growing feeling of chemistry between them as they planned their wedding. But they held back, as committed Christians should. He said: "When a Christian man and woman systematically deny their own physical desires as an expression of mutual faith and submission to Jesus Christ, they are laying a solid spiritual foundation for their marriage."[2]

After the wedding, however, the joy of married sex is available and not merely as a form of physical release: "[God] could have made the means by which we procreate as brief and boring as sneezing. Instead He gave it more sizzle than the Fourth of July. And when a husband and wife revel in and thank God for the gift of sex, they glorify Him. Their love-making becomes a jubilant, two-person worship service!"[3]

Harris's 2000 book was the latest iteration in the genre of glowing evangelical treatises on marital sex. In addition to an awkward sex talk with my mom over a sundae at Dairy Queen when I was about twelve, I had gotten a lot of my sex education from Tim LaHaye, the Christian writer of an earlier generation, and his wife, Beverly. However hostile he was to gay sex, he was hugely enthusiastic about sex between married straight couples.

As a young teen, when my parents were away from the house, I would slip upstairs to their bedroom, slide open the bottom drawer of my father's walnut dresser, and pull out the LaHayes' paperback book *The Act of Marriage.* I was intrigued by the detailed descriptions of the mechanics of sex, and another unfamiliar word: orgasm. To its credit, the book spent a fair amount of time instructing Christian husbands about how to locate the clitoris, and what to do with it.

Listening for the hum of the garage door opening downstairs, I flipped through the pages, greedily imbibing this new information: "Generally, a thoughtful husband may gently massage his wife's neck, shoulders, and breasts to arouse her until blood rushes to the nipples and they become firm and erect. . . . Any tender fondling and kissing on the upper body will help to arouse her."[4]

I was learning so much! I had no idea nipples were involved in anything but breastfeeding. The descriptions of a woman's arousal right before penetration were even more evocative than the romance novels I'd found at the drugstore down the street: "Her heart will palpitate, her skin becomes warm, and almost every part of her body becomes sensitive to the touch. Her breathing will be more rapid, her face may grimace as if in pain, and she may groan audibly—and her husband finds this all very exhilarating."[5]

And so did I.

For Emily Petrini, the messages about sexual purity before marriage were counterbalanced by strong messages about the goodness of sex within it. Petrini, who now lives in North Carolina with her husband and children, told me when we first spoke by phone after connecting on social media that while she wouldn't "advocate for it," she also doesn't regret her decision to wait.

"It ended up being good for me, I think," Petrini said. "But I think that I am unique in that, from lots of folks that I've talked to."

She remembers hearing a consistently positive view of sex articulated by her parents, especially her father.

"Not really much more than that, but like—it's good. It's not bad," she said. "So I didn't go into marriage feeling super ashamed about sex or anything like that."

Even so, almost exactly a year after our first conversation, Petrini reached out again. She was rethinking some things, she said, and trying to more fully come to terms with the realization that as much as she loves her husband, waiting for marriage felt like something that had been decided *for* her.

"That was not a conscious choice that I was ever able to make, because there literally was no other choice," Petrini said. "I think I'm just processing that I never felt like I had any autonomy with my sexual choices."

Recently, she told me, she's been trying to get more comfortable with her sexuality and her body: going running in a sports bra, wearing a crop top, buying a bikini. She said her husband, who was not raised in purity culture, is supportive but sometimes slightly bewildered. They've been having more frank conversations, which can feel freeing as well as confusing for both of them.

"The other night he asked, 'So, how long are you going to be doing this? How long are you going to keep unraveling things? Are you going to be deconstructing when you're forty?'" she said.

Petrini said she told her husband that it's not really something that has an "end date" because of how profoundly purity culture and other aspects of evangelicalism had shaped her life.[6] For others raised in purity culture, the emphasis on waiting and the dangers of premarital sex overshadowed the joy of it, or delayed natural self-exploration and discovery.

That was the case for Jocelyn Howard, who grew up in Virginia and attended Bob Jones University. It took a few years after leaving the conservative Christian college to come to terms with their identity as a bisexual and non-binary person.

"I was so deep in the closet, I was in Narnia," Howard told me with a laugh.[7] "I was never allowed to even consider being attracted to women."

Howard dealt with those feelings, for a while, by trying to "hyper-focus" on their attraction to men.

"All those years people have the opportunity to figure that out, I was steeped in purity culture," Howard said. "I was like, 'Oh, I really like guys!' But it was all theoretical."

It wasn't until graduate school, when Howard finally started dating and experimenting with kissing, that their queer identity became clear.

For a woman in her midthirties who asked me to call her Louise, the fear of exploration meant many years of sexual frustration and dissatisfaction, even in marriage.[8] Louise grew up on the West Coast, "steeped in purity culture," and met her eventual husband at an evangelical college. He was the only person she'd ever kissed.

"On our wedding night, we didn't know how to have sex," Louise told me. "We thought we knew how, but then it didn't really work."

That experience is not unusual for young evangelicals who begin their honeymoons with little or no sexual experience, and, often, years of sexual shame. Tori Williams Douglass, an anti-racism educator based in Oregon, grew up largely in white evangelical spaces in the 1980s and '90s, heavily influenced by the purity movement of the time. In a Twitter thread in July 2022, Douglass argued that even critical discussions of purity culture often fall short by failing to fully capture the trauma of being expected to suddenly begin a robust sexual relationship on the wedding night. It doesn't require newlyweds to "flip a switch," Douglass said, but to completely reform the way they interact with their own bodies and each other: "You're being expected to defuse a bomb. With no skills. Naked. While someone watches," Douglass wrote.[9] After years of expending tremendous mental and emotional energy to hold back sexual impulses, to avoid even sexual thoughts, Douglass said, many young couples have no idea what they like, or what they want, creating incredibly difficult conditions under which to explore sex and form a physical bond.

"Marriage cannot magically become an emotionally safe place to discover your sexuality, never mind emotional intimacy with another person, because sexuality requires exploring a body you're terrified of," she wrote. "Your body is inherently, fundamentally, structurally UNSAFE."[10]

As Linda Kay Klein describes in her 2018 book, *Pure: Inside the Evangelical Movement That Shamed a Generation of Young Women and How I Broke Free,* growing up in purity culture can produce a persistent, if not permanent, fusion of sex and shame inside the mind. "Even if we eventually come to understand that our sexual nature is natural, normal, and healthy," Klein writes, "we may find that our upbringing in purity culture, which has dedifferentiated shame and sex over years of messaging, observation, and experience, ensures that our brains fire those shame neurons when the subject of our sexuality arises, with or without our permission, trapping us in a shame spiral."[11]

Despite their awkward wedding night, Louise and her husband eventually figured it out. But for years, she said, sex was painful. Louise struggled with negative feelings about her body, and a belief that as a woman, sex wasn't really meant for her pleasure.

"The messages that I got from the church were that men want sex, and you need to give sex to your husband to keep him interested, and that's your job as the woman," she said. "It was never really for me, and I didn't feel like it was for me because it wasn't enjoyable."

But something shifted for Louise after she gave birth and began breastfeeding her son.

"I was like, 'Oh my gosh, my body could do that; I made that human inside of me,'" she said. "It felt very empowering, and I started to see my body very differently."

She gathered the nerve to tell a therapist a secret—that she'd never had an orgasm.

"She was like, 'You need to go buy a vibrator right now! That's going to be your goal; I prescribe orgasms to you.'"

Louise bought a vibrator, but for a couple of years, was too ashamed to try it.

"I didn't really believe in masturbation, and I felt uncomfortable," she said.

Until, at age thirty-four, she was home alone watching TV one day and got inspired.

"It was *Bridgerton*," Louise told me with a laugh, alluding to the Netflix series famous for its gorgeous cast of characters and steamy love scenes. "That was the impetus, yes. The first season."

She was shocked at how easily it happened and how much she'd been missing.

"It was right away and I was like, 'Oh my God! God is a woman! This is amazing!'" she said.

Louise's deconstruction of her evangelical faith had come in phases, she said. In college, she began to feel uncomfortable with the conservative politics of many of the evangelicals around her and later, with the reluctance of one of her pastors to affirm LGBTQ+ Christians. And then, the pandemic—and the refusal of many white evangelicals to use masks and vaccines—felt like another breaking point.

"I saw the responses of Christians, many Christians, and it made me want nothing to do with Christianity," she said, though she told me she may eventually "come around."

She found support and community from other former evangelicals on social media, working through their own deconstruction processes.

And now, there's more to figure out. Louise said having her first orgasm in her midthirties has surfaced new feelings, and raised new questions, including the possibility that she might be attracted to women.

"I was thinking about what actually turned me on and what didn't," she said. "It was like everything was opened up. I'm still very much exploring it, but seeing things very differently right now."

She's sorting through it mostly on her own for now, with some help from a therapist.

"How do you do that, when you're in your thirties and you have a child?" Louise said. "I'm scared of what will happen."

My own honeymoon in California and the early days of marriage, in a small apartment in suburban Chicago, felt awkward and surprisingly lonely. Fresh out of college, far from our families and with many of our friends beginning to disperse, my husband and I tried to figure out not only sex but also adulthood—how to rent a car, pay our bills, and join our finances, and what to do with these strange, new, unchaperoned days and nights together.

We had followed the rules: he'd asked my father for permission to date me and we'd saved sex for marriage, doing little more than deep kissing and some heavy petting before our wedding in August 2003, three months after our college graduation.

But from the earliest days of our marriage, we'd begun to discover gaps between us, our desires and dreams. We'd tried hard to bridge them, through date nights and getaways; two babies and cross-country moves and job changes; visits to our respective therapists; and increasingly long, late-night conversations that dissolved into arguments and tears.

By 2016, as I was crisscrossing the country covering the presidential campaign and feeling disconnected from home, a news story caught my eye. Joshua Harris had been hearing from many adults who'd grown up reading his books in their evangelical homes and were now wrestling with some kind of pain—marrying the wrong person in haste and feeling sexually or emotionally unfulfilled; holding back for years only to discover that they were queer; feeling shame about their bodies after being told to cover up; or putting off dating for so long that they felt they'd missed out on important life experiences, and might never find a spouse.[12]

Over the next couple of years, I reached out to Harris and wound up spending some time with him, working on a story for NPR in 2018 about his evolving thought process. I visited his film crew at a church outside Pittsburgh, where they were working on a documentary about his soul-searching. I asked Harris how he and his wife were thinking about their own marriage, in light of that process.

"I think it's made us realize how there's heartache and there's pain no matter what pathway you choose in life," he told me. "There's no path you can choose that can protect you from that."[13]

The next year, some colleagues at NPR's *All Things Considered* reached out to me about working with them on a piece for a series about sex. Someone had pitched a story about people who save sex for marriage, and, knowing my evangelical background, they wanted my help. I tracked down a young married couple, Laura and Adam Hardin, and my colleague Kat Lonsdorf and I arranged to visit them at their small home in Maryland. They were a sweet couple, very involved in their church, with an adorable family: two toddlers underfoot, and Laura was heavily pregnant with their third child.

They told us about meeting each other at church and committing to save sex for marriage. There was some awkwardness, they said, in figuring out how to have sex for the first time on their honeymoon. But like Petrini, they'd benefited from refreshingly frank and encouraging conversations about sex with people in their church community, particularly a pastor and his wife.[14] Laura and Adam seemed in sync and happy.

A couple of months after that story aired, in July 2019, Joshua Harris and his wife, Shannon Bonne, posted a photo of the two of them on Instagram, with a caption that began, "We're writing to share the news that we are separating and will continue our life together as friends."

I felt a wave of sadness, mixed with relief. I had known for some time that I was ready to take the same step, but I'd felt stuck, afraid to unravel years of history with the same person, and equally afraid of what our families would say. But for me, divorce had begun to feel inevitable. And now, seeing an icon of the very movement that I'd put my faith in struggle and fail in the same way felt like a strange and bittersweet vindication of my own experience.

There are parts of that story that are not mine alone to share. When someone agrees to get married—or divorced—they don't agree to reveal all of the details leading up to those events. And as in any divorce, there are versions of the story that would make me look better or worse, depending on the telling.

But none of that really matters to me now. Fundamentally, we were not happy, at least not enough for me. But we were honest. We managed to do a very difficult and painful thing—unwind a sixteen-year marriage with two children while remaining civil, most of the time.

Several months later, I finally gathered up the nerve to tell my parents that my marriage was over. I broke the news in an email, which read in part:

*I know this will be hard to absorb and concerning for you. I want you to know that we arrived at this point after a long and difficult process. The reasons are many and personal, but I want to say clearly that there was no cheating, no betrayal, no major drama, just many years of unsuccessfully trying to make our marriage work. . . . I know you will disagree with this decision in principle, but as your daughter, I would ask for as much love and support as you can muster.*

They responded with concern for my soul and for the well-being of my children, and with considerable anger. The support I'd requested did not materialize.

As hurtful as that was, it was not entirely unexpected. My parents believe deeply that divorce is a violation of God's design for human flourishing and a destructive force in a family. I, too, grieve the dream of the intact family for my children, which I chose to relinquish. I feel that grief alongside a quiet confidence that I made the right decision, and that I didn't make it lightly or hastily. I also understand that my decision may seem unthinkable for people like my parents, who've enjoyed a long, committed marriage and invested many years in trying to instill that same value in me.

Despite the divorce, I value marriage, so much so that I got married again, and rather quickly, as many people may have quietly observed. Greg and I met while I was in Washington for work, felt an immediate connection, and suddenly found ourselves testing a newly minted love in a global pandemic. He was coming off possibly the most amicable divorce in human history, enjoying the dating scene as an empty nester with his youngest off to college, fully in his professional stride after many years as a civil servant, free of a mortgage for the first time in decades. And *I* felt like a mess, recovering from the fallout of the end of my marriage and the rejection of my parents, helping two children through virtual learning, facing sudden uncertainty at work amidst the economic downturn, and navigating homeownership hassles, including a leaky roof that launched an unplanned double bathroom renovation.

And yet Greg was still there, showing up and loving me unblinkingly through every chaotic moment. Four decades into my life, after a long first marriage and giving birth twice, I was well past *most* of the shame about sex and my body. Still, I had my occasional moments of guilt about the divorce and fear that the joy I felt in my connection with Greg was a mirage, and that he would suddenly disappear. But he didn't. He approached my history with patience, curiosity, and kindness. And he reassured me that at least in his version of Judaism, sex is a gift to be celebrated. On the Sabbath, he told me, it was traditional for married couples to go home and mark the holiest time of the week with sex—a mitzvah, he said.

We knew we had something special. And when you're in your forties and fifties, and you tell your friends that you know you have something special, the good ones embrace you and your joy.

We were married Thanksgiving weekend of 2021 under a chuppah, after the desert sun set on the Jewish Sabbath. My parents did not attend, but we were surrounded by a small circle of close friends and family.

I wore a long ivory dress, with a small train and eyelet lace. Uncouth, some might say, for a forty-year-old second-time bride. But I loved the dress. Not to mention the groom. My younger son asked to walk me down the aisle and to sing a song at our reception. The caterer brought the alcohol, but forgot the soda. We all survived.

Nothing was the way I would have imagined or planned my wedding to be as a little girl—and yet, it felt warm, loving, peaceful, exactly as it should be.

Or as Greg says, "*Beshert.*"


Around the time of our wedding, Greg and I moved into a house a few blocks away from my ex-husband. The goal was to make co-parenting simpler, and ease the stress on our sons involved in alternating between their dad's house and mine. Over a drink at a pub near our neighborhood, we caught up.

My ex and I see each other often, in passing, but it had been a while since we'd really talked. We had been civil, cooperative, and sometimes talked about trying to rekindle some form of a friendship, for old times' sake. The conversation turned to the boys and, eventually, to the end of our marriage. We both felt that it had been fundamentally over for a long time. But I was the one to pull the plug first, and on that day I told him, again, that I was sorry for the pain I knew it caused him. I told him I was still in pain, sometimes, from the weight of all of it.

"We followed all the rules," I said, tearing up in frustration. "They told us to follow the rules so we wouldn't get hurt."

"We're not hurting because we broke the rules," he said. "We're hurting because we followed the rules."

# 12

# BE FRUITFUL AND MULTIPLY

D espite all of its emphasis in evangelicalism, fulfilling married sex was not the end in itself but a means to a larger goal: a Christian family and, within it, a God-given role for each individual, promising structure and purpose for life. The divine order was set out in the Garden of Eden, as described in the book of Genesis: a man first, then a woman, then children, from whom all of humanity would flow, with a hierarchy in that order.

As a girl, my upbringing was to prepare me for my ultimate role as a wife and mother. In *Dare to Discipline*—the 1970 parenting manual that's sold millions of copies over multiple reprintings—Dr. James Dobson advises parents of teenage girls who might be tempted to engage in sexual activity to teach them that doing so will reduce their prospects when it's time to look for a husband.

"The natural sex appeal of girls serves as their primary source of bargaining power in the game of life," Dobson writes. "In exchange for feminine affection and love, a man accepts a girl as his lifetime responsibility—supplying her needs and caring for her welfare. . . . Therefore, a girl who indiscriminately gives away her basis for exchange has little left with which to bargain."[1]

Evangelical parents like mine were encouraged to begin conveying those messages to their daughters from an early age. Among the children's books that sat on my shelf when I was growing up was a retelling of Proverbs 31—the famous Old Testament chapter describing a "virtuous woman"—illustrated for little girls and published by Moody Bible Institute in 1984, the year I turned three.

*When I'm a Mommy,* the front cover read, above a picture of a blond little girl, eyes closed and smiling as she dreamed about her future. Inside, in large font above an illustration of the girl with her cat and dog, it said, "When I grow up I want to be a mommy—a very good mommy—the VERY BEST mommy!" The book goes on to paraphrase the Bible passage, heavily emphasizing the parts about motherhood, alongside illustrations of the little girl imagining herself engaged in various domestic chores, such as sewing, cooking, and grocery shopping.

My mother loved being a homemaker. She was an avid follower of Phyllis Schlafly, embracing her opposition to abortion and the Equal Rights Amendment, as well as her advocacy for traditional gender roles, which were seen as a fulfillment of God's design for the family. The culture was in crisis, the thinking went, partly because too many women were in the workforce rather than at home raising their children.

My mom often quoted from the New Testament book of Titus,[2] where older women were instructed to model feminine virtues: they should "urge the younger women to love their husbands and children, to be self-controlled and pure, to be busy at home, to be kind, and to be subject to their husbands, so that no one will malign the word of God."*

These ideals were also promoted in our Christian school curriculum. In Heritage Studies for Christian Schools, a Bob Jones University textbook series for first graders of my era, traditional gender roles are portrayed as God's will. "Fathers work to provide for their families," reads one section, alongside pictures of a man reading the Bible to his wife and children, and men engaged in various types of labor, including carpentry and agriculture. "God tells mothers to help fathers," it says, next to pictures of women grocery shopping, doing laundry, and caring for a sick child.[3]

I received somewhat mixed messages about how to imagine my future life: I should prepare to go to college, mostly so that I would have a "marketable skill," as my mother put it, on the off chance I didn't get married. (She'd attended for two years, she told me, while praying about whether to continue college or marry. Then my dad came along.) I should think first and foremost about how to serve God with my work and as a woman, that work would likely mean serving my family above all else. I should be involved in activities outside the home that helped fulfill a larger mission, like participating in political organizing for Christian candidates or volunteering at the church, but paid work for women was more questionable.

The women in our circles who *did* work often did so part-time, explicitly because they needed to contribute to the family income.

---

* I never made the connection until I began writing this chapter that a few verses later is the infamous instruction that has been used in attempts to justify slavery: "Teach slaves to be subject to their masters in everything, to try to please them, not to talk back to them, and not to steal from them, but to show that they can be fully trusted, so that in every way they will make the teaching about God our Savior attractive."

We were fortunate that Dad's corporate job throughout most of my childhood freed my mother from those concerns. When I heard one day from a classmate that her mother became a teacher after her younger children had gone to school, I excitedly told my mom about it. As I buckled my seat belt for the ride home, I said I'd figured out a way to have a career one day and still be a good mom: I'd teach during the day and, like my friend's mother, be off in the summers to be with my children. My mom was quiet for a moment. "I don't know," she said. "It's still good for a mom to be at home."

I thought about that conversation again, many years later, sitting around a cafeteria table with some college classmates. A friend of mine—a popular, handsome male student—was hosting his parents for a couple of days, taking them around to meet his friends. As my roommate and I, both single women at the time, ate our lunch, his mother asked us about our future plans. I was studying English, I said, and thinking about going to law school. It seemed like the surest path to working in politics and influencing the culture and the political system for Christian values, as I'd been taught. My roommate was studying science and thinking about going on to medical school to become a medical missionary.

"I don't know," she said, shaking her head. "If you go to grad school, it will always pull you away from your families."

Christian families, led by godly patriarchs and devoted homemakers, played a critical role in society: shielding children from the influences of secular society while preparing them to one day influence the culture for Christianity. Evangelical parents, pastors, and teachers saw it as their God-given duty to carefully shape the worldview of the next generation, preparing us to carry on the larger mission of aligning society with the conservative Christian vision of God's design for the family and nation. My evangelical alma mater,

Trinity International University, chose as its motto: "Forming students to transform the world through Christ."[4]

For decades, evangelical leaders painted a picture of a nation in decline. As a solution, they proffered a return to supposedly bygone days when women were wholesome and men only had sex with women. Writing in 1987, Dobson wistfully looked back on his teenage years in the 1950s: "Occasionally a girl came up pregnant, but she was packed off in a hurry and I never knew where she went. Homosexuals were very weird and unusual people. I heard there were a few around but I didn't know them personally."[5]

Reflecting on those words a few years later in *Children at Risk: What You Need to Know to Protect Your Family*, his book with religious right leader Gary Bauer, Dobson said it was possible that "those earlier years were not as tranquil or moral as I recall. Nevertheless, the cultural gap between that time and this is a million miles wide, and most of the changes occurring in the world of children have been for the worse."[6] Dobson and Bauer were sounding an alarm about what they perceived as encroaching godlessness in media, education, and the culture at large, and called on conservative Christian parents to get involved in political activism on behalf of goals like school vouchers, opposing the "gay rights agenda," promoting abstinence-based sex education, and ending abortion.[7]

Decades later, many white evangelicals—led by Bauer, Dobson, and other figures who were still active in American politics—would come to see Trump as the unlikely hero capable of reversing the cultural changes that now seemed unstoppable to "Make America Great Again." A February 2023 survey by the Public Religion Research Institute found pervasive acceptance of Christian nationalist ideals within members of the Republican party and among white evangelical Protestant Christians. Nearly two-thirds of white evangelicals expressed either sympathy for or adherence to ideas like, "The US government should declare America a Christian nation" and "Being Christian is an important part of being truly American." The poll also found strong correlations between support for Christian nationalism and approval of Trump.[8]

As historian John Fea notes in his analysis of the relationship between Trump and white evangelicals, *Believe Me,* his election was "the latest manifestation of a long-standing evangelical approach to public life. This political playbook was written in the 1970s and drew heavily from an even longer history of white evangelical fear. It is a playbook characterized by attempts to 'win back' or 'restore the culture.' It is a playbook grounded in a highly problematic interpretation of the relationship between Christianity and the American founding."[9]

Indeed, the groundwork was being laid long ago, as leaders like Dobson wielded ever-growing power over both the politics and the personal lives of millions of evangelical parents and their children. In 1996, when I was fifteen and avidly supporting the Republican nominee for president, I remember Dobson lashing out at the party for "abandoning moral issues" like abortion. Dobson threatened to withdraw his support from Bob Dole at the GOP convention, after Dole said he would consider a running mate who did not share his opposition to abortion rights. In a July 1996 piece for the *Washington Post,* reporter Marc Fisher profiled Dobson and documented those tensions. Conservative activist Howard Phillips described Dobson as "one of the best-kept secrets in America. . . . He's extremely well-known and respected everywhere except the secular world of Washington, New York and Hollywood. That makes him extremely influential."[10]

To a readership that had yet to fully realize the force of Dobson's influence, the piece noted that his radio audience was on par with that of broadcast giants Rush Limbaugh and Paul Harvey, and that his mailing list included 3.5 million families. Dobson "didn't buy a single name from the telemarketing industry," the *Post* said. "They all came to him, for advice, for the love and biblical wisdom he dispenses on the radio."[11]

Throughout my childhood, there was no political cause more urgent than abortion. The urgency of the issue was deeply tied to our view of the family—of sex as something reserved for marriage, the idea of children as a gift from God, and the role of women as nurturers.

Opposition to abortion was the energizing force that drove my parents to put up signs for Pat Robertson—one of the architects of the Christian right who had harnessed the anti-abortion movement—in our front yard; volunteer at phone banks for Republican Congressional candidates; and, along with hundreds of people from our church and other local evangelical congregations and Catholic parishes, join anti-abortion marches through the streets of Kansas City, holding signs with slogans like "Abortion Hurts Women" and "Choose Life."

As a younger child, I was told not to look inside the top drawer of my parents' nightstand. But one evening, when my parents were in another room, I did exactly that. Inside was a glossy pamphlet, filled with photos of aborted fetuses mangled and bloody, their eyes closed, organs and bones visible through their shiny translucent skin.

I knew immediately what they were; I'd already spent many Saturday mornings standing with my mother outside the abortion clinic, holding signs and "picketing" as women went in for procedures. Sometimes members of our group would call out to women as they pulled up in cars, often driven by men. My mom had explained to me that they were killing babies inside that building, and that we were trying to persuade them not to. I had watched my mother as her pregnancies progressed, and looked on in awe as she held my sisters in the rocking chair and tenderly breastfed them. Being a woman, and having a body that could produce life, was such a beautiful gift. Babies were so lovely. Why would anyone kill them?

There were people in the movement who believed that violence could be justified to save these babies, my mom told me one day. She struggled with it: if you knew for sure, for example, that someone was preparing to kidnap a two-year-old and kill her, wouldn't you be justified in killing that person to protect the child? How was an unborn child any different, she reasoned? The only difference was time. And yet, she didn't believe that killing was the answer. That's why we worked to elect lawmakers who would one day overturn *Roe v. Wade.* It had been little more than a decade since the 1973 decision legalized abortion nationwide, but my mother had faith that it would one day be overturned. And if it wasn't, she told me, she believed that eventually the country would find itself in a civil war over the issue, much like it had over slavery.

The two issues were, and still are, often compared by anti-abortion activists who see abortion as a modern moral evil on the scale of slavery. But often, abortion was treated as an urgent issue for today, while racism was seen as largely a thing of the past. In one Christian high school text first published in 1984, *American Government in Christian Perspective,* the three-fifths compromise—which counted enslaved people as only three-fifths of a person for purposes including taxation and representation in Congress—is described in one paragraph, under the heading "Other important compromises," without discussion of the legal and moral implications of that policy for enslaved Black people.[12] In a chapter about how legislation becomes law, the textbook features a discussion of the filibuster. A headshot of the segregationist South Carolina senator, Strom Thurmond, appears in the upper right-hand corner, noting that he "set the record for filibusters in 1975 when he held the floor for 24 hours."[13] Nowhere does it mention that Thurmond set that record in an effort to stop the passage of the Civil Rights Act, something I wouldn't learn until one of my own trips to Washington.[14]

Abortion, meanwhile, is featured prominently in a section on the history and function of the US Supreme Court. It describes *Roe v. Wade* as "ignoring 3,500 years of Judeo-Christian civilization, religion, morality, and law," and compared it to the *Dred Scott v. Sandford* decision of 1857 that deemed enslaved people the legal property of their enslavers. The book calls abortion a "usurpation of God's role" and urges young Christians to strive to end access to the procedure through the political process: "The need has never been greater for Christians to urge their elected representatives to pass legislation removing such cases from the Court's jurisdiction," the text read, decades before conservatives would successfully take over the court itself and reverse the *Roe* decision.[15]

So at sixteen, feeling driven to help in some way, I offered to volunteer at a local crisis pregnancy center, one of many such centers often set up near abortion providers or family planning clinics to try to persuade women not to have abortions. Ours, about a tenminute drive from my parents' house in Kansas City, was in a strip mall across from a White Castle. The nuns who ran the place told me they wouldn't normally let a teenager work there—sometimes alone—but I seemed mature enough.

On my first day, they walked me through a brief training: how to ask a woman for a urine sample, then carefully hover the dropper over the test. While she waited for the results, we'd ask her to view *The Silent Scream,* an anti-abortion film that has been criticized by members of the medical community for making inaccurate claims about fetal development. If the pregnancy test was positive, we'd try to persuade her to continue the pregnancy, pointing to the plastic models of fetal development we kept in the office, asking her to consider the life of her "baby," promising free diapers and clothing, and giving her information about public safety net programs like Medicaid and food stamps.

I had expected the work would be exciting, that I would feel like I was saving babies. But many Saturday mornings when I volunteered, the office was quiet, with only one or two clients, or none at all. The women who did come in often seemed to simply want a pregnancy test. They were not usually eager to talk much about it, or at least not with a sixteen-year-old.

So it was strange, twenty years later, to find myself in the thick of covering the very issues to which my family had devoted so much time and energy.

As the 2016 campaign wound down, I decided to dive in headfirst. I couldn't stay in Washington—my then husband had taken a job in coastal Virginia. But I wanted to keep a hand in politics. The abortion beat had become available, so I asked for it, which is how I found myself, in the days after the overturning of *Roe v. Wade,* inside an abortion clinic in Louisiana, watching as workers scrambled to take calls from women desperate to get in while bans worked their way through the state court system.

Decades had passed since I was a teenager pleading with young women to keep their babies. If I could go back and talk to her, I'd tell her about the people I'd met since: people close to me— some with similar religious backgrounds—who'd faced troubled relationships or medical complications and the wrenching decisions that come with being pregnant in those circumstances. I'd also tell her what it feels like to carry a baby to term: the absolute wonder of a new life taking shape and growing and moving inside your body, coupled with the tremendous toll a pregnancy—even a healthy one—can take on a woman's body and mind. And I'd tell her about the indescribable feeling of both joy and heavy responsibility that washes over you in the moment you hold the baby your body has just brought forth.

At the clinic in Shreveport, I met a young mother who'd driven with her family from their small town in Texas, racing against time as a court ruling temporarily blocked Louisiana's abortion ban. She was thin and looked tired. At twenty-seven, she already had three young boys. She told me she was a stay-at-home mom, that she was lonely, and that each of her pregnancies had made her severely ill, often leaving her hospitalized.

She couldn't imagine going through that again.

"I don't think that my overall health can take it, let alone my mental health," she told me.[16]

This time, as I sat in another quiet room with a woman facing an unwanted pregnancy, I offered no advice, no answers—only questions.

# 13

# SUFFER THE LITTLE CHILDREN

Once children are born in an evangelical family, they are to be guided with a firm hand. Evangelical leaders teach young parents that it's God's will to guide kids' minds, hearts, and souls in the way of Christ. To do that, the thinking goes, the Bible teaches that they must physically discipline their children as a means of training them for life and for eternity, preparing them to submit not just to the will of their parents but to the will of God. In the evangelical view of the Bible, the admonition in Proverbs that "whoever spares the rod hates their children, but the one who loves their children is careful to discipline them" must be taken literally.[1]

Dobson's *Dare to Discipline* is among the earliest and best-known examples of what became a genre of Christian parenting manuals offering an evangelical alternative to secular experts like Dr. Benjamin Spock, the pediatrician whose 1946 bestseller *The Common Sense Book of Baby and Child Care* became the parenting Bible for many families for decades. Dobson, and others who would follow him, promised a vision of parenting rooted in Scripture, the guide for all aspects of life for evangelical Christians.

In retrospect, what these books were promoting was a culture of systematic and spiritualized child abuse. Along with other conservative Christian writers such as Michael and Debi Pearl, who came to prominence in the 1990s, many advocated spanking children as young as fifteen months old as an essential method of teaching appropriate behavior.[2] In *Dare to Discipline,* while advising that discipline should be "administered in a calm and judicious manner" and cautioning against punishing children "too frequently or too severely," Dobson nonetheless stresses that "the spanking should be of sufficient magnitude to cause the child to cry genuinely." Later, he says that if a child cries for longer than five minutes, the parent should "require him to stop the protest crying usually by offering him a little more of whatever caused the original tears."[3]

Others, like the Pearls, took it further. On her blog in 2013, the late writer Rachel Held Evans, whose work inspired countless evangelical young adults to rethink their faith, wrote about the tactics advised in the Pearls' guide to "biblical discipline," *To Train Up a Child.* As Held Evans notes, the couple advocated spanking children with plastic tubes, and doing whatever was necessary to punish defiant children, even if it meant holding them down and sitting on them.[4] As the *New York Times* had reported in 2011, the Pearls' methods came under heightened scrutiny after three children whose parents had been influenced by their teachings died of apparent abuse. The Pearls have insisted that they oppose disciplining children in anger or causing physical harm.[5]

In "Ministry of Violence," a three-part series published on Substack in 2021, writer Talia Lavin delves into the history—and longer-term impact—of teachings on discipline promoted by a host of conservative Christian writers and speakers, including Dobson and the Pearls. The response to a social media callout asking people from evangelical backgrounds to share their experiences as children on the literal receiving end of these teachings "was immediate, and wide-ranging, and intense," Lavin writes. Lavin heard from scores of people* ranging from their twenties to their sixties, expressing "so much candid anguish I marveled the words didn't etch holes in my screen."[6]

They told Lavin about being spanked with wooden spoons and belts and hands, sometimes dozens of times, sometimes unclothed, sometimes leaving them bruised or even bleeding—all in the name of raising "godly" children.

Dobson had rightfully cautioned against the dangers of lashing out in anger and disciplining too harshly. But even for those whose parents never lost control or left them bloody, the carefully prescribed, intensely religious nature of the discipline could fuel feelings of confusion and shame.

Spanking, according to Dobson, was a unique tool to facilitate bonding and communication between parent and child: "The child will often want to crumple to the breast of his parent, and he should be welcomed with open, loving arms. . . . You can tell him how much you love him, and how important he is to you. . . . This kind of communication is not made possible by other disciplinary measures" such as a time-out.[7]

Most evangelical parents I've known would condemn child abuse *per se* as a betrayal of their God-given responsibility to care for their children. But spanking was viewed as something distinct—God-ordained, and therefore, by definition, not abuse. Abuse, I was told, often involved a parent losing control and becoming violent,

---

* By way of full disclosure, as Lavin was posting on Twitter about research for this series of articles, I reached out and we had a private background conversation about my own experiences and perspective. I was not formally interviewed or quoted in the piece, even with a pseudonym.

rather than calmly and intentionally carrying out God's instructions.

For the child, though, the experience of being hit by a parent, the person responsible for your very survival, was often a "violative and bewildering moment," Lavin writes. "Memories of the infraction fade, but a sense of betrayal lingers, as well as the sense that love and pain flow from the same font."[8]

Hillary McBride, a Canadian trauma therapist who often works with patients from evangelical backgrounds, wrote in a thread on Twitter in October 2022 about repeatedly coming face-to-face with the impact of Dobson's teachings: "On a full day last week, every single adult patient I saw happened to mention the prolific and enduring trauma they experienced because of how their parents disciplined them as children, as instructed by James Dobson. If you were a child parented under this absolute farce of psychological theory, I want you to know that your strong will, your clear bodily knowing, your powerful emotions, and your capacity to resist what you were being taught, was a resource and deserved to be protected."[9]

In an interview, McBride told me her patients often struggle with anxiety, depression, substance abuse, chronic overwork, and other coping mechanisms. She said she recently opened a ketamine clinic to better serve those and other patients. McBride said she's hopeful; she believes "there's no brain that can't change."[10]

Emily Joy Allison, a writer living in Nashville, told me she experienced what she describes as "ritual physical abuse"[11] for more than a decade, in part because of the influence that evangelical teachings about discipline had on her parents. For Allison, the author of #ChurchToo: How Purity Culture Upholds Abuse and How to Find Healing, the methodical nature of the discipline produced its own trauma.

"My parents never once flew off the handle and hit me. Never once was it anything like, 'Oh, I got angry and smacked you,' or something. I could forgive that, because that's fucked up, but it's human at the very least," she said. "I felt like the way that they handled it was inhuman. They would only do it while they were calm. It was with a sanded-down two-by-four with Bible verses written on it—like literally hitting me with the Bible."

For some, particularly women, that intertwining of love and pain—inflicted on an intimate area of the body—produced confusing, shameful feelings. Allison described the ritualized nature of the abuse as having a "psychosexual" undercurrent.

In Lavin's series on evangelical discipline, a forty-year-old woman named Heather described the confusing, intrusive erotic feelings she experienced from being spanked by her parents:

> *There's something about being beaten in such a religious, ritualistic, intimate way that feels almost sexual, even if it's not intended as such. Child me picked up on that too, and started having sensual feelings about it. And felt extremely guilty for that, and wanted it to stop, but those thoughts intruded in my head. So much that I asked God to kill me. He didn't.*[12]

There's no way to know how common this experience is, but I do know that it is real—with lifelong implications.

My own earliest memories of feelings that I now understand as sexual arousal are bound up with my experiences of being spanked, many times over many years throughout my early childhood. Before I ever heard words like "fantasy" or "fetish," I was lying in bed as a very young child, constructing detailed stories in my mind about a blond girl who got into trouble for a variety of reasons.

I imagined these scenes like a scriptwriter: the infraction, the lecture, the discipline. As I would visualize these scenes unfolding, featuring a main character who looked a lot like me, I felt a strange sensation of excitement and pleasure comingled with self-loathing and disgust.

To my great shame, those sensations would return when I was punished by my parents, bewilderingly present alongside a sense of embarrassment, betrayal, anger, helplessness, and fear. Those feelings of humiliation and pain are, for me, forever intertwined with eroticism, in ways that have alternately complicated and enhanced my adult sexual relationships.

In my house, the "rod" took many forms: the first one I remember was a thin switch probably pulled from one of the trees in our giant backyard. My parents rotated through different implements: a salad server, a narrow piece of wood, a ping-pong paddle with the ball removed, a hairbrush, and, naturally, a wooden spoon.

Spanking was embedded in the culture of our evangelical community: one of my parents' friends carried around a wooden spoon sticking out of her diaper bag, ready to use on her toddler. Another friend from church had a wooden paddle hanging on her bedroom wall labeled "The Rod." At least once when I was at her house, her father interrupted one of our playdates to take her and the paddle into his bedroom as a consequence for a supposed infraction I don't recall; I could hear her down the hall, crying out with every swat, as I sat nervously on the living-room sofa.

The last time it happened to me, I was twelve years old, fully into puberty, and nearly grown to my adult size. During a junior high choir concert, I had what in retrospect was probably a panic attack. I'd become overwhelmed with obsessive thoughts about going to Hell, and fearful that I would commit the "unforgivable sin"—a mysterious idea mentioned in passing in the New Testament, which had haunted me from the first moment I heard of it as a small child.* The thought that there was something I could do that was beyond the reach of God's forgiveness terrified me, and often kept me awake at night. Intrusive thoughts would slip in randomly, at any moment—during the school day or a summer day at the swimming pool—and suddenly I'd be gripped by fear.

One of these moments came over me as I stood at the top of the risers, with the tall kids, in a festive dress chosen for the concert. I froze, unable to keep singing.

No one seemed to notice, until I got home. My mom had seen and asked me why. Overcome by shame and fear, knowing how strange the answer was, unable to find the words to explain what had happened, and too afraid to utter the words even if I could, I lost control. I began to sob and ran into the kitchen. I flung open the knife drawer and screamed, "I want to kill myself!" I didn't really mean it, but I was out of my mind with anxiety and embarrassment.

My dad ran in and stopped me. The next thing I remember, I was upstairs in their bedroom, both of them wrestling me to the carpeted floor of their walk-in closet, my mother holding me down so my father could hit me with some kind of wooden implement.

Given their influence on my parents and so many others, I reached out to both Focus on the Family and Dobson, who resigned as chairman at Focus in 2009, to ask for comment for this book.[13] Focus is far from the only influence that shaped the actions of a generation of evangelical parents, but it was likely the most prominent and influential. A spokeswoman told me that the current president,

---

* Theologians have debated what this means, but the idea stems from a passage in Matthew 12, where Jesus warns that "blasphemy against the Spirit" will not be forgiven.

Jim Daly, could not make time for an interview but would accept questions via email. I wrote back in August 2022 with several questions, including whether the organization still endorses the use of corporal punishment as promoted by Dobson.

After some hesitation, I decided to add one final question based on personal experience. I described that experience at age twelve and added:

> I had purple and green bruises the next morning. I also remember hearing my younger siblings screaming down the hall as they were disciplined in the same way. I will never be able to erase the sound of their cries, or the sound of wooden implements repeatedly swatting their little bodies, from my memory. At 41, I still have flashbacks and have spent significant time in therapy discussing these events. Based on my research, I know I'm not alone. Do you have a response to this?[14]

Both Focus on the Family[15] and a spokesperson for Dobson declined to be interviewed.[16]

As exvangelicals form their own families as adults, parenting their children outside the strict evangelical framework can feel overwhelming and frightening. Rebekah Drumsta, who runs a website offering life coaching and other resources focused on religious deconstruction, said it's daunting to figure out how to parent differently than the way you were parented.

"You don't want to mess up your kid," she said. "Often people put off deconstructing because they're scared, and they stick with tradition, because that's what they're comfortable with, that's what they know."

As a young mother, what Drumsta knew was, much like my

own childhood, a culture where parents kept "spank sticks" tucked into their bags.

"They would haul the kids out in the middle of a church and you'd hear them in the bathroom, whacking them," she said. "Then the kids would come in with tears streaming down their face and sit down. Talk about public humiliation—you could hear it in the middle of the church service."

As she navigated new parenthood, Drumsta admits to swatting her daughter a few times. But something about it felt wrong.

The breaking point was the moment her young daughter asked why Mommy hit her.

"I was like, 'Mommy didn't hit you. You got in trouble.' And she said, 'No, you hit me,'" Drumsta said. "And in that moment, I realized my child's brain did not know the difference between being hit and being spanked. So why would I be the mom who hits?"

She decided that it would never happen again. And it was a revelatory moment in her parenting. After decades of messages from the church telling her that her emotions would deceive her and lead her astray, away from God's path, she realized that her intuition was providing her with valuable information.

"My gut had always told me something was off," she said. "I started realizing my gut was actually taking me in a healthier direction. I was connecting with my child."

It was even bigger than that. Becoming a mother, and experiencing the love that naturally flowed from her toward her child, became part of her deconstruction. Drumsta began to rethink evangelical teachings about the nature of humanity.

"As I'm laying in bed looking at my precious newborn, I remember having the thought: 'How is my child evil? How is she sinful? How did people think that?'"

Parenting differently than she was parented has meant figuring out a lot of things as she goes, both about being a mom and about what she believes about the world. Without the neat answers that religion can provide, Drumsta said she's had to be honest with her daughter about what she doesn't know and she's willing to learn. Sometimes that means taking her daughter to the library to look for factual answers about science or history or whatever she wants to know.

"So we have been on this journey together," Drumsta said. "And I don't know the outcome yet. I'm seeing the outcome so far. I'm so proud of who my daughter is. I have not tried to break her will, which is what was done to me."

It's a journey that requires vulnerability, Drumsta said, admitting to her daughter that she doesn't have all the answers, and that, sometimes, she might change her mind.

For exvangelical parents, the arrival of a child often means contending in a new way with the big questions. It's one thing to be uncertain or embrace change when it comes to your own beliefs about God and the afterlife, but what do you tell your child, the person you love most, about the meaning of existence?

Holly Fletcher, who grew up as a Southern Baptist missionary kid in Kenya, spent many years slowly shifting her theology in a more progressive direction. She now attends an LGBTQ+-affirming church in the Washington, DC, area. Fletcher told me she wanted to retain a connection to Christianity, but that meant figuring out how to parent as a progressive exvangelical. Fletcher has sometimes required her children to attend church with her, telling them that it's important to her that they participate in their family's tradition.

But she's balanced that requirement with allowing them to decide what to believe.

"Even if you aren't sure about the belief system, it's about being part of something bigger than yourself— spiritually, but also culturally and traditionally," she said. "This is thousands of years that people have been carrying this on. And I think when it's beautiful, it's really beautiful."[17]

Those questions can trigger complicated emotions for parents still struggling with their own answers. Cindy Wang Brandt, author of the book *Parenting Forward,* works with parents dealing with their own religious trauma.[18] When children ask questions like what happens after death, she advises parents to first assess why the child is asking and respond pragmatically.

If it's a philosophical question, she said, offer a range of options: "It's very appropriate to say, 'There are religions that believe this; there are philosophers who believe that; there are poets; there are scientists, and they all have their interpretations.'"

If a child seems to be asking about death out of anxiety and fear, Wang Brandt suggests walking them through some breathing exercises and reminding them that they're safe.[19]

For Emily and Travis Tingley, who live in Nashville and began deconstructing their evangelical faith several years ago, not having answers for their daughter, Daisy, was frightening at first.[20] They worried about not raising her with a firm set of beliefs.

"I was kind of raised, 'If you don't stand for something, you'll fall for anything,'" Emily said. "I was like, 'Oh no, her brain is going to turn to mush because I don't have a rule book or a system.'"

Emily and Travis said they found help from a podcast hosted by Wang Brandt, and from the progressive Christian writer and speaker Rob Bell. Emily said one of his episodes got her thinking about the importance of modeling emotional and mental well-being for Daisy, who's now in her early teens.[21]

"I was like, 'Oh my gosh—the best parenting I can give her is my own healing,'" she said. "That was beautiful and freeing, but it was also really scary. I was like, 'I can do that, but it's a lot of work.'"

At some point, Emily said, she realized she had stopped disciplining her daughter "almost to a fault" and stopped trying so hard to produce a perfect Christian child.

"When I let go of the idea that we were depraved, I started to see her so differently," Emily said. "The more that I let go, the more that it was so easy for me to see her as a gift and something to be enjoyed, and something to treasure and protect."

When Bekah McNeel became a mother, she had to grapple with how much of her conservative evangelical background she wanted to pass on. In her book, *Bringing Up Kids When Church Lets You Down,* McNeel, who now describes herself as a progressive Christian, describes wrestling with how to parent her children and how to talk to them about God, morality, politics, science, and faith. But she came to the conclusion that showing them gentleness and love should be the foundation for the rest of their spirituality.

"Parents are a child's first God-like presence," McNeel writes. "How we treat them is how they will assume God treats them."[22] In my own experience, parenting as an exvangelical has meant stepping out onto an unfamiliar road without a guidebook. It's meant having my boys baptized in the Episcopal Church and asking them to carry the chuppah down the aisle for my wedding to their Jewish stepfather. It's meant long conversations with their dad, friends, teachers, and pediatricians about how to guide them through the twists and turns that growing up inevitably brings. It's meant long conversations with *them*—about how to treat other people, how to think critically, and how to make the most of the gift of life. And it's meant telling them that even adults don't have all the answers, but that asking them is part of what makes us human.

The winding journeys of my parents and grandparents have brought me, and my children, to where we are. But as a parent, I can't keep looking back. I have to step out onto that unfamiliar road, because children are made for the miles yet to come on the journey, not the ones already crossed.

# 14

# BROKEN FOR YOU

The house was unusually quiet one afternoon when Bethany Johnson came home from middle school. There was no sign of her family, except for her mom's jeans and gray button-down sweater draped over the bed in oddly perfect alignment. She remembers[1] the "comfy white sneaker-looking shoes" her mom, a nurse, wore to work, with socks still inside them.

"Like she had been sitting there," Bethany said. "As if she literally—poof!—vanished."

Bethany raced around the house and yard, searching for her.

"I thought, 'Surely this wasn't it! Surely this was not the Rapture—it can't be,'" she said.

Eventually, her mother emerged from hiding, somewhere in the basement, she thinks. Bethany realized she'd been playing a game of hide-and-seek, contrived by her mother in an elaborate effort to make sure she was ready for the Rapture, which her Assemblies of God church in southwest Missouri believed could be imminent.

Her mom asked if she was scared.

"She said, 'Well, if you were scared that the Rapture happened, that means that there's something in your heart that's not right,'" she said. "And we need to come together and see what it is."

Even so, a decade after her mom's death, Bethany still describes her as a "saint."

"She did the best that she could with the information, the beliefs that she had," she said. "As a parent and in the church, your job is to save the souls of your kids, so you're going to do whatever you think necessary."

Bethany, who now lives in Texas, said the experience—and the theology wrapped around it—left scars.

"There is no fear in love. But perfect love drives out fear," the book of 1 John promises.[2]

And yet, the fear of falling out of favor with God, and missing the Rapture, was so strong that Bethany's family prayed each night, asking God to forgive any sins they might not even be aware they committed.

"Because if you sin and you go to sleep, and Jesus comes back, then you're not making the Second Coming, and that's terrifying as a child going to sleep, not knowing if you're going to see your parents that next morning," Bethany said.

Closely tied to that fear was another: being left behind for the Great Tribulation, a seven-year period of terrible suffering and evil that some Christians believe will precede the end of the world. There are many different views of the end-times—or eschatology— within Christianity and even within evangelical Christianity. But Bethany's family subscribed to a view that if they were left behind during the Rapture, their only chance of salvation would come at a very high cost.

There would be a time, Bethany's mother warned, "when people would come to your home and ask you, 'Do you still think you're a

Christian? Do you still love God?' My mom said you'd only go to Heaven if you said yes, and then in that moment they would chop your head off."

I told Bethany that I, too, had grown up with this fear of living through the Tribulation, a time of extreme persecution, when a vicious leader called the Antichrist would take over the world, and Christians everywhere would face the choice of denying Christ or beheading.

"Oh my God, that makes me so happy!" Bethany said, relieved to hear she wasn't alone, before adding quickly, "Well, obviously not."

But Bethany and I were far from alone. Evangelicals have produced at least two film series about these biblical prophecies, which have been shown to countless young churchgoers during Wednesday-night services or, in my case, junior high Bible class at my Christian school.

Many Gen-Xers and older millennials like myself grew up watching *A Thief in the Night* and its three sequels—a low-budget film series produced in the 1970s and early '80s. The title refers to a rather scary passage in 1 Thessalonians that's often quoted in sermons about the end-times, which warns that no one knows when the Lord will return, so we must always be prepared: "For you know very well that the day of the Lord will come like a thief in the night. While people are saying, 'Peace and safety,' destruction will come on them suddenly, as labor pains on a pregnant woman, and they will not escape."[3]

At the beginning of the film series the protagonist, a young woman named Patty, misses the Rapture and is left to endure the Tribulation. Key to the plot is the idea that Patty believes herself to be a Christian until she is left behind and discovers that she and others in her church—clearly a mainline Protestant congregation—are not truly saved.

I don't know about thieves in the night, but I remember plenty of nights without sleep during the weeks after we watched those films. I was particularly preoccupied by one scene where (spoiler alert) Patty is led out the back door of the church, where she and other Christians are being held hostage, to an awaiting guillotine. I'd lie awake in bed, those images flashing through my mind, repeating a passage from the third chapter of Proverbs: "When you lie down, you will not be afraid; when you lie down, your sleep will be sweet. Have no fear of sudden disaster or of the ruin that overtakes the wicked."[4]

Bethany grew up with the more recent iteration of these end-times films, the *Left Behind* series, starring evangelical actor Kirk Cameron, based on novels written by the Christian writer Tim La-Haye. It wasn't until her late twenties that she realized how deeply she'd been traumatized by this belief system. She was trying to fall asleep one night in the summer of 2021, when she says she was jolted awake by a memory from those days.

"If I miss the Rapture, the only way I could go to Heaven is my head being cut off," the thought came, suddenly and out of nowhere. "It was as if I had woken up out of a terrible, terrible dream—the dreams that you can feel and you can't go back to sleep, but I hadn't even slept yet."

Experiences like these have prompted Bethany to begin sharing her experiences, some of them under the hashtag #religioustrauma, on several social media platforms. In response, she said she hears particularly from women who grew up in evangelical purity culture and are wrestling with shameful feelings about their bodies. It's something Bethany has also dealt with.

"[It's] the way we talk to little Christian girls saying, 'Okay, cover up, 'cause that's good,'" she said. "And that's going to impact them when they're adults."

In her 2019 book, *You Are Your Own: A Reckoning with the Reli-*

*gious Trauma of Evangelical Christianity,* Jamie Lee Finch describes feelings of guilt as she physically matured and experienced normal sexual desires, including experimenting with masturbation, as a teenage girl. She writes about fearing that she was "ruining" herself for her future husband, and a resulting "strange and unhealthy comfort with feelings of shame in my physical body. It didn't take long for this to deepen into a comfort with feelings of actual disgust and hatred for my physical body. The more I hated my body and all of Her sensations and emotions, and the more uncomfortable or even disgusted my own body made me feel, the closer I was to ridding myself of my curse of sin . . ."[5]

While many therapists are treating trauma survivors from a variety of religious backgrounds, Finch argues that evangelicalism is a particularly powerful driver of trauma: "What has become more and more apparent to me is that the core doctrines and teachings of fundamentalist Evangelicalism are extremely traumatic because they distort the way the human psyche would naturally function and thrive" by emphasizing the authority of religious leaders to explain and interpret the world, and the intense focus on the afterlife to exclusion of the present. This, Finch argues, results in "disconnection—from self, from other people, and from the outside world."[6]

For Bethany Johnson's exvangelical social media followers, and others, along with young women from her church who reach out privately to discuss their religious trauma, there's often a sense of both relief and secrecy around discussing these experiences.

"'Hey, I'm dealing with this now,'" they tell her. "'I'm too scared to talk about this, so I'm glad somebody is.'"

Sometimes it's comforting to know you're not alone in your trauma. But if the trauma is shared by someone you love and want to protect, it's more complicated. My brother, Danny, is my youngest sibling—eight years my junior—so when I was off to college, he was still in Sunday school and on the swim team. It was at practice one day that he first remembers experiencing a feeling much like Bethany did as she was falling asleep.

"I burst out of the pool [with] this overwhelming panic that came on extremely fast," he said.[7]

Suddenly, he was overwhelmed with the idea of eternity, and the notion of consciousness, never ending. He became preoccupied with a horrifying thought: What if our parents had it all wrong? What if we had the wrong religion, or even the wrong kind of Christianity?

"Because from our point of view, there were other Christians who'd call themselves Christians who go to church every Sunday, who were basically going to Hell, to put it bluntly, and that set in my head like nothing else," he said, not to mention people all over the world who'd never even heard of Jesus. "Okay, so they don't even have a chance? And they're going to burn in Hell forever, in never-ending torture?"

This kept happening, often when his mind was kind of blank and open, engaged in a routine, repetitive activity like swimming or playing a video game. He remembers a time when he was twelve or thirteen, playing *Call of Duty*, when something suddenly clicked in his mind.

"I literally screamed. It was something so fast, I couldn't even register what had happened in my brain, but I threw the chair back from the desk I was at, and had to run out of the room," he said. "Because it immediately clicked for me . . . that cycle of eternity. It will not end. Never, it's just not going to end. That cycle kept going and my brain was like, 'This is what I believe, this is what my parents believe. This is what everyone who matters to me believes, this is reality, this is actually going to happen. I have no say over anything. Some God put me into the world and said, "You're here forever".'"

Eventually, he could sense when the feeling was coming on and learned to conceal it. "I learned to make myself be quiet," he told me.

Danny has been to therapy, but he said it's hard to fully explain this feeling to therapists who may not have any firsthand experience with fundamentalist religion or training in religious trauma.

"I've never had a therapist or anyone I've spoken to really understand it," he said. "At any time of day, any day, it could be years in between, I'll have a recurrence of this sort of circle spiral of thought. . . . And it's kind of a mountain that I can never seem to get over. It's always there, it always seems real and threatening, and it also sounds ridiculous to talk about it out loud."

That's not an uncommon experience, according to Andrew Kerbs, a licensed professional counselor based in Kentucky who has developed a specialty in religious trauma.[8]

"I've heard this from about every single person I have ever worked with—that it's so hard to find a therapist who can take them and their trauma seriously if the only trauma that they do have is religious trauma," he said. "Because a lot of clinicians are like, 'Okay, so you weren't sexually abused, you weren't physically abused. It wasn't domestic violence. It's just this church thing,' and they struggle to, I think, understand it."

That disconnect, Kerbs said, can leave clients feeling even more isolated and misunderstood. When he talks to other clinicians, particularly those who lack training in religious trauma, he tries to explain that "religious trauma *is* trauma physiologically—the way it shows up in the body and the nervous system, it's still trauma."

Laura Anderson, a Tennessee-based psychotherapist and cofounder of the Religious Trauma Institute, said she started the organization in late 2019, after noticing similar patterns in her clients, a majority of whom came from evangelical backgrounds. She was recognizing classic signs of trauma: anxiety and depression, chronic pain and intestinal symptoms, feelings of shame and a tendency toward social isolation. Many didn't have words to describe it.

"What was happening in their bodies was consistent with all of my other trauma clients," she said.[9]

Trauma, according to the American Psychological Association, is, quite broadly, an "emotional response to a terrible event" or series of events, and the resulting, often life-disrupting emotions, experiences like flashbacks, or physical symptoms.[10] But a doctrine or belief alone is not trauma.

"It is how our body and our nervous system experiences those teachings and experiences," Anderson said.

For many people, religion is a source of comfort and community. Anderson said religion has traditionally been seen as a "prosocial" force, or a force for good. That's been an obstacle to fully understanding that religion—particularly what she describes as "high-demand" religions like evangelicalism, which involve a large degree of control and pressure to stay in the group—can also be a source of trauma.

"We're talking about religion, which most people think is a positive influence on a person's life," said Dr. Marlene Winell, psychologist, former evangelical, and pioneer in the treatment of religious trauma.[11] "With religious trauma, it's like a different ball game. There's so much that is mental and emotional."

Winell is the founder of the organization Journey Free, a group for people leaving harmful religious groups. Unlike a car accident or a war, or ongoing trauma like sexual abuse, Winell said the sources of religious trauma can be difficult to pinpoint.

"It's different from other traumas because it's institutionalized . . . as if it's a good thing," she said. "So environmentally, it's completely different from other traumas."

Through an emphasis on teachings about Hell and a person's inborn "sin nature," Winell said evangelicalism and other fundamentalist traditions can convey to children two essential messages: you are not okay and you are not safe. And then, she said, those messages are reinforced by countless symbols, objects, rituals, and respected leaders.

Some who grow up in these environments live in a constant state of low-grade stress, said Brian Peck, a licensed clinical social worker and therapist based in Idaho.

"[The feeling is] 'I never feel safe, I feel a lot of pressure.' All the demands placed on your system regarding sexuality and making sure you're not stepping out of line, that takes a toll as well," Peck said.

This prolonged trauma, or what Peck describes as "developmental trauma," can be more complex and difficult to treat than trauma produced by a single event, he said. It's often compounded by the fact that religious trauma is usually linked closely with trusted, significant adults, like parents, teachers, and clergy.

"One of the most challenging things for a nervous system is when your caregiver is a source of some support and connection, but also a source of abuse and neglect," Peck said. "And so when you want to move towards connection and care, but you also want to move away from adverse experiences—harm, rejection—and that's represented in the same person or the same organization, then your nervous system feels paralyzed by that."

And two people can experience the same situation very differently, Peck said. For example, he said, imagine a brother and sister sitting in church, hearing a message about Hell.

"Maybe the brother has some more power and control because of the patriarchy, and maybe he feels like people deserve to go to Hell, and he feels like he's not going to go to Hell himself because he believes in Jesus or whatever the case is, and so his nervous system is like, 'Yeah, cool.'"

The sister, meanwhile, feels powerless and afraid. She may hope and believe that she's been saved, but fears for the souls of other people. And sitting there in the pew, it all becomes too much, Peck said.

"In that moment, her nervous system goes into a survival response, there's a fight-or-flight response that typically shows up, and then there's no way of escaping," he said.

Such experiences can overwhelm the nervous system, creating what Peck describes as a "mismatch" between the nervous system's "internal and external resources" for coping.

Of course, many people have suffered physical or sexual abuse at church or in the name of God—a problem perhaps most notably first exposed with the Roman Catholic Church's priest sex abuse scandal, but one that is far from unique to the Catholic Church. In 2022, an independent investigation confirmed what a growing number of victims had been describing for years—decades of abuse by pastors affiliated with the Southern Baptist Convention, the nation's largest evangelical denomination.[12] The investigation found that Southern Baptist leaders had maintained a list of hundreds of suspected abusers, while in many cases failing to take appropriate action or even actively concealing allegations.[13] "It's the use of religion to carry out the trauma, to get the job done, so to speak, the use of religion to manipulate, the use of religion to hurt," said Mary Burkhart, a religious trauma life coach based in California. She said many of her clients are dealing with a potent cocktail of sexual, physical, or emotional abuse infused with religion.

Burkhart, now in her late thirties, left her charismatic evangelical church in her early twenties, after feeling disillusioned by what she describes as "the culmination of a lot of contradictions coupled with my eyes opening to a bigger world."

She said she, and many other conservative Christians, also suffered what she describes as "financial trauma" from the constant expectation in many churches to give financially, even at times of financial stress. She said people often blame themselves when they come up short after believing that God would reward their decision to give beyond their means.

"And then they're sitting in lack constantly, and wondering why God is not helping, or why the situation hasn't changed," she said. "'How come I don't have money now? How come my bill isn't paid now?'"

Burkhart, who grew up in a predominantly Black evangelical church and works with evangelical clients from a variety of racial and ethnic backgrounds, eventually found herself questioning her own beliefs after the death of a beloved pastor she'd worked with for years, volunteering hours at the church. After his wife called to say that he'd died, and that he'd seemed afraid at the moment of his death, she was shaken.

"Staying in religion for me was continuing to have an open wound. I couldn't heal, I could not find peace within myself," she said.

But the process was not straightforward or linear. She said leaving left a "void" that made her come close to taking her life, until a friend talked her through a particularly difficult moment, and she eventually sought help from a life coach.

"When you are indoctrinated into religion from a child or for a significant amount of time, religion becomes associated with every part of your life, with everything that you do, with everywhere that you go, with everything that you say, with everything you think, with everything you feel," she said.

Burkhart compares her experience, and that of many of her clients, to the unraveling of a rope made up of many tiny, tightly interwoven strands: "Every fiber is twisted together to make a bigger strand, and then those strands are twisted together to make a rope, to reinforce it. And when you start deconstructing, pulling those fibers at random can really destroy someone."

In her early days after leaving evangelicalism, Burkhart said everything seemed okay at first. She had a terrific job as a network engineer and knew that she felt better outside the church. But something still felt off, unstable.

"I still felt like there was a hole," she said. "Like I was missing something."

Over time, she worked with a life coach and learned to find a new community, outside the church. She's found connection through an online group for Black people who've left religion. She advises her clients to cultivate interests in activities like meditation that can help build a sense of peace and centeredness.

"Because deconstruction is not a destination, it's a journey. You have to continue it on, and it doesn't matter how far you come, you will still be pulling threads, being triggered, but knowing that you have the strength and the solid foundation that you're not going to unravel the whole world."

Laura Anderson said that's a common feeling for her clients, who may be fearful and struggle to imagine a life after evangelicalism.

"We're talking about this all-encompassing way of living, feeling, thinking, acting, believing. All of our relationships are tied to it, everything we do is tied to it," Anderson said. "There's a lot that we risk in that we could lose connection, we could lose our closest relationships, we might lose our job or place in the community, we might be told that we'll go to Hell. . . . That fear doesn't leave our body simply by shifting our beliefs."

This is true for many exvangelicals who've been steeped in a religious identity that stresses a "personal relationship" with Jesus, Winell said. The loss is particularly traumatic for people who've deeply embraced their faith.

"That emphasis means that when you leave the religion it's like breaking up, it's like getting divorced and you're breaking up with God, breaking up with Jesus," Winell said. So, much like a dysfunctional relationship, many exvangelicals initially try to "make it work," Winell said, by embracing Christian apologetics in an effort to overcome troubling intellectual or moral objections.

Leaving conservative evangelicalism means giving up the security of silencing some of life's most vexing and anxiety-inducing questions with a set of "answers"—about the purpose of life, human origins, and what happens after death. It also means losing an entire community of people who could once be relied on to help celebrate weddings and new babies, organize meal trains when you're sick or bereaved, and provide a built-in network of support and socialization around a shared set of expectations and ideals.

It's often felt, for me, like a choice between denying my deepest instincts about truth and morality to preserve that community, or being honest with myself and the rest of the world and risking that loss.

Working through it is not easy, Mary Burkhart said, "but if you don't try . . . you'll fester in the remains of religion."


Religious trauma therapists acknowledge that religion is far from uniformly traumatic; in fact, multiple studies have found correlations between religious observance and psychological well-being.[14] But Marlene Winell said many fail to tease out which aspects of religion are helpful, such as the structure and community support, from those that may be damaging, such as telling children that they are intrinsically sinful and at risk of eternal damnation. For those who find their experiences with religion to be painful, Winell notes that "there are other ways of getting community," such as getting involved in local organizations and connecting with other people who've been on a similar religious journey.

Laura Anderson said because religion is often viewed as a force for good, there's a tendency to minimize its negative effects.

"Experiences of abuse, harm, and adversity have been chalked up as a 'bad church experience' or the 'one bad apple' myth," she said. "Many people are told that because humans are sinful, things like abuse and harm can happen but that it's not a reflection of who God is. To that end, religious abuse, harm, and trauma have been dismissed or invalidated in a lot of cases or it is only validated in the most extreme of cases" such as clergy sexual abuse.

Anderson teaches against "binary thinking"—that religion is either good or bad. And, like Winell, she says religion can be a valuable way of finding meaning and support, but "I don't think that this is something that religion has the corner market on."[15]

Trauma related to religion is nothing new, but Anderson said she saw a notable shift around 2016 in evangelicals speaking out on social media and discovering they were not alone in their feelings.

"That is when we started to see really a mass exodus of people from these high-demand, high-control religions, evangelical Christianity, fundamentalism," she said. "We saw a lot of people going, 'I don't know what quite happened, but this is not what I was taught, and all these people that I've looked up to, these people that I've trusted to guide me to have my best interest and to lead me towards God, they made these really weird choices and there's something not quite right.'"

Kerbs said he's also seen an influx in recent years of evangelical clients leaving church out of frustration with the association between their faith leaders and the far right, and a sense that white supremacy has become deeply enmeshed in white American evangelicalism. Kerbs said for some exvangelicals, their church's response, or lack of response, to the death of George Floyd was a breaking point.

"I've seen a huge number of people leaving church with no intention of coming back," Kerbs said. "And they are becoming more aware of, like, 'This really affected me,' and saying, 'Maybe I need professional help for some of the things I'm dealing with.'"

For others, the turning points come in smaller ways, through nagging doubts and interactions with people outside the evangelical world. Brian Peck, the therapist in Idaho, said his own departure from evangelicalism began more than two decades ago, during his college years. Peck grew up in Ohio and Pennsylvania in the Holiness movement, one of the many flavors of conservative evangelicalism. He tried Bible college for one year, he said, before transferring to Penn State, where he began to meet people from a wide variety of backgrounds.

"I met secular folks who were ethical and moral and compassionate, and all the things, the caricatures and stereotypes that I learned in church, that I discovered weren't true," he said.

One turning point for Peck was a literature class, where he found himself, as a white heterosexual Christian male, in the minority for the first time.

"I was hearing stories, both reading the literature as well as hearing personal stories, about the way my religious beliefs were hurting other humans," he said. "And there's a lot of cognitive dissonance in that experience. I discovered that I could either be the compassionate human that I wanted to be in the world, or I could maintain my same religious beliefs and be part of my religious community. And I realized that I couldn't do both."

Now in his forties, his practice focuses almost entirely on religious trauma survivors, including former evangelicals, ex-Mormons, and ex–Jehovah's Witnesses.

The study of religious trauma is still relatively new, but there's growing attention to the issue by clinicians and organizations like Peck and Anderson's Religious Trauma Institute. They're leading efforts to promote research into religious trauma and related topics like the psychological impact of purity culture, and offer support and training to mental-health care providers.

And it's not only about leaving religion; for some patients, it's a process of reimagining their relationship with it.

"Religion can be a source of health and safety for some folks and also a source of harm for others," Peck said. "I think it behooves us to talk about it in ways that acknowledge: what are the protective factors inside of a religious community, what are the adverse experiences, how do we acknowledge this, how do we support folks who have been harmed?"

Anderson said her group is not opposed to religion but focused on training clinicians to help people recover from trauma inflicted in religious contexts, and assist clients in finding a path forward—with or without religion.

"I certainly do not want to diminish other people's experiences, where they really have found something that is powerful or profound within a religious system," Anderson said. "I am not anti-religion. If you can find something that honors authenticity and autonomy and being able to have choices, and it's within a religious or spiritual context—great."

Treatment and recovery from religious trauma are similar to therapies for other types of post-traumatic stress, Kerbs said. And it may require more than talking with a therapist. Trauma gets wrapped up in the "survival part of your brain," Kerbs told me, and even if you've long ago reached a place where you've intellectually moved beyond certain beliefs, they can still have a grip on the nervous system.

"Okay, so maybe this fear of Hell is irrational, but the survival response that is being activated by those thoughts, it's a different part of your brain," Kerbs said. "And so when it comes to trauma treatment it's definitely not so much about going through the narrative and identifying, 'Oh, this is an irrational thought.' It's definitely more about learning to feel safe in your body again."

Trauma therapists are using a variety of methods to help patients do that, including eye movement desensitization and reprocessing, or EMDR, a technique that's been used to help PTSD sufferers such as military veterans.[16] Others advocate incorporating techniques like yoga or meditation into a larger treatment program. Those techniques, which involve both the body and the mind in the treatment process, are important, Peck said, because it's not often possible to think your way out of trauma.

"Our nervous system doesn't speak English," he said. "It doesn't care about our story, it really doesn't. I wish that it did."

Peck said when someone suffers a single traumatic event, part of treatment can include working back mentally and emotionally, thinking about a time that felt more safe and secure. But for people who grew up in stressful home environments, being fed theological messages that undermine any sense of safety, the healing process can be more complex.

"If I'm saying, at the moment you're born, 'you're sinful and you're broken; there's something wrong with you,' and that's reinforced in the very earliest messages that you receive as a child," he said. "Talking to exvangelicals, if you ask the question, 'What does it feel like to be safe?' Often, they don't have a really good answer. They know how to survive, but they don't know how to feel safe."

Healing, he said, requires rebuilding a sense of safety "from the ground up."

But that requires reaching out for help, which may be challenging at first for some exvangelicals who've come from backgrounds where seeking mental health care itself was stigmatized. In many evangelical circles, mental health problems are seen as possible signs of spiritual weakness, best dealt with through prayer and pastoral care or mentoring from other church members.[17] This reluctance to seek professional help can exacerbate mental health problems and fuel shame around getting help for religious trauma, Peck said.

"I think certainly that kind of skepticism of therapy that exists in a lot of churches is preventing folks from getting the kind of healthcare that they need," Peck said. "To venture into a therapist's office for the first time with all of that uncertainty, you can know rationally, 'This is what I need to do; this will be helpful for me.' But you're still bringing with you that previous baggage."

The growing awareness of religious trauma, driven in part by online hashtags like #exvangelical and conversations about religious deconstruction, represents a significant advancement since the beginning of Winell's career. Winell is the author of the 1993 book *Leaving the Fold,* which offered advice for people leaving fundamentalist backgrounds at a time when "no one was talking about" religious trauma.

Her work grew out of her own experience, growing up in the 1950s and '60s as a Christian missionary kid in Hong Kong and Taiwan. As she moved into her therapy practice, Winell realized that many of her patients were tortured by fears and anxieties grounded in their own religious upbringings, and were exhibiting classic trauma symptoms. She and some colleagues began to use the term "religious trauma syndrome."

"People have really resonated with it. There was a need for a name," she said. "It's interesting how sometimes a name helps a lot with helping people not feel alone, or feel crazy, like they've made it up."

Winell said the label also has been important for advancing research into religious trauma, and developing treatments for people suffering from it. But she said the field of psychology has been relatively slow to embrace the study and treatment of religious trauma, because religion is so deeply "institutionalized" and intertwined with other concepts like culture and diversity.

"Talking about it is a taboo, criticizing it is a huge taboo," she said. "You have a client and you're supposed to respect their culture, and you're also supposed to respect their religion."

Even so, Winell said that's gradually shifting with the growing secularization of culture and aided by the rise of podcasts and social media. Winell said the internet has made it possible for her clients to pursue questions about their faith.

"There are powerful forces that keep people in so when you find out from more information that's around that people do make a change, and leave their religion, then that gives you more options and more hope," she said. "And I think that possibility of freedom spreads."

For my brother, Danny, and for myself, healing is an ongoing journey. We've each seen several therapists, none of whom specialize in the relatively new area of religious trauma but who've listened sympathetically nonetheless. We've both tried ketamine, a relatively new psychedelic therapy that's shown some promise for treating trauma of all kinds.

Danny said he's been working on trying to make sense of both the good and the bad from our evangelical childhood.

"That's kind of the ultimate insurmountable problem that I run into all the time," he said. "Trying to marry the two ideas that I generally had a fine childhood, but also, I still deal with repercussions from it. That is the thing that therapists have not been able to help me with—reconciling those two feelings that I have."

That's very much how I feel, but we're both learning to live with it.

When we talked about this recently, I asked Danny how often he finds himself thinking about something from our childhood that felt traumatic. Nearly every day, he said, less when he's busy, but it's always there, lurking somewhere in the background.

# 15

# INTO THE WILDERNESS

With newfound freedom comes new challenges—and questions.

In one of her "Church Kids" graphic stories on Instagram, Stephanie Stalvey, the Florida-based art teacher, features a young woman who appears deep in thought: "We are the church kids all grown up," it reads. "Where do we go from here?"[1]

It's a question I ask myself almost every day: Once you've discovered that the world you called home is no longer a place you can comfortably reside in, where do you go? What will you find along the way? And who might you become? For those of us wandering out of evangelicalism, we can find ourselves in a foreign—and often frightening—spiritual and emotional wilderness.

Doug Pagitt, a longtime progressive evangelical activist and pastor, told me he hopes younger exvangelicals can find ways to disentangle their faith from white evangelical politics and abusive church environments while still maintaining some connection to their Christian faith. But he acknowledges that many are "exhausted" by their experiences and feel the need to step away entirely.

"They want to not think about it for a while: 'Can I just get these thoughts out of my head? Can I stop having those songs run through my head for a while and not feel like I have to be arguing with the lyrics running through my brain?' They just want a break," Pagitt told me over coffee recently in Washington, DC.[2] "That's the forty days in the wilderness. And then you start to remake something else."

Pagitt is executive director of the group Vote Common Good, whose mission is to persuade evangelicals and Catholics that they don't have to vote Republican to be faithful Christians.

"I think it's healthy to be able to find those things that others have joined together that should have never been joined together," Pagitt told me. "Power is not in stopping or quitting; spiritual power is the ability to be in your agency and realize that you don't have to go along with that deal that was made on your behalf by someone else."

Stalvey's comic depicts several of the key tension points that are pushing many evangelical adults out of a movement that had once carefully and purposefully nurtured them: disillusionment with "the gap between our Christ and our Christian culture" and an unavoidable awareness of what Stalvey calls the "toxicity" that's embedded in much of white evangelicalism. In a later frame, the woman asks if it's possible to "separate and salvage the good from the bad."[3]

Stalvey told me that for herself, and many of her exvangelical peers, there's a feeling of being "forced to choose between this world that we knew and our conscience."

Leaving behind that world often also means leaving behind friends and family, making the choice all the more excruciating. Stalvey told me that she tries to avoid talking politics with her Trump-supporting parents, but she knows other exvangelicals who've been unable to draw that boundary with their evangelical family members.

"And so they don't even have relationships with their parents anymore," she said.

This is a reality for many exvangelicals, Promise Enlow Councill thinks, that many people outside the evangelical world can't fully understand. Councill, who broke with the faith of her high-profile pastor father, notes that evangelicalism is not merely a set of religious ideas. White American evangelicalism—and the parallel universe it creates for many of its adherents—shapes virtually all aspects of life: how people dress, whom they marry, sometimes the kinds of careers they choose, their politics, and whom they consider to be friend or foe.

"It is a culture. It is a way of life. It consumes everything," Councill said. "There are so many little things that can deeply offend and upset the rest of your family that haven't left that culture. It comes at a huge cost for a lot of people to leave that, and most of us have to sacrifice something."

For my friends Kate and Andy Blair, leaving behind evangelical teachings about issues including homosexuality meant losing relationships both with relatives and members of the church they'd started in 2008 in Savannah, Georgia. Their decision to fully welcome a lesbian couple into their church sparked a quick backlash; within days after Kate officiated at the couple's wedding, Andy was stripped of his ministerial credentials by their evangelical denomination. Some church members stopped coming, and some new visitors didn't come back after realizing that the congregation included LGBTQ people.

That was painful, but what's even worse is the broken relationships with some relatives who've disapproved of Kate and Andy's spiritual evolution.

"The biggest loss for us has been family—the rejection that came with thinking differently is what has just been the hardest part," she said. "It's a struggle."[4]

The sacrifice is often too much. Terry Shoemaker, who teaches in the religious studies department at Arizona State University and has researched both American evangelicalism and exvangelicals, describes evangelicalism as a "social system to keep people committed over and over and over again." Many of the adults he's interviewed who were raised evangelical express doubts about their faith but remain affiliated with it for other reasons.

"The thing you have to understand about evangelicalism is that it is so rooted in an insular social network of family and church, that many of the people that I interview couldn't imagine leaving," he said. "This is their entire life."

Perhaps not surprisingly, a 2022 survey published by the American Enterprise Institute found that while evangelicalism has for years enjoyed one of the lowest disaffiliation rates for people raised in any faith, those who leave report feeling lonely or isolated at higher rates than people who'd left other faiths: 39 percent of former evangelicals said they felt that way all or most of the time, compared with 28 percent of mainline Protestants and 23 percent of former Catholics.[5]

For many exvangelicals, closeness with their families becomes elusive or impossible after they shift away from the faith of their childhood.

In an email[6] dated July 21, 2022—with the subject line, "Do you wish this was an email from your adult child?"—Focus on the Family addressed followers of the organization whose grown children had become distant or estranged.

"They won't return your calls," the message begins. "They ignore your texts and emails. Either you have little to no idea of what they're actually doing, or their only communication is to rub in your faith the sinful lifestyle they've embraced. It wasn't supposed to turn out this way."

The email goes on to describe the hypothetical perspective of a parent who believes they'd raised their children to follow Christ, who as adults "would accomplish amazing things, and would reach out often with all the updates, and with sincere gratitude for all you sacrificed to help them succeed. Instead, your child has grown into an adult who rejects you, and everything you believe in." The email links to an online course designed to help parents reconnect with their adult children.[7]

Atop a screenshot of the message, the Portland, Oregon–based writer D. L. Mayfield tweeted, "Good lord conservative Christian boomers are not ok." Mayfield, a millennial who grew up evangelical, continued with an imagined response to these frustrated baby boomers who'd raised their children by the tenets of Dr. Dobson and Focus on the Family only to see them walk away from it all. In a thread, Mayfield writes: "Listen your kids don't want to talk to you because your love is conditional and it is very painful!!!! To not be loved for who you are!!! By the people who were supposed to love you unconditionally!"

Mayfield's thread garnered thousands of retweets and tens of thousands of likes, and responses poured in from other adults raised in evangelical families under Dobson's heavy influence.

"Dear FoTF," wrote a woman in South Dakota, who said she'd cultivated a deep Christian faith and enjoyed many accomplishments as an adult. "But thanks to you my mother believed I was living a sinful lifestyle because of how I voted. Why would I reach out with updates to someone whom I could never please?"[8]

"Literally nobody else in my life sees me as a failure . . . except my parents, because of the religion," came a reply from another account.[9]

In a phone conversation,[10] Mayfield told me there should be no surprise that groups like Focus on the Family would see a need to help their longtime followers cope with a rising sense of disillusionment, as many of their children come of age and forge their own paths in an increasingly diverse and interconnected world.

"In a pluralistic society with access to social media, you're going to have this tidal wave of kids saying, 'No, we reject this and we're our own people,'" Mayfield said.

Mayfield, who was raised as a pastor's daughter and home-schooled before going off to a Bible college with the hope of becoming a missionary, looked like "a poster child for white evangelicalism and how to raise your kids so that they continue on in the faith."

"My goal in life was to be a really good Christian. That's how I got love, and care and attention and safety and security," Mayfield said. "It's [difficult] to be honest about how I actually feel and to risk losing relationships with the people who I wanted to love me for who I am."

Mayfield believes many evangelicals come to the movement with good motives, only to be taken advantage of by leaders who have "exploited people who have a desire to think about God, think about theology, and who want communities." Mayfield, who uses they/them pronouns, told me their writing had, for years, been aimed at well-meaning evangelicals.

"I thought, 'People will want to know about this gap between their supposed beliefs and what's actually happening,'" they said. "We live in unequal and unjust communities, and if we don't change the status quo, it's going to get worse."

But over time, Mayfield realized: "'Oh shit—white evangelicals love the status quo.'"

Mayfield said the last several years have marked a breaking point for many people with deep ties to the evangelical world who've found themselves increasingly at odds with their community over politics, issues of racial justice and gender equality, and the pandemic response.

"People don't have the emotional energy anymore to lie to their parents to get love and acceptance, and to get a slightly less awkward holiday," Mayfield said. "But there is such deep grief there."

\*   \*   \*

"Grief" was also the way David Gushee described the experiences of the many exvangelicals he's taught as a Christian ethics professor at Mercer University.

"[They're facing] alienation from parents and siblings and extended family networks and churches and Christian schools," Gushee said. "That's a lot of losses. So there's a lot of grief."

My friend the writer Jeff Chu thinks that sense of alienation has intensified in recent years, as many evangelicals have found themselves "at a different kind of crossroads." In the past, Chu told me, when people left evangelicalism, often their family and friends would stay in touch, hoping they'd eventually return: "[They'd think], 'Maybe this is a phase. Maybe the Lord will work miracles in their hearts and they'll repent.'"[11]

But now, he said, the divisions that shape the larger culture are also cutting through many churches. And the differences over COVID vaccines, racial injustice, and partisan politics seem insurmountable.

"We're talking about pastors advocating for candidates that are espousing lies; we're talking about during the Trump administration separating families; we're talking about what it means to have a pro-life ethic when women are going to die because of a shift in the right to an abortion. And for a lot of us here, it's like more and more bricks in the walls that divide us from loved ones," Chu said. "There's a lot of pain that results in families because of all these different things that I don't think were felt so acutely ten or fifteen years ago."

Another writer, Jared Yates Sexton, grew up "deeply evangelical" in Indiana, wanting to be a preacher, until a pastor he admired had an affair with the wife of a staff member, sparking a crisis in his own faith. Yates Sexton has worked as a writing professor and author, and his work in recent years has focused on the intersections of evangelicalism, white supremacy, and far-right extremism. He told me the fallout from his work has often been intensely personal.

"The more that I've published and the more that I've spoken out about this, there are people I've known and cared about and trusted who now see me not just as an apostate, but as an agent of 'the deep state,'" he said. "That's a different type of excommunication."

For my childhood friend Daniel Doss, existing as a gay man without sacrificing a relationship with his conservative evangelical family has meant negotiating an invisible boundary. He hasn't been cut off from his relatives, but there are major parts of his life that can never be shared. During those times when many people would lean on family members for support—for example, when his boyfriend was deployed to Iraq early on in their relationship—Daniel suffered alone, in silence.

"I waited all this time to meet somebody, and I met somebody, and now he's going to war for a year," Daniel said. "I desperately wanted to talk to somebody about how terrifying that was, someone in my family. And I couldn't bring that subject up."

He thinks his family must know, on some level, that he's gay: they've welcomed his "roommate" to family holidays and other events. It wouldn't seem difficult, he suggests, to read between the lines.

"I conduct musical theater for a living," he jokes. "What more do you need? Do you need a sign? Do I need to wear bells? I mean, there it is, folks!"

And yet, they've never had a direct conversation about his sexuality.

"I've never wanted to cause my parents the sadness that that would create," Daniel said. "Part of me wants to think that there's an understanding that it's happening, but we don't have to talk about it."

So he's spent years sitting by quietly while his mom disparages a "homosexual" couple, or his uncle expresses his feelings of disgust about gay people during Thanksgiving dinner. And yet, he appreciates and holds on to the loving, warm, irreplaceable moments: hours passed playing board games during the pandemic; the way the family came together when his mother was severely ill with COVID.

"I couldn't imagine a life without family," Daniel said. "I don't want to be the person to push them away. I love them despite their crazy [beliefs], and I hope they do the same for me if they were ever to find out."

Along with the alienation, grief, and loss of relationships, there's often a sense of confusion about how to make sense of what Stalvey describes as the "terrifying complexities" and "gradients" of the world—those shades of gray that the evangelical belief system had worked strenuously to paint as black and white.[12]

For me, striking out on my own meant navigating those grays and testing waters I'd been warned to stay out of. We'd kept popular culture at arm's length, but evangelical culture had its own set of familiar rhythms and shared expectations that felt normal to me. The rules were often unstated but understood, and there was a clear structure for most gatherings.

Home Bible studies, or potlucks after the Sunday-morning service, and even baby and bridal showers began and ended with a prayer. The practice of sharing prayer requests created a vehicle for potentially fraught social interactions, a way to subtly reach out for emotional or material support, celebrate an achievement, or even exchange gossip ("Please pray for Karen's daughter. She and her fiancé are expecting a baby and they're moving up the wedding."). Teenage interactions were smoothed over by gatherings around the campfire to sing, or around a picnic table for a White-Castle-burger-eating contest. (For some reason, my parents had declared a family day of prayer and fasting; I arrived at youth group famished and won easily.)

Outside of that familiar world, many of us feel unmoored, awkward, and out of place. When I went away at sixteen to spend a semester in Washington as a Senate page, and again the summer after college to intern for my US Senator, I felt an intense other-worldliness. Many of my peers already were having experiences I could barely imagine, experiences that frankly seemed sinful and almost frightening to me in their foreignness. There was no mother or older sister or close friend to call for advice about how to dress or flirt with boys, or even how to behave at parties, where people were drinking, or dancing and listening to "secular music."

One night in the summer of 1999, a fellow Senate intern invited me to a party in Georgetown. I anxiously agreed, fearful that I'd be somehow drawn into sin or give in to the "peer pressure" I'd so often been warned about in youth group. When we arrived at the small single-family house, everyone was standing in the kitchen and the backyard, holding red Solo cups of beer.

A girl offered me one. I tried to play it cool: "No thanks, I'm actually underage and I don't really like to drink," I said nervously, expecting pushback and shunning.

"Oh, okay, cool!" the girl said, smiling.

Much to my surprise, there was no shunning. No one seemed to care what I did, which itself felt unfamiliar.

"We were all trying to be good people," Jocelyn Howard told me about growing up evangelical in Virginia. "We were given an easy definition: this is how you are a good person."

Howard had similar experiences after leaving Bob Jones University, as a developing young artist living in an artists' community for a couple of years after college, and in graduate school. After graduating in 2006, Howard discovered a "huge gap between myself and those who grew up in mainstream culture," they told me.

In graduate school, it was awkward having to admit they'd never seen a movie directed by Quentin Tarantino. Howard became adept at faking their way through conversations that involved unfamiliar pop culture references.

"I put on this little face to say, 'Please keep going with your story,' so I don't have to be under the freak-show microscope," Howard said. "I feel like an alien sometimes. I feel so out of place."

Howard told me that "'assimilate' feels like the wrong word," and yet, that's kind of how it feels—like "a wonderland where everything is upside down and backwards. . . . There are so many ways in which I still feel like I don't get it, or I don't know how to connect with 'normal' people. I learned how to socialize, I learned how to function in a very particular type of society, and then when you leave that society, there are no rules for the outside world."

Howard thinks the fear of losing all of that—a way of organizing life, a community of support, and maybe even a family—is a major reason why many people spend years deconstructing, struggling to hold on to their beliefs and stay within evangelical churches, despite discomfort with their theology or politics.

"You are asking a group of people to completely deny their entire culture," Howard said. "Their entire worldview, their family structure, and just walk away from it. It is not easy. It's a Herculean effort."

A lot of that effort involves forming a new sense of values, identity, and community, to replace what was lost.

For Jared Yates Sexton, even after leaving the church, the evangelical "programming" was hard to shake.

"I saw myself as a fallen sinner," he told me.[13] "Even though I didn't believe in the mythology of it anymore, I still viewed the world as if I had failed, as if I had come up short, or fallen victim to some sort of temptation."

While his work has alienated some of his longtime friends, Yates Sexton told me that writing about the growing authoritarianism he's observing in white evangelical Christianity forced him to make a choice about how to move forward with his own thinking, and in his own spiritual life.

"I was either going to descend into full-blown nihilism and pessimism, or I was going to rediscover more faith," he said. "I've been able to find solace, not in religious faith but in a religious-like faith in other people. The idea that we are not fundamentally stained by some original sin or wickedness, and we are not fallen, but we're actually a pretty incredible species."

Yates Sexton told me that while he doesn't attach a religious label to himself these days, he finds inspiration in the interconnectedness of human beings.

"If you want to consider that a manifestation of God," he said, "that's totally fine."

On TikTok, Abraham Piper projects a generally happy-go-lucky vibe as he muses about making sense of life outside the church as the son of a famous evangelical preacher. In a post from August 2022, Piper reflects on the years of experiences and personal growth that many former evangelicals feel they've missed during their years in the movement. Wearing a plaid sport jacket with his graying hair tied up in a man bun, Piper announces he's had a recent "epiphany" about this specific exvangelical regret. Piper warns that spending too much time contemplating the lost years is a train of thought that will take a person directly to what he calls "Desolation Station." Piper says he's been through there, and he doesn't recommend getting on that train.

"You're no less alive than you were at any previous time," he says. "Life is not the amount of time remaining. This is it. You have exactly as much life right now as you ever have."

The key to navigating what's left of that life, Piper seems to suggest, is not to focus on where you've been, but on where you are now—and where you could go next.

In the Bible, the wilderness is a place for transition and for growth. The Israelites wandered in it as they fled from slavery and looked for the Promised Land, encountering God along the way. John the Baptist goes to the wilderness, a dry and empty place, to announce the coming of Jesus. It's there that Jesus encounters the Devil and resists temptation.

Of course, it's easier to navigate with other sojourners. Terry Shoemaker said finding people with a shared experience can be critical for those struggling on their way out the door.

"Once they discovered there were other people questioning their faith, who are experiencing very similar kinds of life experiences at that moment, it was easy for them to transition," Shoemaker said. "There's strength in knowing that other people were wrestling and grappling with the same questions and sometimes the same trauma that they were grappling with."

That may mean finding support in explicitly "exvangelical" spaces, or seeking out other forms of community built around the idea of deconstruction and reimagining religious faith.

Jeff Chu told me that while he is a former evangelical, and no longer embraces much of that theology, he doesn't use the term "exvangelical," which he thinks holds a "tinge of bitterness" that doesn't resonate.

"I don't want to be stuck," he said. "Having had so much of my life already defined by evangelicalism, I don't want to spend the rest of my life now that I'm out of it defining myself in opposition to it."

Still, as a queer person, Chu has had to look outside the evangelical church for community and acceptance. Until recently he co-led Evolving Faith, an organization that describes itself as a place for "misfits" and spiritual "wanderers," which hosts conferences and other opportunities for connection, mostly for people who've left evangelical backgrounds.[14]

As Jeff thinks about the new communities he's formed, he talks a lot about compassion—both the compassion of the people he knew in church growing up, however imperfect that community was, and compassion he wants to cultivate going forward.

"The sense of being cast out made me more compassionate toward other people," Chu said. "I think it gave me a particular tenderness for people who find themselves on the margins of a group. All of these things about evangelicalism helped make me who I am, and I don't regret those things."

Many of us who've been cast out are surveying the wilderness around us, and finding that we're anything but alone.

# 16

# WRESTLING AGAINST FLESH AND BLOOD

To be an American evangelical is to be often at war—a Christian soldier, moving ever onward into an invisible battle with the highest possible stakes. As I learned in many sermons about "spiritual warfare," while on this Earth we Christians were called upon to be engaged in a fight for our souls, for the souls of our friends and neighbors, and for the soul of America and the world.

"Our struggle is not against flesh and blood," my pastors would preach, quoting from the New Testament book of Ephesians, "but against the rulers, against the authorities, against the powers of this dark world and against the spiritual forces of evil in the heavenly realms."

This threat was seen as real and ever-present. In one history textbook from Bob Jones University Press, the Salem Witch Trials are described in all of their horror, including the swirling accusations that led to hangings and other brutal executions of people, mostly young girls, deemed guilty of "witchcraft." Setting aside what to modern eyes seems like the obvious misogyny of that historical moment, the book asserts that the girls "began acting strangely after dabbling in witchcraft" and that town leaders "took steps to determine who was responsible for the witchcraft."[1]

The section notes that several potential explanations have been suggested for the girls' supposed unusual behavior, including physical or psychological illnesses. It then concludes: "While there may be truth in some of these explanations, they all overlook an obvious explanation. Some of the people in Salem may have been demon possessed. The Bible clearly shows that this can happen."[2]

From that somber vision of the world flowed the urgent call to action for Christians: "Put on the full armor of God, so that when the day of evil comes, you may be able to stand your ground, and after you have done everything, to stand."

In my conversations with fellow exvangelicals, I often remember that we'd been trained for this army from our earliest days. In Sunday school, we colored pictures of soldiers, labeling each detail of their armor as described in the passage from Ephesians: "Stand firm then, with the belt of truth buckled around your waist, with the breastplate of righteousness in place, and with your feet fitted with the readiness that comes from the gospel of peace. In addition to all this, take up the shield of faith, with which you can extinguish all the flaming arrows of the evil one. Take the helmet of salvation and the sword of the Spirit, which is the word of God."[3]

We had it all: the Truth, certainty about how to live righteously; the Gospel, to preach to everyone we met; our faith, to shield us from danger; salvation from sin and eternal damnation; and the "sword of the Spirit": the word of God.

It was daunting to hear about all we'd been called to do as a small child, but there was also a sense of being part of something dramatic and important. I have two distinct memories from one of my first summer Vacation Bible School sessions at a friend's church.

The first was being given a brightly colored plastic kazoo, which I deeply enjoyed playing, and the second was learning to sing:

> *I may never march in the infantry, ride in the cavalry, shoot the artillery*
> *I may never fly o'er the enemy, but I'm in the Lord's Army!*

We sang, making choppy marching motions with our arms, pulling in our imaginary horse reins, slapping our hands together to make a loud "shooting" sound, and spreading out our arms to "fly" high above the enemy.

*"I'm in the Lord's Army—YES, SIR!"* we shouted, making a dramatic salute with our right hands.

In elementary school, teachers would entertain us on slow days with "sword drills"—a reference to the Bible, the Sword of the Spirit, which we were to always have in our hearts and close at hand. The teacher called out a chapter and verse, and counted down as we held our Bibles by the spine—no cheating!—pages toward Heaven, waiting for our chubby fingers to flip through with as much speed as possible. Whoever could find the designated passage first and begin reading it aloud would win that round. It was fun, or at least more fun than our standard lessons, and it served a purpose—to prepare us to know God's Word, forward and backward.

But even for those soldiers who wish to lay down their swords, the battle is never far away. Scars linger, and defectors are seen as the worst kind of enemy by their former comrades.

"It is time that we declare war against this deconstruction Christian movement," John Cooper, the front man for the Christian rock band Skillet, told an audience in 2022. Covered in sweat and wearing a leather vest, Cooper called the movement a "false religion" and blamed the decline in Christian faith for alarming rates of depression and suicide among young people.[4]

\* \* \*

Writer Rachel Held Evans was arguably one of the pioneers of what would become an exodus of evangelicals of her generation. The author of six books and numerous blog posts, she wrestled openly with doubts about the evangelical faith of her childhood including the politicization of the movement. When she died suddenly at age thirty-seven after a brief illness in 2019, the most vicious responses came from her fellow self-described Christians—evangelicals and other theological conservatives who saw in her work an affront to their belief system and way of life. In the days after Rachel's death, Jeff Chu, who was among Rachel's closest friends, wrote about his grief on Twitter. He described Rachel's work as tearing down the church's "facades and false walls, built to exclude so many of us. She realized that what seemed like the center wasn't the center, and what we'd made to be the margins weren't actually the margins"— gay people, women who wanted to be pastors, people who loved Jesus but had doubts about conservative Christian beliefs.[5]

And when she died, many prominent, and not-so-prominent, evangelicals felt compelled to announce their belief that she was in Hell. Lori Alexander, who maintains an online following devoted to her vision of traditional Christian womanhood under the moniker the Transformed Wife, appeared to gloat, "She has met her Maker. . . . He is True and now she knows for sure." In screenshots of social media posts shared by Bruce Gerencser, a former pastor turned atheist who wrote a blog post rounding up some of these responses, one of Alexander's followers responded, "She is burning in Hell." In another screenshot, a woman named Emily Thomes wrote, "Life is so very short. Eternity is long. Rachel has now seen the Lord face to face and no longer has an opportunity to repent."[6]

What was most painful for me about this episode was not merely the sentiment that unbelievers would face certain damnation—to be fair, it's arguably an honest reflection of what many Christians have seen as standard beliefs, even if those beliefs aren't often discussed in such detail in polite company. What hurt the most was seeing this kind of vitriol directed at Rachel, someone who, from my standpoint, was never trying to offend or provoke; someone who was trying so hard to bridge the chasm between her community and her conscience; someone who had sincerely wrestled with the God she'd been taught to worship and tried to remain in the evangelical fold but ultimately found doing so untenable.[7]

I never met Rachel in person, but I identified with her and her project in many ways. We were both born in 1981, graduates of evangelical colleges in the middle of the country, each with two children. By 2014, when Rachel finally publicly severed ties with the movement, I'd already, years before, walked away from evangelicalism over what felt like a similar but expedited path—an early period of adulthood marked by struggle with evangelical positions on issues like science and LGBTQ+ issues, followed by a few years trying out mainline Protestant churches, before settling in as a rather half-hearted Episcopalian, the church Rachel publicly aligned with in 2015.[8]

I, too, had been accused of "apostasy"—by a member of my own family—for my support of LGBTQ+ Christians and my acceptance of my grandfather's sexuality, and warned that I was leading them to Hell. I knew what it was like to puzzle over the incongruity between what I'd been taught in my church, Christian school, and home, and what I observed and learned in the larger world. I'd followed Rachel's career throughout my adult life with interest, as well as some envy and frustration. How, I wondered, did she muster the courage and clarity, at such a young age, to wrestle so publicly and thoughtfully with her doubts and misgivings about our faith? And why, in the face of so many challenges, did she keep trying for so long to hang on to some form of an evangelical identity even as she so openly struggled with it?

In a pained post on her website announcing her decision to relinquish the fight to remain evangelical, Rachel wrote, "I think it's time to focus on finding and creating church among its many refugees—women called to ministry, our LGBTQ brother and sisters, science-lovers, doubters, dreamers, misfits, abuse survivors, those who refuse to choose between their intellectual integrity and their faith or their compassion and their religion. . . . Instead of fighting for a seat at the evangelical table, I want to prepare tables in the wilderness, where everyone is welcome and where we can go on discussing (and debating!) the Bible, science, sexuality, gender, racial reconciliation, justice, church, and faith, but without labels, without wars."[9]

But Rachel's decision to leave the table, to lay down her sword and walk away from the war, had infuriated and enraged many of her fellow Christians. Their comments layered cruelty on top of the horrific tragedy of this brilliant young writer taken so suddenly from her children, family, friends, and followers. I asked Jeff Chu about it during an interview on NPR tied to the posthumous publication of Rachel's final book, *Wholehearted Faith,* in 2021. As a labor of love, Jeff completed the book for her, piecing it together from her notes, social media posts, and conversations with friends and family.[10]

Why did Rachel's ideas seem to enrage some evangelicals so greatly, I asked Jeff?

"Somehow, much of American evangelicalism has become a place where you're not allowed to ask questions," Jeff told me. "Rachel was unafraid about asking questions. . . . In the churches of our childhoods—because Rachel and I both grew up evangelical—you couldn't question those interpretations because to question them would somehow be a sign of a lack of faith."

Jeff went on: "But here's the question Rachel had and that I have and that I think many of us have: What kind of scripture and, really, what kind of God, can't stand up to the questioning of mere mortals like us?"

I believe God can handle our questions. But as the response to Rachel—and to the larger exvangelical and deconstruction movements—suggests some evangelicals do not. In a blog post on *Medium* in 2021, writer Sarah Stankorb noted that several scholars who research evangelicalism, and whose work sometimes calls out racism, patriarchy, and other problems, had become the focus of criticism and sometimes harassment online.

For example, the Council for Biblical Manhood and Womanhood, a group that holds to complementarianism—the view that God created men and women to play different roles, with men as the leaders—had used criticism of the work of two female scholars at evangelical colleges to whip up a fundraising effort.

"Much of the anxiety around these scholars' work seems centered on fears of evangelical deconstruction," Stankorb observed, noting that writers like Chrissy Stroop, Blake Chastain, and others were giving voice to an experience that until recently had often taken place quietly and in relative isolation, among people "raised with strict, evangelical teachings that placed firm rules around their sexuality, relationships, politics, and faith. To interrogate a worldview so central to one's identity can be immensely painful. The public smearing of those who interrogate American evangelicalism is also a warning for the common deconstructing believer: you may be categorically attacked too. This is going to hurt, maybe double."[11]

To put it another way, evangelicals are not going down without a fight.

\* \* \*

This sense of embattlement, scholars of evangelicalism have argued, is not only a hallmark of the movement but is essential to its success. In 1998—my junior year of high school, the year I began as a Senate page serving Republican members of the US Senate as part of a larger vision of service to God—sociologist Christian Smith wrote: "American evangelicalism . . . is strong not because it is shielded against, but because it is—or at least perceives itself to be—embattled with forces that seem to oppose or threaten it." Without that tension, Smith writes in *American Evangelicalism: Embattled and Thriving,* "evangelicalism would lose its identity and purpose and grow languid and aimless."[12]

Smith, who received his undergraduate degree from the evangelical Gordon College, described a movement that was strong and thriving, both in terms of raw numbers and political influence, and yet perceived itself as under threat. One of the great ironies of American evangelicalism, Smith argues, is the function that this very perception serves in strengthening the sense of evangelical identity and the sense of urgency to both *preserve* the subculture and *exert* influence on the larger culture. Smith documents a long history, stretching back to at least the Puritans, of American conservative Protestants' belief that their Christian identity was in danger of being replaced by a series of threats, including Catholicism, immigration, science, and secularization.

These laments from evangelical leaders typically were followed with calls to action aimed at the project of preserving conservative Christian beliefs and ways of being, and defending those paradigms as the default for American life through social, cultural, and certainly political engagement.[13] "After reading enough of these narratives," he writes, "one begins to develop the distinct sense that evangelicalism actually feeds upon such engagement, tension, and crisis for its own vitality."[14]

In *Jesus and John Wayne,* Kristin Kobes Du Mez similarly describes an evangelicalism characterized over many decades by a sense of being ever under threat, and unified by that sense despite internal divisions between, among other things, fundamentalist versus modernist impulses. The waning threat of the Cold War, she argues, gave way to "a new war—a culture war—demanding a similar militancy. . . . For conservative white evangelicals, a militant faith required an ever-present sense of threat."[15]

You don't have to be a famous exvangelical or academic to face censure from the evangelical institutions and leaders who see themselves as messengers of God and guardians of the Truth. In a November 2021 piece for the Gospel Coalition, writer and pastor Joshua Ryan Butler took broad aim at those going through the deconstruction process, claiming it was often generated by the "desire to sin" or, as he put it, "street cred." He opined: "Doubt is hip. The desire to fit in with the cultural ethos of our moment is strong. That's why so many deconversion stories sound like everyone's reading off the same script—its well-worn clichés signaling conformity to accepted norms."[16]

In an opinion piece for Baptist News Global, Mercer divinity student Amy Hayes pushed back, expressing a feeling of being dismissed and gaslit by such responses.

"No one vivisects their faith on a whim," Hayes wrote. "Usually triggered by painful religious trauma, deconstruction engulfs a person, forcing them to confront all the ways in which the current form of their faith has failed or hurt them. For some, this vivisection results in a reimagining of their faith. For others, it soundly destroys it. For everyone, it comes with grief and pain. Because, above all, deconstruction is a loss—of certainty, of community, of comfort. It's a process that requires tenderness and trust."[17]

The idea that people leave evangelicalism out of nothing

more than a desire to "sin" is frustrating to many of the people I interviewed—and to me. People with little investment in the church are likely to simply walk away, like someone ghosting a party they didn't really feel like going to. But for those of us who took it seriously—who read the apologetics books, did our devotionals, and prayed for clarity—being told to try harder to make all the puzzle pieces fit together feels like a deliberate refusal to truly listen.

For Emily Petrini, an exvangelical in her early thirties who still describes herself as a "person of faith in Jesus," one former pastor's scathing critique of people who deconstruct felt insensitive and cruel. After college, Petrini attended the Village Church in the Dallas area led by prominent evangelical Matt Chandler—who had to take a monthslong leave of absence in 2022 after admitting to an "unwise" online relationship with a woman.[18] He has also been a vocal critic of deconstruction: In a sermon posted online in late 2021, Chandler said that "turning away from and leaving the faith has become some sort of sexy thing to do," before later clarifying that he didn't intend for his comments to cause pain to people dealing with "doubt or theological wrestle or struggling through church hurt."[19]

Petrini said the pushback from evangelical leaders like Chandler suggests an unwillingness to look inward.

"They act like the people who deconstruct aren't the ones who were first in line for every single church thing ever, who'd pored over every theology book, and who really wanted to follow Jesus— the kids who came to youth group every single time," Petrini said. "They act like it's a bunch of people who were really gullible, or who were never believers in the first place, instead of people who were in church leadership, people who went to seminary, people who were raised in this and who had very similar experiences to them."

Brit Fuller, who grew up in a nondenominational charismatic evangelical church in Louisiana before spending time as a missionary kid in Russia and Brazil in the 1990s, believes some church leaders are unwilling to listen to exvangelicals' concerns because doing so would too deeply challenge their point of view. Fuller is one of several people behind an account on Instagram and other social media platforms called @dobetterchurch, where people who say they've suffered a wide variety of forms of abuse and discrimination in churches and other religious settings have anonymously shared their stories.

"It is easier to blame the person who is leaving the environment than it is to self-reflect," she said.

Fuller said she understands that for many pastors and other leaders whose careers have been built around that identity, the exodus from the pews must feel deeply destabilizing.

"That has got to be scary for a pastor, especially if you are in the evangelical moneymaking machine," she said. "They're definitely relying on the book sales and the sermon listens and the people in the seats to keep their livelihoods going. That's got to be a terrifying thing, seeing people leave."

Indeed, exiting the battlefield forces the warrior to find a new vocation. For pastors, leaders, and others involved in ministry who themselves leave, that challenge can be particularly fraught, according to Idaho religious trauma therapist Brian Peck.

"There's a lot of pastors who are realizing that because of their experience in the church, they don't have a lot of marketable experiences or skills because they've invested a lot of their life as a pastor," he said.

In his work as a religious trauma therapist, Peck has run across former evangelical ministry leaders who've tried to repurpose those skills outside the church, offering life coaching or other forms of help to other people who are deconstructing. He calls the phenomenon "Pastoral Counseling 2.0."

But many lack the training to deal with trauma, Peck said, and may end up unintentionally repeating destructive patterns they'd learned in the evangelical world, such as minimizing mental-health challenges.

"It's a slightly different form—and probably a healthier form, I can acknowledge that—of 'just go talk to the pastor,'" Peck said. "If that's helpful and useful and is consistent with what the person needs, that can be a really amazing resource. But when that's a way of not addressing health concerns, or not getting the depression treatment that you need, it can be counterproductive."

At times, there are intramural battles between former evangelicals themselves. Critics have called out the movement for being too focused on the concerns of white evangelicals.[20] And there have been power struggles over who should get to speak for—and profit from—the movement.

After apologizing for the harm done by his Christian bestseller *I Kissed Dating Goodbye,* Joshua Harris, the purity culture guru turned exvangelical, asked his publisher to discontinue printing the book in 2018. Harris had to backpedal again in 2021, after trying to market a $275 "Deconstruction Starter Pack," prompting a variety of angry reactions.[21]

Jamie Lee Finch's 2019 book, *You Are Your Own,* explored the trauma she and others suffered as a result of being brought up in evangelical purity culture under the influence of Harris's teachings. Finch called him out on Twitter, saying he'd privately praised her work but then failed to cite it in his course.[22] And, as someone with the Twitter handle @TruthBy_JN put it: "Joshua Harris made bread from Christianity and is still making bread in his 'deconstructing' of the Faith."[23]

Writer D. L. Mayfield told me there's some "solace" found in connecting online with other progressive Christians and exvangelicals, but there's also a lot of obvious trauma swirling around those spaces, which are susceptible to the same kinds of pile-ons and toxic group dynamics as any other community on social media.

"It's really a triggered space with lots of really, really triggered people," Mayfield said. "And I would say there's trauma work that needs to be done."

Peck, the trauma therapist, said he sees that in his work with exvangelicals, and getting past it can take time and effort.

"When you've been hurt, when you've experienced trauma inside of a community, it's very hard to build community while you're still processing through that trauma," Peck said.

Over many years as a writer and senior editor at *Relevant* magazine, a mostly online publication that describes its mission as "covering the intersection of faith, life and culture," Tyler Huckabee covered exvangelicals, deconstructing Christians, and the evangelical response to them. In an interview,[24] Huckabee—who is not related to that famous political family from Arkansas—told me he believes the level of pushback from evangelical leaders suggests many see exvangelicals as part of a growing threat to their vision of a Christian way of life for the United States and the world.

"After enjoying many, many years of being the dominant cultural faction in this country and in many countries, they perceive that changing," Huckabee said. "They're trying more and more desperately to try to hold on to it so that they can have some say in the direction of the future."

Huckabee grew up evangelical in Nebraska, where we had overlapping circles of friends while I was a public radio journalist in Lincoln, and attended Moody Bible Institute in Chicago for college. He dates the beginning of his own deconstruction to his early twenties, around 2007, when he began rethinking his views on LGBTQ+ people and other issues. Eventually, Huckabee began identifying simply as a Christian.

When people leave evangelical communities, he told me, that loss means not only lost sinners but also lost cultural currency and political power.

"They're sad about their souls. But that's also money that's leaving," he said. "They perceive the social drift as being losses in a war with the highest stakes imaginable, and they're trying to find a way to fight back."

Huckabee, born in 1984, came of age at a time when "evangelicals were obsessed" with a vision of strong, white, Christian masculinity that was embodied in characters like those in the Mel Gibson film *Braveheart* in 1995 or in Christian books like John Eldredge's *Wild at Heart: Discovering the Secret of a Man's Soul* in 2001, which drew heavily on themes from the film.[25]

"They love the idea of men—of white men—being these barrel-chested, hairy, very Western, medieval warriors," Huckabee said. "But real life doesn't give you a lot of opportunities to really live that out. So the idea was you're in the Lord's Army, in sort of a cosplay mentality."

The great irony is that (predominantly white) American Christianity is seeing its numbers shrink at the same time its political power as a movement has arguably achieved its apex—in the election of Trump, the long-sought-after overturning of *Roe v. Wade,* and growing support for Christian nationalist ideas on the right. At the same time, the Pew Research Center predicts that numerical decline, largely toward an affiliation with no faith at all, will escalate in the coming decades, with a majority of Americans no longer identifying as Christians within about half a century.[26]

Some conservative Christian leaders have tried to keep these exvangelicals in the fold by responding to their concerns. Writing for *Christianity Today* in November 2021, Russell Moore, a former Southern Baptist leader, observed of the exvangelical phenomenon that "what looks like rebellion might often be pain and despair."[27]

Moore is someone I've occasionally written about and interviewed in my work for NPR. He's always struck me as the real deal—someone whose conscience guides him and whose compassion is as enduring as his theological conservatism. He wrote about what church has meant to him and how different it felt to his late father, who'd grown up as a pastor's kid and had seen some of the worst the church has to offer throughout his childhood.

"To me, my church meant home and belonging and acceptance," Moore wrote. "If I so much as smell something similar to my church foyer or a Sunday school room or those vacation Bible school cookies, I immediately calm down. And the hymns we sang together week after week after week bring to my mind, every time I hear them, whatever the opposite of trauma might be. But I had not grown up in a parsonage; my father had."[28]

His father's sometimes-complicated relationship with church eventually led Moore to realize that he "chalked up to deficient spirituality what was mostly the result of pain." So it was with many exvangelicals he'd met and taken the time to talk with, Moore said.

"Not one of them walked away because they wanted to curry favor with 'elites' or because they wanted to rebel," Moore said. "If anything, the posture of many of these people was not that of the Prodigal Son off in the far country so much as that of his father, waiting by the road for a prodigal they loved and wanted to embrace again: their church."

Moore warned evangelical readers not to assume that those who walk away from their churches do so out of a flawed understanding of the faith or a desire to sin, but to empathize with their pain.

But Moore's calls for empathy and understanding have often

seemed out of step with the prevailing sentiment among his fellow evangelicals; that essay was published mere months after Moore had parted ways with the Southern Baptist Convention, following years of facing slings and arrows for his opposition to Trump.

Some exvangelicals, like Promise Enlow Councill, warn that those who remain in the movement appear to be doubling down on what she describes as the most "toxic" aspects of their belief system.

"I think things are actually getting more culty, because as they shun people and feel shunned by people that have left, they're kind of tightening their circle up," Enlow Councill said. "They feel like this is the persecution that they all thought they were going to have. It's really other people choosing a different life path, but that feels like persecution to them."[29]

A growing body of evidence backs up Councill's observation, and suggests that some may be ready for more than a spiritual battle. In surveys commissioned by the American Enterprise Institute[30] and the Public Religion Research Institute[31] in the aftermath of the January 6, 2021, insurrection at the US Capitol, white evangelicals expressed stronger support than other groups for the idea that political violence may be necessary to protect the country. And even as some are driven away from conservative Christianity by its extremism and fusion with right-wing, nationalist politics, others are drawn into the evangelical movement because of it."[32]

As writer and religion scholar David Gushee put it in *After Evangelicalism,* the "moralistic, politicized conservative evangelicalism continually creates and then sheds dissidents. This has been going on for a while. But it certainly seems that the dissident population is growing from all racial and ethnic groups within evangelicalism. The all-powerful, mostly male, white, and American evangelical power structure is being challenged as never before."[33]

All of this leaves white evangelicalism in the midst of powerful crosscurrents, with important implications for where it could take both the evangelical movement and the larger culture.

For many soldiers, the sense of threat remains long after they've left the battlefield.

In one of his TikTok videos under the hashtags #exvangelical and #deconstruction, Abraham Piper warns against the danger of leaving evangelicalism only to embrace "a new brand of fundamentalist." As he conceptualizes it, fundamentalist impulses aren't limited to religion: "I mean the personality type," he says, calling out "black and white . . . hyper-confident" thinking.[34]

Writing on Substack, progressive Lutheran minister Nadia Bolz-Weber also warned against trading one set of fundamentalist impulses for another. In her early years after leaving her conservative religious background, Bolz-Weber says her sister told her she was difficult to have a relationship with: "The unwavering level of devotion and commitment I demanded from myself and others, the being so sure about who was right and who was wrong, who was good and who was bad—well, decades later I see how much it smacked of the same kind of arrogance and dualism I was trying hard to leave behind." As an antidote, she advises exvangelicals to remain humble and curious, open to learning and trying to understand others, and to avoid becoming "equally as strident against [conservative Christianity] as they were against *liberals* years earlier."[35]

Wounded people have a natural instinct to push back, to protect themselves. And for those of us who grew up in the culture wars—who've been trained to fight, and to fight hard—laying down the sword, taking off the armor, and tending those wounds is one of the biggest battles of all.

# 17

# INTO ALL THE WORLD

The moment I'd feared the most as a child, as we gathered around our family dinner table and prayed for my grandpa's soul, seemed imminent. Grandpa was dying and there was nothing I could do.

The afternoon sunlight streamed in, illuminating Grandpa's vanishing frame, as I sat beside his bed in the quiet of the back bedroom. A blue blanket covered his torso and legs as he lay cradled in pillows, barely moving, drifting in and out of light sleep.

On the wall, near the foot of the hospital bed that nurses had set up in his room, was a reminder of the man he'd been—a portrait taken sometime near the end of his neurosurgery career. This was how I'd known him as a young girl in the early 1980s: serious eyes above a soft smile on his round face, hair still mostly full and red, at age sixty or so.

He'd joked to me a few years before, "If I'd known I was going to live this long, I'd have taken better care of my body." But that body had carried him for ninety-seven years: through medical school, marriage and children, the loss of his wife, and on to a second phase as a widower, finally coming out in the 1980s and forming a decades-long relationship with his partner, Ernie. He'd lived to see so much: my fortieth birthday; the birth of several great-grandchildren, including my two sons; and my recent remarriage to Greg. Only a year before, I'd brought Greg to Kansas City to meet the family. Grandpa had come to the table for lunch and sat upright in a straight-backed dining-room chair to eat with us and quiz Greg about his legal career.

But now, I could see Grandpa almost visibly fading in front of me. On this spring afternoon in 2022, I'd come to say what I was pretty sure would be our last goodbye. My two siblings who'd also moved away had been making plans to visit. The rest of the family was in and out of the house frequently, my dad and his brother and sister taking turns sitting by the bed in the house where Grandpa and Ernie had lived for almost as long as I could remember.

Long ago, when I'd pictured this moment, I'd imagined eternity hanging in the balance. I'd prayed that Grandpa would change, that he would get saved while he still had a chance. I'd imagined feeling a great deal of fear for his soul.

Instead, as I sat quietly next to him, I was struck by the almost quotidian nature of imminent death. Grandpa asked, haltingly, for a sip of the ginger ale at his bedside table. I tipped it against his lips from a sippy cup, like the ones my boys had used as toddlers.

He asked me to rub his feet. I went searching for them under the covers.

"Be gentle," Ernie cautioned from his chair near the doorway to an adjoining room. "If you get too firm, he'll let you know."

It was strangely intimate. During all the years of distance and tension between my father and my grandfather during my childhood, I had never spent a night at this house, even though we lived across town. I remembered seeing Grandpa in his pajamas only once, on a road trip that my parents let me take with him when I reached my late teens. While Grandpa was always kind, he wasn't exactly warm; even at home he carried himself with stiff sophistication.

And yet here I was, sitting by the bed where he was slowly dying, rubbing his feet. Over the past several weeks, Ernie had told me, Grandpa had been talking about seeing people from the past, even some of the beloved cats he'd kept as companions over the years. Sometimes, he would call out for my grandmother Mary Ellen, who'd been gone now for close to forty years. It could be hard to tell if he was dreaming or hallucinating.

One day, not long before my last visit, Grandpa told Ernie that he was riding a train. Ernie could hear him talking with his fellow passengers, but it was unclear where they were going. After a while, Grandpa had said it was time to get off—they had arrived at the final stop.

Ernie slipped out of the room, leaving Grandpa and me to sit together quietly. It had been years since I'd felt any compulsion to try to convert him or pray for his soul. I wasn't even sure how to pray for my own at this point.

But, for whatever it meant, and whatever it was worth, as he slept I said a silent prayer in my mind—for peace, for Grandpa and for me. I'm not sure what Grandpa would have thought if he knew, but I don't think he would object to me doing something that would bring me comfort.

*I love him so much,* I thought. *How could God not love him, too?*

Grandpa asked that there be no religion at his memorial service, held over Memorial Day weekend 2022. Only music and eulogies.

In front of our family and a few friends—most of his peers were long dead—I repeated aloud much of what I'd told Grandpa on his deathbed: that he'd inspired me to love learning and to strive for excellence. There were many implicit reminders of his impossible drive to achieve. My dad played a recording he'd made of Grandpa in 2006, then eighty-one, playing Chopin on the grand piano, one of his many hobbies when he wasn't doing brain surgery. At the end of the recording, ever the perfectionist, Grandpa could be heard letting out a heavy sigh. "Eh, not very good."

My dad reminisced about hearing his father play the piano in the home while he was growing up; visiting the hospital with his dad, who had a habit of taking the stairs two at a time, as an "ad hoc exercise program" he could fit into his demanding work schedule; and his impact on the patients whose lives he'd saved, especially the "little patients" he cared for at Kansas City's children's hospital.

"The Fifth Commandment says to honor your father and mother," my dad slipped in at the very end of his eulogy. "I hope I've been able to do that for both Dad and Mom a bit this morning."

Honoring your parents when you don't see eye to eye on some of life's most fundamental questions is not easy. For Josh Scott, who grew up Baptist, his shifting beliefs have come at a personal cost, even though he's a pastor leading his own congregation, Grace-Pointe Church in Nashville. He and his parents don't really discuss what he does for a living.

"In the beginning," Scott said, "there would be questions about my salvation, about all of that, but now we just don't talk about it, which is hard."[1]

This is a near-universal experience, at least to some degree, for exvangelicals, on a spectrum that ranges from awkwardness to total estrangement. There's a lot my own parents and I don't talk about, that we *can't* talk about. When we have tried over the years, the conversations inevitably end in misunderstandings, tears, and an ever-widening distance. They spent years building a world for me that was intended to protect my spiritual safety and warning me not to leave it, only for me to feel anything but safe inside.

I heard about Scott's church from my friend, writer Tyler Huckabee, who told me it had become a haven for many exvangelicals like us. Scott describes it as a "progressive Christian church" that's also home to atheists and agnostics and people of a variety of beliefs. He tries to create space for exploration and curiosity without dogma, or what many Christians would consider traditional theology.

"One of my favorite comments I've ever gotten was at the end of one of the sermons. An older gentleman came up to me and said, 'That was very Buddhist of you,' and high-fived me," Scott told me.

When I walked into the sanctuary—a bar and performance space the rest of the week—it felt exactly like a typical evangelical service: soft music, low lights, heartfelt choruses with lyrics projected on a big screen. But if you listen closely, it's not exactly what it appears. For one thing, the songs aren't standard praise choruses at all, but rather, compositions by stars like Brandi Carlile.

As the music winds down, Scott, who's in his early forties, is wearing jeans and a short-sleeved button-up. He takes the stage and perches—megachurch-pastor-style—on a stool, where he begins his sermon.

"Practically all of us, I would say, have experienced some sort of faith shift," Scott tells the audience. "Which raises lots of questions about all the things we've been taught, all the categories we've been given, all the doctrines and dogmas that have been handed down to us."

The audience is spread out around the venue, some sitting in chairs set up in rows, others at small tables, most casually dressed like their pastor—a long way from the smocked dresses and patent leather shoes of my own early Sunday school days.

The week I visit,[2] Scott is talking about Baptism, a Christian sacrament, but rather than a discourse on the correct theology, it's an exploration. Scott delves into Jewish history, talks about the ritual bath called the mikveh, and then delves into the ways early

Christians might have understood Baptism. He offers an unortho-
dox and expansive view of its meaning, stressing it as a symbol not
necessarily of cleansing or holiness but of inclusion and introduction into a community.

"We're not doing this because you need to be washed clean,
we're not doing this because you need to be saved," Scott said.
"We're not offering this because there's something inherently bad
and broken about you. We're offering this as a way for so many of
us who have been told again and again that because of who we are,
because of who we love, because of our theology and our faith shift,
because of all these many reasons, we no longer belong."

After so many years away from evangelicalism, I'd wondered if
being in this place—so evangelical in style and feel—might trigger
some intense emotions. I thought that I might feel the sense of
warmth and closeness to God that could sometimes come over me
in a worship service, or almost as likely, the irritating sense that the
lights and the music and the pastor's soothing, low tones were all
part of a giant manipulative sales pitch, an elaborate production
calculated for maximum emotional impact. But I was surprised at
how uneventfully I experienced the service; it felt neither upsetting
nor particularly inspiring.

I asked Scott why bother starting a church that questions some
of the most fundamental orthodoxies of Christian faith and practice? Particularly when there are, as he'd alluded to, many other
spiritual traditions already available beyond evangelicalism, such as
mainline Christianity, Unitarianism, Buddhism, or nothing at all.

For many of the exvangelicals and other Christians who attend
on Sundays, or watch the service streaming online, Scott said it's
about building a "somewhat nostalgic community," a space to learn
about Jesus and try to follow his teachings "in a place where they
don't have to turn off their brain and pretend they believe stuff they
don't."

That made sense. No one wants to have to pretend, and no one wants to go out into the world alone. But the world often feels lonely for the exvangelical who may be unable to go home, who never feels fully at home in the world we've been taught to fear. The exvangelicals I've met are rebuilding that lost community in a variety of ways—online and in the real world, by exploring new ways of being spiritual and by building connections in nonreligious spaces. Jocelyn Howard told me that connecting with fellow artists, other queer people, and self-described "nerds" has helped provide the support they once found at church.

"There's so much fear when you decide to deconstruct, of all the things you're going to lose, because I think the church convinces you that you can't find this anywhere else," Howard said. "But then you get out into the outside world and realize, 'Oh wait, these are basic human needs, and because they're basic human needs, there will be and there are other places where I can find that.'"

They've run across fellow exvangelicals in places you might expect—a Facebook group for "survivors" of Bob Jones University, for example—and in unexpected places, including a social media group for fans of a favorite television show.

"A lot of the groups that I have found outside of the church somehow tie back to 'we were once church people,'" Howard said. "For me, a lot of the connection has been exvangelicals that I keep finding."

In place of Bible studies and prayer groups, Howard said they've found what feels like a "much healthier" version of community, wherever they look for it.

"Instead of encouraging me to fit in and change myself to fit in, each group I've found has been about embracing your individuality, embracing who you are," they said. "Instead of replacing that hive-mind experience of the church with another hive mind, I've instead found groups that are the opposite of that."

Mel Kulenski, an exvangelical in her early thirties living in the Philadelphia area, told me that as a trained social worker, she thinks a lot about how people form a sense of identity, particularly after leaving a community where identity is so deeply intertwined with a specific set of values and beliefs.

"I think it's really important for exvangelicals to find themselves and to define themselves, not just by what they're not anymore but also by who they are," she said.[3]

Kulenski said finding new hobbies and interests has helped. She's into crochet, fantasy young adult novels, and *Game of Thrones*—"really nerdy stuff" that makes her happy.

"It's not healthy for us to think about this stuff all the time, about Hell theology," Kulenski said. "That's really heavy stuff that has made an impact on our nervous system, and it's good for our brain to make new neural connections outside of that and learn who we are here as a person."

Kulenski said she's learned a lot from spending time with people who do *not* share her background, and who can offer an entirely new and fresh perspective on the world.

Kulenski describes these new connections as "healing in community," which has helped her to envision another path: "[I've realized], 'Hey, I'm capable of that, too. I'm capable of forging my own identity, because these other people are doing great.'"

My own marriage to someone of a different faith has provided some of that same kind of fresh perspective. I love my husband for many reasons, but the fact that he's Jewish—a tradition that is at once familiar and new—often feels like a gift, maybe even a gift from God. I have not converted, but he's generously shared his culture and traditions with me, and when I want to pray, I very often ask to go to synagogue with him.

The traditions are still new for me, and I struggle with the liturgy. When I go, I am a guest, one who is very much learning. But to the extent that I've felt what I believed to be God's presence in church, I have felt that presence equally in synagogue beside my husband.

A few months after Grandpa died, at the service on the eve of Yom Kippur, I listened as the cantor performed the Kol Nidre. According to some traditions, the centuries-old statement was once recited by Jews who were being forced on pain of death to convert to other faiths, in an effort to nullify those vows, which cut them off from their Jewish identity.

"Let them all be relinquished and abandoned, null and void, neither firm nor established," the cantor sang in the original Aramaic. "Let our vows, pledges, and oaths be considered neither vows nor pledges nor oaths."[4]

I thought about the powerful desire to remain connected, to retain identity, and to feel reconciled to God. I thought about the pain of alienation, and the difficulty of knowing which promises to keep, and which to let go.

On the doorway of our home, in keeping with Jewish tradition, Greg and I mounted a mezuzah, a scroll inside a case made of the melted-down glass Greg had stomped to bits at the end of our wedding. (In a nod to egalitarianism, he offered to let me help, but I didn't want to mess up my ballet flats, or my feet).

On the tiny scroll are several verses from Deuteronomy, including a passage from chapter six, which I heard often growing up in my evangelical home.[5]

In English, it reads in part, "Love the Lord your God with all your heart and with all your soul and with all your strength. These commandments that I give you today are to be on your hearts. Impress them on your children. Talk about them when you sit at home and when you walk along the road, when you lie down and when you get up. . . . Write them on the doorframes of your houses and on your gates."[6]

I know that this is what my parents, and so many of the evangelical parents who raised generations of us who are now adults, were trying to achieve: to love God as they understood him to be, and to impress that devotion on their children so that we would carry it forward into our own families. At a time when American culture was experiencing tremendous transformation, fueled by advances in technology and burgeoning diversity, a massive regime of white evangelical leaders emerged to promise spiritual direction, marital satisfaction, parenting support, a welcoming community, and a strong sense of identity and mission. This was all available in exchange for signing on to a vision of a divinely ordered America in which Christian families would exemplify and carry out God's will. Christian ethics professor David Gushee believes that movement has distorted the very meaning of what it is to be a Christian.

"Evangelical political organizers kept using the word 'evangelical' to organize for a certain kind of political change," Gushee said. "And in the end, what changed was them."

Perhaps the best statistical evidence for this shift lies in the 2021 Pew Research Center survey that found a growing tendency among white supporters of Donald Trump to newly adopt an evangelical identity.[7]

"In the end, their own movement was redefined as a reactionary, angry, white Christian, storm-the-Capitol movement," Gushee said. "People who don't have any idea about classical evangelical doctrines, but by God, they like Trump and they're white, so therefore they're evangelical. That is a complete collapse of moral and religious identity that evangelicals brought on themselves."

Some exvangelicals see that collapse as an opportunity, or an obligation, to take action.

Charla Arnold told me she was motivated to found the Recovering Evangelicals group a couple of years into the Trump administration, after observing that most churches in her area were unfriendly territory for anyone who didn't support him.[8] Born in 1974, Arnold married young and had children by the 1990s, when she first began noticing what she now sees as the early links between evangelicalism and the far right.

"The seeds of this were laid in the eighties and nineties with the Moral Majority and the Christian Coalition," Arnold told me. "When they attached themselves to Ronald Reagan's campaign, it created what we are seeing the aftereffects of now."

Arnold believes it's particularly urgent for exvangelicals concerned about the growing intersections between evangelicalism and extremism to speak out and push back.

"I don't think that we have enough people who were former [evangelical] leaders looking back saying how genuinely sad it is to see this stuff," she said. "We did this. We're the ones who created the cracks that are eroding the foundation of the American Constitution at this moment."

Arnold said she's started an offshoot of Recovering Evangelicals for former pastors. She hopes that some of the members of her groups will get involved in trying to repair some of those cracks.

"We need to be sad. But we also need to be energized enough to start looking for ways to bring healing," she said. "I'm hoping that people are starting to see, 'Okay, this is bad. How can we fix it?'"

Diane Bolme, an exvangelical now in her thirties, decided to become more vocal about her support for abortion rights in the aftermath of the US Supreme Court decision overturning *Roe v. Wade*. Writing about her evolving views on the issue for the feminist publication *Jezebel,* Bolme described a series of personal experiences with her own reproductive healthcare that slowly softened her opposition to abortion, which she'd been taught to staunchly oppose as an evangelical.

Bolme describes a moment at an abortion rights rally, where she zeroed in on some counterprotesters holding anti-abortion signs: "With a few different decisions," Bolme writes, "I could have easily been the women speaking with fervor into a bullhorn about how 'God knits together children in your womb' and offers forgiveness for the sin of abortion. In many ways, she was the pinnacle of where I had been headed: a bold, brave leader for the Evangelical Christian community."[9]

But Bolme found her ideological shift somewhat isolating and wrote that she sometimes felt like an "alien" around her liberal friends, especially as she tried to sort through some of her lingering discomfort with abortion.

Of the rise of the term "exvangelical," Bolme wrote, "I'm relieved that there appears to be a more robust social network of people who have departed Evangelical Christianity to provide support and validation to each other. My journey may have been easier or quicker if I had more people like me to engage with."[10]

In an interview,[11] Bolme told me she hopes more exvangelicals will begin to write and speak openly about their experiences, as well as their unique understanding of the mechanics of the religious right. She points to the continuing decline in numbers that American Christianity, including white evangelicalism, has experienced in recent years.[12] Bolme believes there are many more people like her who may still be afraid to go public with their dissent from their white evangelical communities of origin.

"There's this huge group of people who have knowledge about how it works, who understand the indoctrination," Bolme said. "I think it is a community that needs to be speaking out more, that needs to be sharing the insights that they have, because I really think there's a lot more of us."

David Dark, a writer and religion professor at the historically Baptist Belmont University in Nashville, said the conversation around deconstruction among his students and Twitter followers has been escalating and underscoring the deepening rifts in the evangelical movement.

"I think it has hit critical mass because many of us have realized that we have perpetuated or abided a network of bigots—abusive people. I think that Trump is kind of an apocalypse because it unveiled something that was there all along," Dark said. "A lot of people younger than me found out that their parents, who held a certain moral line, have abandoned that moral line in the name of this movement."

Dark, who was described to me by an exvangelical I met online as the "bishop" of Nashville's deconstruction community, told me that for those who've been deconstructing for years, there's also a sense of responsibility.

"Many of us are realizing we are the adults in the room," Dark said. "We have to say something now."

Dark often asks his students if they believe they are responsible to hold loved ones accountable for "the lies" people say in their presence.

"The quiet presumed answer to that is 'yes, if I would not let my mom or dad say something if there was a Black person or a gay person or a Muslim in the room, I need to say something. I need to stop being shy,'" Dark said. "I think we are also realizing that because of our soft coddling of abusive people, there's been a cost."

But as he observes the upheaval within evangelicalism, and the new communities being formed by those leaving it, Dark has hope for exvangelicals, and those they encounter.

"I sometimes think that people who have been through it and who have remained curious and loving and in relationships with people are some of the freest people who have ever walked the Earth," Dark told me.[13] "Exvangelicals, ex-fundamentalists—we know the text. We know the tradition. I sometimes say you have to hate the tradition to love it properly, to really see what's wrong.

"There will be those who emerge from that but have a deeper appreciation that there's a way of loving sacred scripture without viewing it as your property, with which you can judge other people."

In a Substack post before the 2022 midterm elections titled "Evangelical Wreckage," Diana Butler Bass—a historian and progressive Christian writer with an evangelical background—described an event she'd recently attended, where people came together to discuss theology over beer. The speaker asked participants to identify their religious backgrounds by a show of hands. As Bass describes it, few hands went up when the speaker named several mainline Protestant traditions—Presbyterian, Methodist, Episcopalian. Frustrated, the speaker asked, "Who are you people anyway?" The answer: "We're exvangelicals."[14]

Bass went on to describe this room of otherwise "fun, energetic, smart, and enthusiastic" younger adults—mostly in their thirties and forties—pouring out their stories of pain and rejection by friends and family members for coming out as LGBTQ+, supporting female clergy, opposing Donald Trump, or simply asking the *wrong* theological questions. "Beer flowed," she wrote, "but so did tears."[15]

Bass concluded her post by writing what she wished she'd said when asked at another public event if there's anything good in white evangelicalism. She wished she'd directed the questioner to ask the young adults in that room:

Ask THEM the question—the people, the human beings who were treated as litter by evangelical leaders and institutions on a crusade for religious, social, and political power, a quest that wrecked their souls and their sanity. Spend three days with those wounded, joyful thrivers, those who were kicked out, fled, crawled out, or backed slowly out the rear door. Those who are hanging around the edges for dear life, those deconstructing and reconstructing their lives, those who are still haunted by nightmares of heresy trials, purity culture, and rapture fears.

Go ask them if there's any good in evangelicalism.[16]

When I read Bass's words, I felt deeply seen. Like so many exvangelicals I've met, I've spent much of my adult life slowly crawling away, trying to hang on to something for dear life, often feeling like a wrecked—or shipwrecked—soul, swimming for solid ground. Even now in middle age, nearly two decades out of that world, the nightmares still haunt me, as they do so many others. And it's all made so much worse by the feeling of being seen as the problem, as evil or foolish for not remaining within those walls. But we are holding on and reconstructing our lives—finding each other and, maybe, God.

Along with the mezuzah by our front door, Greg was kind enough to hang up a picture of Jesus on our dining-room wall. I bought it from the Georgia folk artist Panhandle Slim, whose work I ran across while I was living in Savannah. He has a habit of making religious art that probably wouldn't sell too well at your typical Christian bookstore. In bright splashes of paint on a piece of plywood, the painting depicts Jesus with dark hair, alongside a quote from the New Testament: "Be on your guard against false prophets:

they come to you looking like sheep on the outside, but on the inside they are really like wild wolves."[17]

But who are the wolves, and who are the sheep? Who are the false prophets, and who is to be believed? How can you tell the difference—and what if the people you came from see sheep where you see a wolf? Or worse, they see *you* as one of the wolves?

These are the questions that still sometimes wake me up in the middle of the night, with a jolt and a sudden tight gasp of air, so much like those nights when I was a little girl, praying to God to save my grandpa's soul and begging him to make sure mine was really saved, too. There are times I wonder if I have it all wrong, or if my parents have it right, and this is all an illusion, an elaborate deception from the Enemy.

These days, I ask God if he is there. And why, all these years later, I'm still filled with questions about what it all means and what is true.

Sometimes I panic and wake up my husband: "Is God mad at me?" I whisper, or sob, in the dark. "Why did he even put me here? What does he want?"

Greg believes in God, but not as some kind of man behind the curtain, directing everything down to the smallest detail. He reminds me that his religion has been around a lot longer than mine, and that people have been struggling with these ideas for even longer than that.

"I believe God gives us the tools," he always tells me—and that includes our minds. "It's up to us to use them."


The weekend after Yom Kippur, I went home to Kansas City again, for another memorial service. While we'd been preparing ourselves for years to say goodbye to Grandpa, no one expected Ernie, who was a generation younger, to follow only months later.

Our family had just finished going through my grandpa's belongings, and my aunt Emily gave me a letter she'd found among his papers, which I'd long forgotten about. In the letter, Grandpa was helping me with a philosophy assignment I'd been given in college, to interact with someone from outside the Christian worldview, and ask them about their ideas about the meaning of life and what comes afterward. My half of the exchange is long gone, but in a few pages, Grandpa summed up his beliefs, circa 2000.

Reading Grandpa's words with the memory of his death still fresh, I lingered over his thoughts on the afterlife. A person lives on "through the things he has done in life and the people he has influenced in one way or another," Grandpa wrote. He did not believe in a bodily resurrection or a physical heaven, which he saw as "mythologies" people had created to try to explain things that were beyond understanding.

"I would rather not subscribe to any in which I cannot have a deep and abiding faith," Grandpa wrote. "To do so is a betrayal of one's own integrity."

Though not religious, Grandpa said he believed there could be a place for faith—at least, outside of organized religion—particularly when it comes to questions that science is not intended to answer.

"I just don't feel that I have to accept a structured dogma . . . to live a full life," Grandpa wrote. "I am quite willing to admit and live with the fact that I do not know all the answers rather than have the blanks filled in arbitrarily by someone else (who doesn't know either)."

Abraham Piper recently expressed a similar sentiment in a Twitter thread. He said people often insist that because he doesn't believe in the traditional monotheistic view of God as advanced by Judaism or Christianity, he must be an atheist. But Piper rejects that label, too.

"Any predetermined sectarianism is too restrictive,"[18] Piper explains. "Adherents of every ideology have cute little stories they tell themselves to make the world make sense, and I want to have a bit more of a sense of freedom with the cute little stories I tell myself."[19]

As for me, I'm still attached to the story of Jesus. The thought of God inhabiting the human experience, knowing the joys and deep suffering and vulnerability of embodiment, resonates with me. I'm moved by Jesus's love for the weak and the needy. I'm inspired by his call to sacrifice one's own comfort because of a commitment to a larger good, and I see that kind of selflessness as essential for a functional community. I'm convicted—to use an evangelical word—by his warnings about how easy it is to be distracted from that mission by selfish desires, and the pull to accumulate things that won't last.

But the evangelical impulse—the idea that "people need the Lord," that we have been given a unique understanding of the Truth about the most complex questions about reality, and which we must impose through persuasion or coercion—has never made much sense to me when I survey the complexities of the world, and the diversity of experiences and points of view. Even worse, that way of thinking seems to be at the root of so many evils that have been perpetuated throughout human history by religious fundamentalists and other extremist ideologues. I fear that same impulse is currently laying the groundwork for irreparable harm in our country and the world, and I fear that some of the people I have known and loved, and who've loved me, are being persuaded to aid and abet that evil.

To use Grandpa's words, to subscribe to such a project—even out of a desire to maintain family and community ties—would be "a betrayal of one's own integrity."

So what mission can I subscribe to in good conscience, as an exvangelical? Knowing his audience when he wrote that letter to me in college, Grandpa noted that the purpose of life was something Jesus had also worried about. His advice was simple, even biblical: help others.

"This is the one thing that brings the most meaning and satisfaction to existence," Grandpa wrote. "I think we are here to help our fellow man," he said. "To do this we must be accepting first of ourselves and our imperfections, and then, of other people and their differences. To overcome our intolerance and fear of others, and to appreciate and even emulate their good qualities, gives us a feeling for the fullness of life."

As I read this, I think about what Grandpa's own journey of self-discovery and acceptance must have been like: from a closeted medical student in the 1940s, to a retired physician in a partnered relationship, volunteering to help AIDS patients during some of the worst years of the crisis. I think back over the years I'd spent trying to understand and accept my family, with all of our imperfections and differences, and to love and feel loved by them. I think about my struggle to overcome my own intolerance and fears: of hurting people through selfishness or ignorance, of losing the love of my family, of getting it all wrong, of angering God.

And I hope that struggle to overcome will be enough.

Grandpa hadn't changed, but I had.

If God has given us the tools, as Greg believes—and I think he's got that right—then I've come to believe that we're responsible for carrying out the tasks suited to those tools. As I see them, these tools are beautiful but also rudimentary. We've been given minds that can reason and inquire, but that can only understand so much. We have hearts that can feel compassion and empathy but are always constrained by the limitations of our own experiences and observations. I've asked God again and again to "open the eyes of my heart," as we used to sing in one of the praise choruses projected on the big screen at church. But those eyes can only see so far. And

I can't pretend to know with certainty what's beyond my field of vision.

Peace, when I have found it, has come from accepting that I don't have to solve the riddle of the universe or uncover any magical answers. That life isn't an elaborate calculus problem, and that God isn't waiting to punish us if we make an error. I don't have the answers, but I'm not sure I'm meant to.

I've relaxed, most of the time, into the understanding that I didn't have to save Grandpa, and that I don't have to save anyone. That I, like everyone else, was somehow born naked into this world, knowing nothing, a tiny bundle of flesh and blood and bones pulsating with needs and desires—and that someday if I'm very fortunate, I will be lying in a quiet, sunlit room, in a withering body, holding the hand of my grandchild, gently fading away.

# ACKNOWLEDGMENTS

As I've told several people while writing this book, I feel like I've spent my entire life—certainly my adult life—working on it. The concept has been gestating in my mind for some time, and in particular, the last several years. It would have stayed there, a half-formed idea, were it not for the love and encouragement to conquer my fears (and careful proofreading) of my husband, Greg. Thank you, my love, for relentlessly believing in me.

Along the way, countless friends and family members have offered encouragement, feedback, and gentle questions (often impressively self-aware ones along the lines of, "Is it okay to ask how the book is coming?"). I can't possibly thank you all. But for starters, thank you to Rasheeta for your enthusiastic support when I was drafting the book proposal, to Melanie Simón for your inspiration and encouragement, to Jarred and Ari R. for reading the manuscript, and to Arden for saying, "You should write a story about your life, Mom."

I've also benefited from the advice and support of colleagues—many of whom I am fortunate to count as friends—who've offered guidance on putting together a book proposal, provided feedback on my writing, or simply encouraged me to keep going. In particular, thank you to Barbara Bradley Hagerty, Eliza Griswold, Steve Inskeep, Aarti Shahani, Celeste Headlee, Elise Hu, Mary Louise Kelly, Korva Coleman, and Lauren Hodges, but also to so many others.

Many thanks to Robert P. Jones, Samuel Perry, and Kristin Kobes Du Mez for lending their time and expertise to help me understand some of the key data and scholarship without which this book would not be possible.

I'd also like to thank my publishing team at St. Martin's Press and William Morris Endeavor, particularly my brilliant literary agent, Margaret Riley King; my research assistant, Victoria Dominguez; and my empathetic and incisive editor, Hannah Phillips, for sharing my vision for this book and helping me to make it a reality.

And finally, thank you to the exvangelical, post-evangelical, progressive evangelical, disillusioned evangelical, and evangelicalism-adjacent writers, academics, podcasters, and fellow travelers who provided the inspiration for this book, and who've shared their insights, expertise, and experiences with me.

# FURTHER READING AND LISTENING

## THE EXVANGELICAL/POST-EVANGELICAL EXPERIENCE

Tim Alberta, *The Kingdom, the Power, and the Glory: American Evangelicals in an Age of Extremism*

Emily Joy Allison, *#Church Too: How Purity Culture Upholds Abuse and How to Find Healing*

Laura E. Anderson, *When Religion Hurts You: Healing from Religious Trauma and the Impact of High-Control Religion*

Nadia Bolz-Weber, *Shameless: A Case for Not Feeling Bad About Feeling Good (About Sex)*

Diana Butler Bass, *Christianity After Religion: The End of Church and the Birth of a New Spiritual Awakening*

Jeff Chu, *Does Jesus Really Love Me? A Gay Christian's Pilgrimage in Search of God in America*

Glennon Doyle, *Untamed*

Shannon Harris, *The Woman They Wanted*

Rachel Held Evans, *Searching for Sunday: Loving, Leaving, and Finding the Church*

Jamie Lee Finch, *You Are Your Own: Reckoning with the Religious Trauma of Evangelical Christianity*

David Gushee, *After Evangelicalism: A Path to a New Christianity*

Aaron Hartzler, *Rapture Practice: A True Story About Growing Up Gay in an Evangelical Family*

Jeanna Kadlec, *Heretic: A Memoir*

Linda Kay Klein, *Pure: Inside the Evangelical Movement That Shamed a Generation of Young Women and How I Broke Free*

Lyz Lenz, *God Land: A Story of Faith, Loss, and Renewal in Middle America*

Charles Marsh, *Evangelical Anxiety: A Memoir*

Beth Moore, *All My Knotted-Up Life: A Memoir*

R. Scott Okamoto, *Asian American Apostate: Losing Religion and Finding Myself at an Evangelical University*

Dante Stewart, *Shoutin' in the Fire: An American Epistle*

Chrissy Stroop and Lauren O'Neal, *Empty the Pews: Stories of Leaving the Church*

John Ward, *Testimony: Inside the Evangelical Movement That Failed a Generation*

Marlene Winell, *Leaving the Fold: A Guide for Former Fundamentalists and Others Leaving Their Religion*

### HISTORY OF EVANGELICALISM

Beth Allison Barr, *The Making of Biblical Womanhood: How the Subjugation of Women Became Gospel Truth*

Kate Bowler, *Blessed: A History of the American Prosperity Gospel*

Ryan P. Burge, *The Nones: Where They Came From, Who They Are, and Where They Are Going*

Anthea Butler, *White Evangelical Racism: The Politics of Morality in America*

Jim Davis and Michael Graham with Ryan P. Burge, *The Great Dechurching: Who's Leaving, Why Are They Going, and What Will It Take to Bring Them Back?*

Angela Denker, *Red State Christians: Understanding the Voters Who Elected Donald Trump*

Kristin Kobes Du Mez, *Jesus and John Wayne: How the Evangelicals Corrupted a Faith and Fractured a Nation*

Christina Barland Edmonson and Chad Brennan, *Faithful Antiracism: Moving Past Talk to Systemic Change*

John Fea, *Believe Me: The Evangelical Road to Donald Trump*

Frances Fitzgerald, *The Evangelicals: The Struggle to Shape America*

Sheila Wray Gregoire, *The Great Sex Rescue: The Lies You've Been Taught and How to Recover What God Intended*

Ben Howe, *The Immoral Majority: Why Evangelicals Chose Political Power Over Christian Values*

Robert P. Jones, *The End of White Christian America*

Anne Nelson, *Shadow Network: Media, Money, and the Secret Hub of the Radical Right*

Bradley Onishi, *Preparing for War: The Extremist History of White Christian Nationalism—and What Comes Next*

Philip S. Gorski and Samuel L. Perry, *The Flag and the Cross: White Christian Nationalism and the Threat to American Democracy*

Jeff Sharlet, *The Family: The Secret Fundamentalism at the Heart of American Power*

Isaac B. Sharp, *The Other Evangelicals: A Story of Liberal, Black,*

*Progressive, Feminist, and Gay Christians—and the Movement That Pushed Them Out*

Bob Smietana, *Reorganized Religion: The Reshaping of the American Church and Why It Matters*

Katherine Stewart, *The Power Worshippers: Inside the Dangerous Rise of Religious Nationalism*

Jemar Tisby, *The Color of Compromise: The Truth About the American Church's Complicity in Racism*

Daniel K. Williams, *God's Own Party: The Making of the Christian Right*

## THEOLOGY/OTHER

Rob Bell, *Sex God: Exploring the Endless Connections Between Sexuality and Spirituality*

Sarah Bessey, *Out of Sorts: Making Peace with an Evolving Faith*

Peter Enns, *The Bible Tells Me So: Why Defending Scripture Has Made Us Unable to Read It*

Brian D. McLaren, *Faith After Doubt: Why Your Beliefs Stopped Working and What to Do About It*

Russell D. Moore, *Losing Our Religion: An Altar Call for Evangelical America*

Doug Pagitt, *Outdoing Jesus: Seven Ways to Live Out the Promise of "Greater Than"*

## PODCASTS

Cindy Wang Brandt, *Parenting Forward*

Blake Chastain, *Exvangelical*

Brenda Davies, *God is Grey*

Glennon Doyle, *We Can Do Hard Things*

Peter Enns, *The Bible for Normal People*

Adrian Gibbs and Josh Link, *Dirty Rotten Church Kids*

Brady Hardin, *The Life After Podcast*

Jen Hatmaker, *For the Love*

Daniel Miller and Bradley Onishi, *Straight White American Jesus*

Tim Whitaker, *The New Evangelicals Podcast*

# NOTES

## INTRODUCTION

1. "In U.S., Decline of Christianity Continues at Rapid Pace," Pew Research Center, October 17, 2019, https://www.pewforum.org/2019/10/17/in-u-s-decline-of-christianity-continues-at-rapid-pace/.

2. "Blake Chastain: writer & podcaster," Blake Chastain personal website home page, last retrieved March 18, 2023, https://blakechastain.com/.

3. Stef W. Kight, "The Exvangelicals," *Axios,* September 19, 2021, https://www.axios.com/2021/09/19/evangelical-exvangelicals-church-religion-christianity.

4. Tim Whitaker, interview with the author, June 21, 2021.

5. David Bazan, "When We Fell," Barsuk Records, September 9, 2009, available at David Bazan-Topic, YouTube video, last updated December 1, 2014, https://www.youtube.com/watch?v=k-syIAC6t4w.

6. Robert P. Jones, email exchange with author, August 11, 2023. Data drawn from the American National Election Study, Pew Research Center, and Public Religion Research Institute.

7. Isaac B. Sharp, *The Other Evangelicals: A Story of Liberal, Black, Progressive, Feminist, and Gay Christians—and the Movement That Pushed Them Out* (Grand Rapids, MI: Wm. B. Eerdmans Publishing Co., 2023), xviii.

8. Ryan Parker, "'Rope. Tree. Journalist' Shirts Pulled after Image Goes Viral at Trump Rally," *Hollywood Reporter,* November 7, 2016, https://www

.hollywoodreporter.com/tv/tv-news/rope-tree-journalist-shirts-pulled
-image-goes-viral-at-trump-rally-944763/.

## 1. PEOPLE NEED THE LORD

1. Psalms 127:3 and 128:3, respectively (NIV).
2. Proverbs 22:6 (NIV).
3. "More Precious than Silver," Lynn DeShazo, copyright 1982 by Integrity's Hosanna! Music, information from Hymnary.org, last retrieved March 18, 2023, https://hymnary.org/text/lord_you_are_more_precious_than_silver.
4. John 14:27 (NIV).
5. 1 John 1:9 (NIV).
6. Stephanie Stalvey (@stephanie.stalvey.artist), image caption: "Evangelism. A weird way to be taught to relate to other human beings," Instagram, January 29, 2021, https://www.instagram.com/p/CK9vYV8Mv7V/.
7. Stephanie Stalvey, phone interview with the author, March 18, 2021.
8. Stephanie Stalvey (@stephanie.stalvey.artist), image caption: "The good stuff was really good," Instagram, February 10, 2021, https://www.instagram.com/p/CLHlz6yM7EA/?utm_source=ig_web_copy_link.
9. Micah 6:8 (NIV).
10. David P. Gushee, *After Evangelicalism: The Path to a New Christianity* (Louisville, KY: Westminster John Knox Press, 2020), 1.
11. Daniel Cox, "Are White Evangelicals Sacrificing the Future in Search of the Past?," *FiveThirtyEight,* January 24, 2018, https://fivethirtyeight.com/features/are-white-evangelicals-sacrificing-the-future-in-search-of-the-past/.
12. Gushee, *After Evangelicalism,* 1–2.
13. Ibid., 6–7.

## 2. A "PARALLEL UNIVERSE"

1. Jon Meacham, "The Editor's Desk," *Newsweek,* November 12, 2006, https://www.newsweek.com/editors-desk-106637.
2. Randall Balmer, *The Making of American Evangelicalism: From Revivalism to Politics and Beyond* (Waco, TX: Baylor University Press, 2010), 55.
3. Kristin Kobes Du Mez, *Jesus and John Wayne: How White Evangelicals Corrupted a Faith and Fractured a Nation* (New York: Liveright Publishing Corporation, 2020), 106.
4. Tom Gjelten, "How Positive Thinking, Prosperity Gospel Define Donald

Trump's Faith Outlook," NPR, August 3, 2016, https://www.npr.org/2016/08/03/488513585/how-positive-thinking-prosperity-gospel-define-donald-trumps-faith-outlook.

5. Matthew 19:23–24 (NIV).

6. Balmer, *The Making of American Evangelicalism,* 57.

7. "The Fall of Jimmy Swaggart," *People,* March 7, 1988, https://people.com/archive/cover-story-the-fall-of-jimmy-swaggart-vol-29-no-9/.

8. Lauren Effron, Andrew Paparella, and Jeca Taudte, "The Scandals That Brought Down the Bakkers, Once among US's Most Famous Televangelists," ABC News, December 20, 2019, https://abcnews.go.com/US/scandals-brought-bakkers-uss-famous-televangelists/story?id=60389342.

9. Sarah McCammon (@sarahmccammon), Twitter, 1:27 p.m., August 25, 2020, https://twitter.com/sarahmccammon/status/1298311055811260416?s=20&t=MmV7nnrtewqrthiRrPFTA.

10. Molli Mitchell, "Where Is Giancarlo Granda Now? Jerry Falwell Jr.'s Pool Boy," *Newsweek,* November 1, 2022, https://www.newsweek.com/where-giancarlo-granda-now-jerry-falwell-jr-god-forbid-1756053.

11. Alvin McEwen, "Family Research Council Evades Regarding Ugandan Anti-gay Bill Lobbying Efforts," *HuffPost,* updated December 6, 2017, https://www.huffpost.com/entry/family-research-council-e_b_602594.

12. James Dobson, *The Strong-Willed Child* (Carol Stream, IL: Tyndale House Publishers, 1978), 46–47.

13. Duane T. Gish, *Dinosaurs: Those Terrible Lizards* (Green Forest, AR: Master Book Publishers, 1978).

14. Claude Brodesser-Akner, "Smurf Conspiracy-Theory Roundup: Are They Racist? Misogynist? Closet KKK?," *Vulture,* July 25, 2011, https://www.vulture.com/2011/07/smurf_conspiracy_theories.html.

15. "Creation Duet from Mister Rogers' Neighborhood," Jordan Magill YouTube account, posted March 27, 2018, last retrieved March 19, 2023, YouTube video, https://www.youtube.com/watch?v=BdlOOLT3Foc.

16. "Part 8: Religion in American Life" in *The 2004 Political Landscape,* Pew Research Center, November 5, 2003, https://www.pewresearch.org/politics/2003/11/05/part-8-religion-in-american-life/.

17. Robert P. Jones, email interview with author, Aug. 11, 2023. Data drawn from sources including the American National Election Study, Pew Research Center, and PRRI.

18. Rachel C. Larson, *The American Republic,* 3rd ed. (Greenville, SC: BJU Press, 2010), xiii.

19. Ibid., xi.

20. Du Mez, *Jesus and John Wayne,* 7–12.

21. D.L. Mayfield (@d_-_mayfield), now-defunct Twitter account, last retrieved September 10, 2022, https://twitter.com/d_l_mayfield/status/1568408861 132070912?s=27&t=Te7nsAxULzOKOJj5DXVe8g.

22. "PRRI 2022 Census of American Religion," Public Religion Research Institute, February 24, 2023, https://www.prri.org/spotlight/prri-2022-american -values-atlas-religious-affiliation-updates-and-trends/.

23. Justin Nortey, "Most White Americans Who Regularly Attend MI Voted for Trump in 2020," Pew Research Center, August 30, 2021, https://www .pewresearch.org/fact-tank/2021/08/30/most-white-americans-who -regularly-attend-worship-services-voted-for-trump-in-2020/.

24. https://www.prri.org/research/2020-census-of-american-religion/.

25. "PRRI 2022 Census of American Religion: Religious Affiliation Updates and Trends," Public Religion Research Institute, February 24, 2023, https://www.prri.org/spotlight/prri-2022-american-values-atlas-religious -affiliation-updates-and-trends/.

26. Gregory A. Smith, "About Three-in-Ten US Adults Are Now Religiously Unaffiliated," Pew Research Center, December 14, 2021, https://www .pewforum.org/2021/12/14/about-three-in-ten-u-s-adults-are-now-religiously -unaffiliated/.

27. Marina E. Franco, "Mapped: Power of Latino Protestants," *Axios,* August 6, 2022, https://www.axios.com/2022/08/06/latinos-protestants-catholics -republicans.

28. Meaghan Winter, "The Fastest-Growing Group of American Evangelicals," *The Atlantic,* July 26, 2021, https://www.theatlantic.com/culture/archive /2021/07/latinos-will-determine-future-american-evangelicalism/619551/.

29. "Religion and Congregations in a Time of Social and Political Upheaval," Public Religion Research Institute, May 16, 2023, https://www.prri.org/research /religion-and-congregations-in-a-time-of-social-and-political-upheaval/.

30. Gregory A. Smith, "More White Americans Adopted than Shed Evangelical Label During Trump Presidency, Especially His Supporters," Pew Research Center, September 15, 2021, https://www.pewresearch.org/fact-tank/2021 /09/15/more-white-americans-adopted-than-shed-evangelical-label-during -trump-presidency-especially-his-supporters/.

31. Jim Davis and Michael Graham with Ryan P. Burge, *The Great Dechurching: Who's Leaving, Why Are They Going, and What Will It Take to Bring Them Back?* (Grand Rapids, MI: Zondervan Reflections, 2023), 32.

32. Lydia Bean, "Why America's White Evangelical Christians Turn Out at High Rates in Midterm Elections," Scholars Strategy Network, March 7, 2016, https://scholars.org/contribution/why-americas-white-evangelical-christians-turn.

33. Robert P. Jones, phone interview with the author, June 15, 2022.

34. Samuel Perry, phone interview with the author, February 15, 2022.

## 3. AN EXODUS

1. Promise Enlow Councill, phone interview with the author, July 8, 2021.

2. Jenni Fink, "Pastor Johnny Enlow Says Trump Support Is Measure of One's Dedication to God," *Newsweek,* June 7, 2021, https://www.newsweek.com/pastor-johnny-enlow-says-trump-support-measure-ones-dedication-god-1598339.

3. Sarah McCammon, "Trump Presents Dilemma for Evangelical Women, Once Reliable GOP Voters," NPR, November 1, 2016, https://www.npr.org/2016/11/01/500183772/evangelicals-face-a-gender-split-over-trump.

4. Deirdre Sugiuchi, "I Grew Up Evangelical and the Christian Nationalist Insurrection Did Not Surprise Me," *Religion Dispatches,* January 28, 2021, https://religiondispatches.org/i-grew-up-evangelical-and-the-christian-nationalist-insurrection-did-not-surprise-me/.

5. Kevin Max, phone interview with the author, June 21, 2021.

6. Ruth Graham, "A Pastor's Son Becomes a Critic of Religion on TikTok," *New York Times,* April 12, 2021, https://www.nytimes.com/2021/04/12/us/abraham-piper-tiktok-exvangelical.html.

7. Derek Webb, phone interview with the author, July 7, 2021.

## 4. UNRAVELING

1. "Felicia Galas Munn Brenner on Her Parents," USC Shoah Foundation, University of Southern California, last retrieved March 19, 2023, https://sfi.usc.edu/video/felicia-galas-munn-brenner-her-parents.

2. Andrew L. Wang and *Tribune* reporter, "Felicia Brenner: 1925–2008," *Chicago Tribune,* May 27, 2008, https://www.chicagotribune.com/news/ct-xpm-2008-05-27-0805260209-story.html.

3. "Oral History Interview with Felicia Brenner," United States Holocaust Memorial Museum, interview recorded November 24, 1985, last modified July 28, 2022, https://collections.ushmm.org/search/catalog/irn507439.

4. "Felicia Brenner Obituary," first published by the *Chicago Tribune* May 25 and 26, 2008, last retrieved from Legacy.com on March 19, 2023, https://www

.legacy.com/us/obituaries/chicagotribune/name/felicia-brenner-obituary?id =2817519.

5. Wang and *Tribune* reporter, "Felicia Brenner: 1925–2008."

6. Carmen Mendoza, in a series of private Facebook messages exchanged with the author, November 2022.

7. "Oral History Interview with Felicia Brenner," United States Holocaust Memorial Museum.

## 5. "WERE YOU THERE?"

1. Psalms 8:3–4 (NIV).

2. "Bill Nye Debates Ken Ham," Answers in Genesis YouTube account, YouTube video, February 4, 2014, https://www.youtube.com/watch?v=z6kgvhG3AkI.

3. Sarah Treadwell, phone interview with the author, March 6, 2022.

4. The complexities of the evangelical and fundamentalist responses to Darwinism—and the overlap between those groups—have been explored by historians and religion scholars with far better academic credentials than my own. For my purposes, I'm broadly referring to opposition to evolutionary theory from theologically and culturally conservative Christians who took a literal, inerrantist view of Scripture and believe, among other things, that salvation through belief in Jesus Christ is the only way to Heaven. For a much more thorough discussion of this history, I recommend George M. Marsden's 1991 book *Understanding Fundamentalism and Evangelicalism* (Grand Rapids, MI: William B. Eerdmans Publishing Company, 1991).

5. Richard Hofstadter, *Anti-intellectualism in American Life* (New York: Alfred A. Knopf, 1963), 121–129.

6. Ibid., 125.

7. Marsden, *Understanding Fundamentalism and Evangelicalism,* 153–181.

8. Andrew Hartman, *A War for the Soul of America: A History of the Culture Wars* (Chicago: University of Chicago Press, 2015), 100.

9. Clyde Wilcox and Carin Robinson, *Onward Christian Soldiers?: The Religious Right in American Politics* (New York: Westview Press, 2011), 160.

10. Daniel K. Williams, *God's Own Party: The Making of the Christian Right* (New York: Oxford University Press, 2010), 191.

11. "A History of Private Schools and Race in the American South," Southern Education Foundation, last retrieved March 19, 2023, https://southerneducation .org/publications/history-of-private-schools-and-race-in-the-american -south/.

12. The publisher originally spelled its name "A Beka," which is the format that appears on textbooks from my grade school and high school years.

13. Katherine Stewart, *The Power Worshippers: Inside the Dangerous Rise of Religious Nationalism* (New York: Bloomsbury Publishing, 2019), 205.

14. Chrissy Stroop (@C_stroop), Twitter, 9:58 a.m., March 26, 2019, last retrieved May 16, 2023, https://twitter.com/C_Stroop/status/1110541510880186369?s=20.

15. *Science 6 for Christian Schools: Home Teacher's Edition* (Greenville, SC: Bob Jones University Press, 1995), 49.

16. Ibid., 32.

17. Rebekah Drumsta, phone interview with the author, February 28, 2022.

18. Colin Schultz, "The Pope Would Like You to Accept Evolution and the Big Bang," *Smithsonian Magazine,* October 28, 2014, https://www.smithsonianmag.com/smart-news/pope-would-you-accept-evolution-and-the-big-bang-180953166/.

19. Sarah McCammon, author's personal collection.

## 6. ALTERNATIVE FACTS

1. Ibid.

2. Molly Worthen, *Apostles of Reason: The Crisis of Authority in American Evangelicalism* (New York: Oxford University Press, 2014), 251–253.

3. Ibid., 252.

4. Sarah McCammon, author's personal collection.

5. Proverbs 3:5–7 (NIV).

6. Isaiah 55:8–9 (NIV).

7. John 10:10 (NIV).

8. Shannon Montgomery, phone interview with the author, March 10, 2022.

9. "Conway: Press Secretary Gave 'Alternative Facts,'" *Meet the Press,* NBC News, January 22, 2017, https://www.nbcnews.com/meet-the-press/video/conway-press-secretary-gave-alternative-facts-860142147643.

10. Linda Qiu, "Donald Trump Had Biggest Inaugural Crowd Ever? Metrics Don't Show It," *Politifact,* January 21, 2017, https://www.politifact.com/factchecks/2017/jan/21/sean-spicer/trump-had-biggest-inaugural-crowd-ever-metrics-don/.

11. "Meet the Press 01/22/17," *Meet the Press,* NBC News, https://www.nbcnews.com/meet-the-press/meet-press-01-22-17-n710491.

12. Christopher Douglas, "The Religious Origins of Fake News and 'Alternative Facts,'" *Religion Dispatches*, February 23, 2017, https://religiondispatches .org/the-religious-origins-of-fake-news-and-alternative-facts/?utm_source =Religion+Dispatches+Newsletter&utm_campaign=c14407befd-RD _Daily_Newsletter&utm_medium=email&utm_term=0_742d86f519 -c14407befd-42414197.

13. Ibid.

14. David Roberts, "Donald Trump and the Rise of Tribal Epistemology," *Vox*, May 19, 2017, https://www.vox.com/policy-and-politics/2017/3/22 /14762030/donald-trump-tribal-epistemology.

15. Mark A. Noll, *The Scandal of the Evangelical Mind* (Grand Rapids, MI: William B. Eerdmans Publishing Company, 1994), 3.

16. Ibid., 13.

17. Ruth Braunstein, interview with the author, March 21, 2022.

18. Ibid.

19. Samuel L. Perry, Ruth Braunstein, Philip S. Gorski, and Joshua B. Grubbs, "Historical Fundamentalism? Christian Nationalism and Ignorance about Religion in American Political History," *Journal for the Scientific Study of Religion* 61, no. 1 (December 7, 2021), https://onlinelibrary.wiley.com/doi /abs/10.1111/jssr.12760.

20. Tom Nichols, *The Death of Expertise: The Campaign Against Established Knowledge and Why It Matters* (New York: Oxford University Press, 2017), 3.

21. Ibid., 55–58.

22. Ibid.

23. "Understanding QAnon's Connection to American Politics, Religion, and Media Consumption," Public Religion Research Institute, May 27, 2021, https://www.prri.org/research/qanon-conspiracy-american-politics-report/.

24. Will Sommer, "QAnon Star Who Said Only 'Idiots' Get Vax Dies of COVID," *Daily Beast*, January 7, 2022, https://www.thedailybeast.com/qanon-star -cirsten-weldon-who-said-only-idiots-get-vaccinated-dies-of-covid.

25. "Competing Visions of America: An Evolving Identity or a Culture Under Attack? Findings from the 2021 American Values Survey," Public Religion Research Institute, November 1, 2021, https://www.prri.org/research/competing -visions-of-america-an-evolving-identity-or-a-culture-under-attack/.

26. Elizabeth Dwoskin, "On Social Media, Vaccine Misinformation Mixes with Extreme Faith," *Washington Post*, February 16, 2021, https://www .washingtonpost.com/technology/2021/02/16/covid-vaccine-misinformation -evangelical-mark-beast/.

27. Sarah McCammon, "'Love Your Neighbor' and Get the Shot: White Evangelical Leaders Push COVID Vaccines," NPR, April 5, 2021, https://www.npr.org/2021/04/05/984322992/love-your-neighbor-and-get-the-shot-white-evangelical-leaders-push-covid-vaccine.

28. Jarvis DeBerry, "White Evangelicals Dying of Covid after Denouncing Vaccines Are Wasting Martyrdom," MSNBC, December 26, 2021, https://www.msnbc.com/opinion/white-evangelicals-dying-covid-after-denouncing-vaccines-are-wasting-martyrdom-n1286581.

29. Kayleigh Rogers, "Why QAnon Has Attracted So Many White Evangelicals," *FiveThirtyEight,* March 4, 2021, https://fivethirtyeight.com/features/why-qanon-has-attracted-so-many-white-evangelicals/.

30. Doug Geiger, phone interview with the author, March 15, 2022.

31. Dalia Mortada, Rachel Martin, and Bo Hamby, "Disinformation Fuels a White Evangelical Movement. It Led 1 Virginia Pastor to Quit," NPR, February 21, 2021, https://www.npr.org/2021/02/21/969539514/disinformation-fuels-a-white-evangelical-movement-it-led-1-virginia-pastor-to-qu.

32. Daniel Wood and Geoff Brumfiel, "Pro-Trump Counties Now Have Far Higher COVID Death Rates. Misinformation Is to Blame," NPR, December 5, 2021, https://www.npr.org/sections/health-shots/2021/12/05/1059828993/data-vaccine-misinformation-trump-counties-covid-death-rate.

## 7. WHOSE "CHARACTER" MATTERS?

1. Kenneth Starr, "Communication from Kenneth W. Starr, Independent Counsel," 105th Congress, 2nd Session, House Document 105–310, September 11, 1998, https://www.govinfo.gov/content/pkg/CDOC-105hdoc310/pdf/CDOC-105hdoc310.pdf.

2. John Fea, "What James Dobson Said in 1998 About Moral Character and the Presidency," *Current,* June 25, 2016, https://currentpub.com/2016/06/25/james-dobson-on-the-character-of-the-president-of-the-united-states/.

3. Ibid.

4. James 3:11 (NIV).

5. Franklin Graham, "Clinton's Sins Aren't Private," *Wall Street Journal,* August 27, 1998, https://www.wsj.com/articles/SB904162265981632000.

6. The Southern Poverty Law Center has since labeled the Family Research Council as a hate group for its anti-LGBTQ+ statements. For more, see "Family Research Council," Southern Poverty Law Center, last retrieved March 19, 2023, https://www.splcenter.org/fighting-hate/extremist-files/group/family-research-council.

7. Edward Walsh, "Bauer Airs Ads Calling for Clinton to Resign," *Washington Post,* September 9, 1998, https://www.washingtonpost.com/wp-srv/politics/special/clinton/stories/bauer090998.htm.

8. Rem Rieder, "The World Is Watching Trump's Attacks on the Press," CNN, August 27, 2017, https://www.cnn.com/2017/08/27/politics/donald-trump-media/index.html.

9. Robert L. Jackson, "Falwell Selling Tape That Attacks Clinton," *Los Angeles Times,* May 14, 1994, https://www.latimes.com/archives/la-xpm-1994-05-14-mn-57626-story.html.

10. Author's personal collection.

11. Jonathan Merritt, "Trump-Loving Christians Owe Bill Clinton an Apology," *The Atlantic,* August 10, 2016, www.theatlantic.com/politics/archive/2016/08/evangelical-christians-trump-bill-clinton-apology/495224/.

12. Stephanie Stalvey, phone interview with the author, March 18, 2021.

13. Angela Denker, *Red State Christians: Understanding the Voters Who Elected Donald Trump* (Minneapolis, MN: Fortress Press, 2019), 179.

14. Amy Snidow, phone interview with the author, March 13, 2022.

15. Edward-Isaac Dovere, "Tony Perkins: Trump Gets 'a Mulligan' on Life, Stormy Daniels," *Politico,* January 23, 2018, https://www.politico.com/magazine/story/2018/01/23/tony-perkins-evangelicals-donald-trump-stormy-daniels-216498/.

16. Asher Stockler, "Evangelist Franklin Graham Defends Trump Against Stormy Daniels Reports," NBC News, January 20, 2018, https://www.nbcnews.com/politics/donald-trump/evangelist-franklin-graham-defends-trump-against-stormy-daniels-reports-n839496.

17. "Dr. James Dobson's Thoughts on President Trump," Dr. James Dobson's Family Talk YouTube channel, YouTube video, May 7, 2019, https://www.youtube.com/watch?v=HhE9Lu9uNr8.

18. Sarah McCammon, "Receptive Audience at Liberty University Praises Trump's Accomplishments," NPR, May 15, 2017, https://www.npr.org/2017/05/15/528419743/receptive-audience-at-liberty-university-praises-trumps-accomplishments.

19. Samantha Raphelson, Vanessa Romo, and Sarah McCammon, "'Free at Last,' Says Jerry Falwell Jr. After Resigning as Head of Liberty University," NPR, August 25, 2020, https://www.npr.org/2020/08/25/905877534/jerry-falwell-jr-resigns-as-liberty-universitys-president.

20. Gabriel Sherman, "Inside Jerry Falwell Jr.'s Unlikely Rise and Precipitous Fall at Liberty University," *Vanity Fair,* January 24, 2022, https://www

.vanityfair.com/news/2022/01/inside-jerry-falwell-jr-unlikely-rise-and
-precipitous-fall?utm_source=VANITYFAIR_REG_GATE.

21. Sarah Rodriguez, "Falwell Speaks," *Liberty Champion,* March 8, 2016, https://
www.liberty.edu/champion/2016/03/falwell-speaks/.

22. Tara Isabella Burton, "The Biblical Story the Christian Right Uses to Defend
Trump," *Vox,* March 5, 2018, https://www.vox.com/identities/2018/3/5
/16796892/trump-cyrus-christian-right-bible-cbn-evangelical-propaganda.

23. Lauren Markoe, "Did God Choose Trump? What It Means to Believe in Divine Intervention," Religion News Service, *Deseret News,* January 17, 2017,
https://www.deseret.com/2017/1/17/20604223/did-god-choose-trump
-what-it-means-to-believe-in-divine-intervention.

24. Sarah McCammon, "Inside Trump's Closed-Door Meeting, Held to Reas-
sure 'The Evangelicals,'" NPR, June 21, 2016, https://www.npr.org/2016/06
/21/483018976/inside-trumps-closed-door-meeting-held-to-reassures-the
-evangelicals.

25. Eugene Scott, "Comparing Trump to Jesus, and Why Some Evangelicals
Believe Trump Is God's Chosen One," *Washington Post,* December 18, 2019,
https://www.washingtonpost.com/politics/2019/11/25/why-evangelicals
-like-rick-perry-believe-that-trump-is-gods-chosen-one/.

26. Yonat Shimron and Adelle M. Banks, "Beth Moore Reignites Debate Over
Whether Women Can Preach," Religion News Service, *Baptist Standard,*
June 7, 2019, https://www.baptiststandard.com/news/baptists/beth-moore
-reignites-debate-over-whether-women-can-preach/.

27. Emma Green, "The Tiny Blond Bible Teacher Taking On the Evangelical
Political Machine," *The Atlantic,* October 2018, https://www.theatlantic.com
/magazine/archive/2018/10/beth-moore-bible-study/568288/.

28. Ruth Graham and Elizabeth Dias, "Beth Moore, a Prominent Evangelical,
Splits with Southern Baptists," *New York Times,* March 10, 2021, https://
www.nytimes.com/2021/03/10/us/beth-moore-southern-baptists.html
?partner=slack&smid=sl-share.

29. Bob Smietana, "Bible Teacher Beth Moore, Splitting with Lifeway, Says,
'I Am No Longer a Southern Baptist,'" Religion News Service, March 9,
2021, https://religionnews.com/2021/03/09/bible-teacher-beth-moore-ends
-partnership-with-lifeway-i-am-no-longer-a-southern-baptist/.

## 8. "LEAVE LOUD"

1. Richard A. Serrano and Tracy Wilkinson, "From the Archives: All 4 in King
Beating Acquitted," *Los Angeles Times,* April 30, 1992, https://www.latimes

.com/local/california/la-me-all-4-in-king-beating-acquitted-19920430-story
.html.

2. *Meet the Press*, NBC, April 17, 1960, transcript available: https://kinginstitute
.stanford.edu/king-papers/documents/interview-meet-press.

3. "1995 Racial Reconciliation," The Evangelical Covenant Church, Commission on Christian Action, https://covchurch.org/resolutions/1995-racial
-reconciliation/.

4. Jane Hong, "The L.A. Uprisings Sparked an Evangelical Racial Reckoning: But It Remains Unfinished," *Washington Post*, April 29, 2022, https://
www.washingtonpost.com/outlook/2022/04/29/la-uprisings-sparked-an
-evangelical-racial-reckoning/.

5. Anthea Butler, *White Evangelical Racism: The Politics of Morality in America* (Chapel Hill, NC: University of North Carolina Press, 2021), 88–90.

6. "Resolution on Racial Reconciliation on the 150th Anniversary of the Southern Baptist Convention," Southern Baptist Convention, June 1, 1995, https://
www.sbc.net/resource-library/resolutions/resolution-on-racial-reconciliation
-on-the-150th-anniversary-of-the-southern-baptist-convention.

7. Butler, *White Evangelical Racism*, 91–95.

8. "Negro Leagues History," Negro Leagues Baseball Museum, Kansas City, Missouri, retrieved March 19, 2023, https://www.nlbm.com/negro-leagues
-history/.

9. Mackenzie Martin, "Meet Henry Perry, the Black Entrepreneur Who Created Kansas City Barbecue in the Early 1900s," KCUR, February 13, 2021, https://www.kcur.org/arts-life/2021-02-13/meet-the-black-entrepreneur
-who-created-kansas-city-barbecue-in-the-early-1900s.

10. Lucille Fisher, *Book 1: Families in America,* Heritage Studies for Christian Schools (Greenville, SC: Bob Jones University Press, 1979), 46–47, 80.

11. Ibid., 112–113.

12. Nathaniel Cary, "Bob Jones University Regains Nonprofit Status 17 years After It Dropped Discriminatory Policy," *Greenville News,* updated February 21, 2017, https://www.greenvilleonline.com/story/news/education/2017
/02/16/bju-regains-nonprofit-status-17-years-after-dropped-discriminatory
-policy/98009170/.

13. Interestingly, the ban on interracial dating initially came in response to a complaint from an Asian family, after their son nearly married a white woman, according to a March 2000 article from Evangelical Press called "Bob Jones University Drops Interracial Dating Ban," published in *Chris-*

*tianity Today,* https://www.christianitytoday.com/ct/2000/marchweb-only
/53.0.html.

14. Butler, *White Evangelical Racism,* 44–45.

15. https://www.abeka.com/AbekaDifference.aspx.

16. Tyler Burns, phone interview with the author, May 17, 2022.

17. Judy Hull Moore, *The History of Our United States* (Pensacola, FL: A Beka
Book, 1998), 206.

18. Dylan Matthews, "9 Reasons Christopher Columbus Was a Murderer,
Tyrant, and Scoundrel," *Vox,* October 12, 2015, https://www.vox.com
/2014/10/13/6957875/christopher-columbus-murderer-tyrant
-scoundrel.

19. Moore, *The History of Our United States,* 38–39.

20. Ibid., 62.

21. Ibid., 64.

22. Ibid., 30–31.

23. Robert P. Jones, *White Too Long: The Legacy of White Supremacy in American
Christianity* (New York: Simon & Schuster, 2020), 73.

24. Tara Isabella Burton, "Before Trump, Churches Were Increasingly Multiracial. What Next?," *Vox,* July 3, 2018, https://www.vox.com/2018/7/3
/17527774/study-churches-racial-diversity-trump.

25. Ibid.

26. Daniel Politi, "Donald Trump in Phoenix: Mexicans Are 'Taking Our Jobs'
and 'Killing Us,'" *Slate,* July 12, 2015, https://slate.com/news-and-politics
/2015/07/donald-trump-in-phoenix-mexicans-are-taking-our-jobs-and
-killing-us.html.

27. Kinsey Clarke, "A Good Read: A White Woman On 'Being an Excuse'
for Deadly Racism," NPR, June 24, 2015, https://www.npr.org/sections
/codeswitch/2015/06/24/417100496/a-good-read-a-white-woman-on
-being-an-excuse-for-deadly-racism.

28. Jones, *White Too Long,* 140.

29. Sarah McCammon, "9 Dead in S.C. Church Shooting; Suspect Hunted
by Authorities," NPR, June 18, 2015, https://www.npr.org/2015/06
/18/415394694/9-dead-in-s-c-church-shooting-suspect-hunted-by
-authorities.

30. Campbell Robertson, "A Quiet Exodus: Why Black Worshipers Are
Leaving White Evangelical Churches," *New York Times,* March 9, 2018,

https://www.nytimes.com/2018/03/09/us/blacks-evangelical-churches
.html.

31. "PTM: What is #LeaveLOUD?" The Witness, *Pass the Mic* podcast, May 5, 2021, https://thewitnessbcc.com/ptm-what-is-leaveloud/.

32. Gregory A. Smith, "More White Americans Adopted than Shed Evangelical Label During Trump Presidency, Especially His Supporters," Pew Research Center, September 15, 2021, https://www.pewresearch.org/fact-tank/2021 /09/15/more-white-americans-adopted-than-shed-evangelical-label-during -trump-presidency-especially-his-supporters/.

33. Gregory A. Smith, Michael Rotolo, and Patricia Tevington, "45% of Americans Say US Should Be a 'Christian Nation,'" Pew Research Center, October 27, 2022, https://www.pewresearch.org/religion/2022/10/27/45 -of-americans-say-u-s-should-be-a-christian-nation/.

34. Jemar Tisby, phone interview with the author, May 13, 2022.

35. "The Fierce Urgency of Now—Jemar Tisby at Grove College," The Witness, A Black Christian Collective YouTube channel, YouTube video, April 28, 2022, https://www.youtube.com/watch?v=25MYHZePbWA.

36. Tyler Huckabee, "Read Jemar Tisby's Challenging Open Letter to Grove City College's Board of Trustees," *Relevant* magazine, May 18, 2022, https:// relevantmagazine.com/faith/church/read-jemar-tisbys-challenging-open -letter-to-grove-city-colleges-board-of-trustees/.

37. "Save GCC from CRT," posted on Petitions.net, November 10, 2021, https:// www.petitions.net/save_gcc_from_crt.

38. *Report and Recommendation of the Special Committee,* Grove City College Special Committee, April 13, 2022, https://www.gcc.edu/Portals/0/Special -Committee-Report-and-Recommendation_0422.pdf.

39. Jemar Tisby, "An Open Letter to the Board of Trustees at Grove City College," *Footnotes by Jemar Tisby,* Substack, May 18, 2022, https://jemartisby .substack.com/p/an-open-letter-to-the-board-of-trustees?r=1513k&s=r &utm_campaign=post&utm_medium=email#details.

40. Sarah Mae Saliong, "#LeaveLoud: What to Know about New Dangerous Woke Anti-church Trend Producing 'Exvangelicals,'" *Christianity Daily,* May 14, 2021, https://www.christianitydaily.com/articles/11852/20210514 /leaveloud-what-to-know-about-new-dangerous-woke-anti-church-trend -leave-loud-exvangelical.htm.

41. John Stonestreet and Maria Baer, "Leave Loud, Blaming Churches," Breakpoint, Colson Center, May 11, 2021, https://www.breakpoint.org/leave-loud -blaming-churches/.

42. Errin Haines, "Darnella Frazier, the Teen Who Filmed George Floyd's Murder, Wins Honorary Pulitzer," *19thNews,* June 11, 2021, https://19thnews.org/2021/06/darnella-frazier-teen-filmed-george-floyds-murder-wins-honorary-pulitzer/.

43. Butler, *White Evangelical Racism,* 147.

44. Jack Jenkins, "Mitt Romney Joins Evangelical Racial Justice March in DC," Religion News Service, *Christianity Today,* June 7, 2020, https://www.christianitytoday.com/news/2020/june/mitt-romney-dc-march-thabiti-anyabwile-christians.html.

45. Mark Woods, "Franklin Graham Branded 'Crude, Insensitive and Paternalistic' for Facebook Comments on Police Shootings," *Christian Today,* March 20, 2015, https://www.christiantoday.com/article/franklin.graham.branded.crude.insensitive.and.patrnalistic.for.facebook.comments.on.police.shootings/50387.htm.

46. Lizzy Long, "Franklin Graham 'Sick to My Stomach' over Death of Black Man in Police Custody," Billy Graham Evangelistic Association, May 27, 2020, https://billygraham.org/story/franklin-graham-sick-to-my-stomach-over-black-man-in-police-custody/.

47. "Race Set Before Us," series landing page, *Christianity Today,* last retrieved March 20, 2023, https://www.christianitytoday.com/ct/departments/race-set-before-us/.

48. Cheryl L. Sanders, "Were You There?," *Christianity Today,* October 30, 2020, https://www.christianitytoday.com/ct/2020/october-web-only/were-you-there.html.

49. In *Shoutin' in the Fire: An American Epistle,* Danté Stewart's 2021 memoir of breaking away from a white evangelical church in Georgia, Stewart describes how a predictable pattern played out after the murder of Trayvon Martin in 2012: "It seemed that after every high-profile event of a Black body being murdered or terrorized, they joined in a chorus of white Christians who wanted to use our voices and bodies not so much to free them both, but to make themselves look better than they actually were. Somehow white people always wanted to make statements and public proclamations of their own progress while using our faces." (New York: Convergent Books, 2021), 79.

50. Tyler Huckabee, "What Role Did White Christian Nationalism Play in the Buffalo Massacre?," *Relevant* magazine, May 17, 2022, https://relevantmagazine.com/current/nation/what-role-did-white-christian-nationalism-play-in-the-buffalo-massacre/.

## 9. WHOM DOES JESUS LOVE?

1. Daniel Doss, phone interview with the author, May 31, 2022.

2. Romans 1:26–27 (NIV).

3. David D. Kirkpatrick, "The 2004 Campaign: The Conservatives; Club of the Most Powerful Gathers in Strictest Privacy," *New York Times,* August 28, 2004, https://www.nytimes.com/2004/08/28/us/2004-campaign -conservatives-club-most-powerful-gathers-strictest-privacy.html.

4. Tim LaHaye, *The Unhappy Gays: What Everyone Should Know about Homosexuality* (Carol Stream, IL: Tyndale House Publishers, 1978), 202.

5. Ibid., 193.

6. Ibid., 112.

7. Ibid., 56–57.

8. Amit R. Paley, "The Secret Court of 1920," *Harvard Crimson,* November 21, 2002, https://www.thecrimson.com/article/2002/11/21/the-secret -court-of-1920-at/.

9. Victoria Whitley-Berry and Sarah McCammon, "Former 'Ex-Gay' Leaders Denounce 'Conversion Therapy' in a New Documentary," NPR, August 2, 2021, https://www.npr.org/2021/08/02/1022837295/former-ex-gay-leaders -denounce-conversion-therapy-in-a-new-documentary.

10. Jeff Chu, *Does Jesus Really Love Me?: A Gay Christian's Pilgrimage in Search of God in America* (New York: HarperCollins, 2013).

11. See James 5:16.

12. David P. Gushee, *Changing Our Mind: Definitive 3rd Edition of the Landmark Call for Inclusion of LGBTQ Christians with Response to Critics* (Canton, MI: Read the Spirit Books, 2017), dedication page.

13. David P. Gushee, phone interview with the author, May 24, 2022.

14. Betsy Cooper, Daniel Cox, Rachel Lienesch, and Robert P. Jones, "Exodus: Why Americans Are Leaving Religion—and Why They're Unlikely to Come Back," Public Religion Research Institute, September 22, 2016, https://www.prri.org/research/prri-rns-poll-nones-atheist-leaving-religion/.

15. Matthew 7:17–20 (NIV).

16. Gabriel Spitzer, "Pushed Away by Their Birth Families, Many LGBTQ People Build 'Chosen Families,'" KNKX Public Radio, February 29, 2020, https://www.knkx.org/other-news/2020-02-29/pushed-away-by-their-birth -families-many-lgbtq-people-build-chosen-families.

17. Ibid.

18. Dory Jackson, "'Jurassic World' Pulled Lesbian Character's Coming Out

Scene, Star Daniella Pineda Says," *Newsweek,* June 20, 2018, https://www .newsweek.com/jurassic-world-lesbian-scene-pulled-985871.

19. Personal email, June 25, 2018, lightly edited for clarity.

20. Chrissy Stroop, phone interview with the author, June 4, 2022.

21. Catherine Allgor, "Coverture: The Word You Probably Don't Know but Should," National Women's History Museum, September 4, 2012, https:// www.womenshistory.org/articles/coverture-word-you-probably-dont-know -should.

## 10. A VIRTUOUS WOMAN

1. Josh McDowell and Dick Day, *Why Wait? What You Need to Know About the Teen Sexuality Crisis* (Nashville, TN: Thomas Nelson Publishers, 1987), 342.

2. Joshua Harris, *I Kissed Dating Goodbye* (Colorado Springs: Multnomah Publishers, 1997), 99.

3. Donna Freitas, *Sex and the Soul: Juggling Sexuality, Spirituality, Romance, and Religion on America's College Campuses*, updated edition (New York: Oxford University Press, 2015), 114–115.

4. Personal letter by the author's mother, October 28, 1998.

5. Ibid.

6. Freitas, *Sex and the Soul,* 86.

7. John Eldredge, *Wild at Heart: Discovering the Secret of a Man's Soul* (Nashville, TN: Thomas Nelson Publishers, 2001), 9–10.

8. Ibid., 231.

9. Katelyn Beaty, "After Atlanta-Area Shooting, Christians Must Rethink Purity Culture That Puts Blame on Women," *Washington Post,* March 18, 2021, https://www.washingtonpost.com/religion/2021/03/18/purity-culture -atlanta-shooter-women-sexuality/.

10. Valerie Bauerlein and Cameron McWhirter, "Atlanta Shooting Suspect Told Police He Targeted Massage Parlors Because of Sex Addiction," *Wall Street Journal,* March 17, 2021, https://www.wsj.com/articles/atlanta-shootings -fbi-investigating-killing-of-eight-at-massage-parlors-11615989454.

11. Beaty, "After Atlanta-Area Shooting."

12. Matt (last name redacted), phone interview with the author, July 18, 2022.

## 11. NAKED AND ASHAMED

1. Joshua Harris, *Boy Meets Girl: Say Hello to Courtship* (Colorado Springs: Multnomah Publishers, 2000), 21–26.

2. Ibid., 151.

3. Ibid., 145.

4. Tim and Beverly LaHaye, *The Act of Marriage: The Beauty of Sexual Love* (Grand Rapids, MI: Zondervan, 1976), 101.

5. Ibid., 102.

6. Emily Petrini, phone interview with the author, May 15, 2023.

7. Jocelyn Howard, phone interview with the author, March 8, 2022.

8. "Louise" (pseudonym), phone interview with the author, June 13, 2022.

9. Tori Williams Douglass (@ToriGlass), Twitter, 1:14 a.m., July 12, 2022, edited for style and format, https://twitter.com/ToriGlass/status/1546724686 523879424?s=20&t=iTOQmeQA8DJ75xcgIwwuzQ.

10. Tori Williams Douglass (@ToriGlass), Twitter, 1:12 a.m., July 12, 2022, https://twitter.com/ToriGlass/status/1546724255097692160?s=20&t =iTOQmeQA8DJ75xcgIwwuzQ.

11. Linda Kay Klein, *Pure: Inside the Evangelical Movement That Shamed a Generation of Young Women and How I Broke Free* (New York: Atria, 2018), 189.

12. Joshua Harris, "Former Evangelical Pastor Rethinks His Approach to Courtship," interview by Rachel Martin, *Weekend Edition Sunday,* NPR, July 10, 2016, https://www.npr.org/2016/07/10/485432485/former-evangelical-pastor -rethinks-his-approach-to-courtship.

13. Sarah McCammon, "Evangelical Writer Kisses an Old Idea Goodbye," NPR, December 17, 2018, https://www.npr.org/2018/12/17/671888011/evangelical -writer-kisses-an-old-idea-goodbye.

14. Sarah McCammon and Kat Lonsdorf, "When Your Wedding Night Is Your First Time," NPR, May 1, 2019, https://www.npr.org/2019/05/01/712882392 /when-your-wedding-night-is-your-first-time.

## 12. BE FRUITFUL AND MULTIPLY

1. Dr. James Dobson, *Dare to Discipline* (Carol Stream, IL: Tyndale House Publishers, 1988), 159–160.

2. Titus 2:3–9 (NIV).

3. Lucille Fisher, *Book 1: Families in America,* Heritage Studies for Christian Schools (Greenville, SC: Bob Jones University Press, 1979).

4. Dahleen Glanton, "Parents Try High Court," *Chicago Tribune,* March 24, 2005, https://www.chicagotribune.com/news/ct-xpm-2005-03-24-05032 40197-story.html.

5. Dr. James C. Dobson, *Parenting Isn't for Cowards: Dealing Confidently with*

*the Frustrations of Child-Rearing* (Nashville, TN: Word Publishing, 1987), 13–14.

6. Dr. James Dobson and Gary L. Bauer, *Children at Risk: What You Need to Know to Protect Your Family* (Nashville, TN: Word Publishing, 1990), 4.

7. Dobson and Bauer, *Children at Risk,* 252.

8. "A Christian Nation? Understanding the Threat of Christian Nationalism to American Democracy and Culture," Public Religion Research Institute, February 8, 2023, https://www.prri.org/research/a-christian-nation -understanding-the-threat-of-christian-nationalism-to-american-democracy -and-culture/.

9. John Fea, *Believe Me: The Evangelical Road to Donald Trump* (Grand Rapids, MI: William B. Eerdmans Publishing Company, 2018), 6.

10. Marc Fisher, "The GOP, Facing a Dobson's Choice," *Washington Post,* July 2, 1996, https://www.washingtonpost.com/archive/lifestyle/1996/07/02/the -gop-facing-a-dobsons-choice/af417df4-cb7b-4d17-8b83-e17a67c70b22/.

11. Ibid.

12. William R. Bowen, George T. Thompson, Michael R. Lowman, and George C. Cochran, *American Government in Christian Perspective* (Pensacola, FL: A Beka Book, 1997), 65.

13. Ibid., 89.

14. "The Racist Filibuster We Can't Afford to Forget," *The Takeaway,* WNYC, August 29, 2016, https://www.wnycstudios.org/podcasts/takeaway/segments /racist-filibuster-we-cant-afford-forget.

15. Bowen et al., *American Government in Christian Perspective,* 151.

16. Lauren Hodges and Sarah McCammon, "After a Reprieve, a Louisiana Clinic Resumes Abortions for Anxious Patients," NPR, June 30, 2022, https://www.npr.org/2022/06/30/1108662002/louisiana-clinic-patients -still-seeking-abortions.

### 13. SUFFER THE LITTLE CHILDREN

1. Proverbs 13:24 (NIV).

2. Dobson, *Dare to Discipline,* 23.

3. Ibid., 45, 23, 38.

4. Rachel Held Evans, "The Abusive Teachings of Michael and Debi Pearl," blog, March 23, 2013, https://rachelheldevans.com/blog/the-abusive-teachings-of -michael-and-debi-pearl.

5.  Erik Eckholm, "Preaching the Virtue of Spanking, Even As Deaths Fuel Debate," *New York Times,* November 6, 2011, https://www.nytimes.com /2011/11/07/us/deaths-put-focus-on-pastors-advocacy-of-spanking.html.

6.  Talia Lavin, "Ministry of Violence," *The Sword and the Sandwich,* Substack, October 25, 2021, https://theswordandthesandwich.substack.com/p/ministry -of-violence.

7.  Dobson, *Dare to Discipline,* 23.

8.  Lavin, "Ministry of Violence."

9.  Hillary McBride (@hillarylmcbride), Twitter, 12:01 a.m., October 29, 2022, https://twitter.com/hillarylmcbride/status/1586206651153285121?s=20&t =QA-ZESO4nzUtkLOktQlJ1g.

10. Hillary McBride, phone interview with the author, December 6, 2022.

11. Emily Joy Allison, in-person interview with the author in Nashville, Tennessee, July 23, 2022.

12. Lavin, "Ministry of Violence."

13. Associated Press, "Dobson Resigns as Chair of Focus on the Family," NBC News, February 27, 2009, https://www.nbcnews.com/id/wbna29431308.

14. Email from the author to Katie Anderson, August 1, 2022.

15. Email to the author from Katie Anderson, September 12, 2022.

16. Email from Brad Mazzocco to the author, September 16, 2022.

17. Holly Fletcher, phone interview with the author, November 28, 2022.

18. Cindy Wang Brandt, Parenting Forward website, https://cindywangbrandt .com/, last retrieved March 20, 2023.

19. Cindy Wang Brandt, virtual interview with the author, August 17, 2022.

20. Emily and Travis Tingley, interview with the author at their home in Nashville, Tennessee, July 24, 2022.

21. Rob Bell, "Launching Rockets," Rob Bell website, https://robbell.com /audio/launching-rockets/, last retrieved March 20, 2023.

22. Bekah McNeel, *Bringing Up Kids When Church Lets You Down: A Guide for Parents Questioning Their Faith* (Grand Rapids, MI: William B. Eerdmans Publishing Company, 2022), 79.

### 14. BROKEN FOR YOU

1.  Bethany Johnson, phone interview with the author, January 30, 2022.

2.  1 John 4:18 (NIV).

3.  1 Thessalonians 5:2–3 (NIV).

4. Proverbs 3:24–25 (NIV).

5. Jamie Lee Finch, *You Are Your Own: A Reckoning with the Religious Trauma of Evangelical Christianity* (self-pub., 2019), 57.

6. Ibid., 66–67.

7. Daniel Fowler, phone interview with the author, January 11, 2022.

8. Andrew Kerbs, phone interview with the author, June 10, 2021.

9. Laura Anderson, phone interview with the author, June 11, 2021.

10. "Trauma," American Psychological Association website, https://www.apa.org/topics/trauma, last retrieved March 20, 2023.

11. Marlene Winell, phone interview with the author, August 23, 2021.

12. Emily St. James, "The Sexual Abuse Scandal Rocking the Southern Baptist Convention, Explained," *Vox,* June 7, 2022, https://www.vox.com/culture/23131530/southern-baptist-convention-sexual-abuse-scandal-guidepost.

13. *The Southern Baptist Convention Executive Committee's Response to Sexual Abuse Allegations and an Audit of the Procedures and Actions of the Credentials Committee,* Guidepost Solutions, May 15, 2022, https://static1.squarespace.com/static/6108172d83d55d3c9db4dd67/t/6298d31ff654dd1a9dae86bf/1654182692359/Guidepost+Solutions+Independent+Investigation+Report___.pdf.

14. "The Mental Health Benefits of Religion & Spirituality," National Alliance on Mental Illness, December 21, 2016, https://www.nami.org/Blogs/NAMI-Blog/December-2016/The-Mental-Health-Benefits-of-Religion-Spiritual#:~:text=Religion%20gives%20people%20something%20to,rates%2C%20alcoholism%20and%20drug%20use.

15. Laura Anderson, email exchange with the author, October 25, 2022.

16. "Eye Movement Desensitization and Reprocessing (EMDR) for PTSD," National Center for PTSD, US Department of Veterans Affairs, last retrieved March 20, 2023, https://www.ptsd.va.gov/understand_tx/emdr.asp.

17. Christopher E. M. Lloyd, Brittney S. Mengistu, and Graham Reid, "'His Main Problem Was Not Being in a Relationship with God': Perceptions of Depression, Help-Seeking, and Treatment in Evangelical Christianity," *Frontiers in Psychology* 13 (April 19, 2022), https://doi.org/10.3389/fpsyg.2022.831534.

## 15. INTO THE WILDERNESS

1. Stephanie Stalvey (@stephanie.stalvey.artist), image caption: "We are the church kids all grown up," Instagram, March 3, 2021, https://www.instagram.com/p/CL-C8iuMnhg/.

2. Doug Pagitt, interview with the author in Washington, DC, September 13, 2022.

3. Stalvey, "We are the church kids all grown up."

4. Kate and Andy Blair, interview with the author, May 2, 2023.

5. Daniel A. Cox, "Generation Z and the Future of Faith in America," Survey Center on American Life, March 24, 2022, https://www.americansurveycenter .org/research/generation-z-future-of-faith/.

6. Danny Huerta, email, July 21, 2022.

7. "Learn How to Restore Your Relationship with Your Estranged Child," Focus on the Family, last retrieved March 19, 2023, https://www.focusonthefamily .com/healing-parent-adult-child-relationships-sign-up/?utm_medium =email&utm_campaign=1447601&utm_source=RevelantResources&seid =116991625.

8. Rea T (@ReaTschetter), Twitter, 9:52 a.m., July 22, 2022, https://twitter.com /ReaTschetter/status/1550479018411102208?s=20&t=PLtOiFcwi9PC25 WCpVXfbQ.

9. Mike Lindell's Brain (@beyond_parody), Twitter, 5:17 a.m., July 22, 2022, https://twitter.com/beyond_parody/status/1550409761929236480?s=20&t =PLtOiFcwi9PC25WCpVXfbQ.

10. D. L. Mayfield, phone interview with the author, July 27, 2022.

11. Jeff Chu, phone interview with the author, May 24, 2022.

12. Stephanie Stalvey (@stephanie.stalvey.artist), "Church Kids Comic," Instagram, August 28, 2021, https://www.instagram.com/p/CTITvhfL2qh/.

13. Jared Yates Sexton, phone interview with the author, March 15, 2022.

14. "About" page, Evolving Faith, https://evolvingfaith.com/about, last retrieved March 19, 2023.

### 16. WRESTLING AGAINST FLESH AND BLOOD

1. Larson, *The American Republic,* 61.

2. Ibid.

3. Ephesians 6:12–17 (NIV).

4. Tyler Huckabee, "Skillet's John Cooper: It's Time to 'Declare War Against This Deconstruction Christian Movement,'" *Relevant* magazine, February 9, 2022, https://relevantmagazine.com/current/skillets-john -cooper-its-time-to-declare-war-against-this-deconstruction-christian -movement/.

5. Jeff Chu (@jeffchu), Twitter, 12:48 p.m., May 4, 2019, https://twitter.com/jeffchu/status/1124717506126594050?s=20&t=NgdPg-cEen4RfiQnpfgj-A.

6. Bruce Gerencser, "Is Rachel Evans in Hell? Pulpit & Pen and the Transformed Wife Say YES!," *The Life and Times of Bruce Gerencser* blog, May 7, 2019, https://brucegerencser.net/2019/05/is-rachel-evans-in-hell-pulpit-pen-and-the-transformed-wife-say-yes/.

7. Rachel Held Evans, "'All right, then I'll go to hell,'" blog, May 23, 2012, https://rachelheldevans.com/blog/huck-finn-hell.

8. Rachel Held Evans, "On 'Going Episcopal,'" blog, March 25, 2015, https://rachelheldevans.com/blog/going-episcopal.

9. Rachel Held Evans, "What now?," blog, April 1, 2014, https://rachelheldevans.com/blog/what-now-world-vision.

10. Sarah McCammon, Elena Burnett, and Justine Kenin, "Author Jeff Chu on Completing the Book Rachel Held Evans Started Before She Died," NPR, October 29, 2021, https://www.npr.org/2021/10/29/1050620569/author-jeff-chu-on-completing-the-book-rachel-held-evans-started-before-she-died.

11. Sarah Stankorb, "'False Teachers,' 'Wolves,' and Other Modern American Evangelical Smears," *Medium,* November 30, 2021, https://gen.medium.com/false-teachers-wolves-and-other-modern-american-evangelical-smears-e03dd755b36.

12. Christian Smith, *American Evangelicalism: Embattled and Thriving* (Chicago: University of Chicago Press, 1998), 89.

13. Ibid., 120–123.

14. Ibid., 123.

15. Du Mez, *Jesus and John*

16. Josh Butler, "4 Causes of Deconstruction," The Gospel Coalition, November 9, 2021, https://www.thegospelcoalition.org/article/4-causes-deconstruction/.

17. Amy Hayes, "Deconstruction Is Not a Disease, and Trying Harder Is Not the Cure," Baptist News Global, November 22, 2021, https://baptistnews.com/article/deconstruction-is-not-a-disease-and-trying-harder-is-not-the-cure/#.YzJlQ3bMLe8.

18. Hojun Choi, "What We Know About Megachurch Pastor Matt Chandler of the Village Church," *Dallas Morning News*, August 29, 2022, https://www.dallasnews.com/news/faith/2022/08/29/what-we-know-about-megachurch-pastor-matt-chandler-of-the-village-church/.

19. Jesse T. Jackson, "Matt Chandler Responds to Deconstruction Controversy,"

ChurchLeaders.com, December 8, 2021, https://churchleaders.com/news/412237-matt-chandler-responds-to-deconstruction-controversy.html.

20. Sorrel Virginia Hester, "The Exvangelical Movement Is Hella White: My Original Critique," *The Generous Pine* blog, January 7, 2019, https://thegenerouspine.com/2019/01/07/the-exvangelical-movement-is-hella-white-my-original-critique/.

21. Jessica Lea, "UPDATE: After 'Valid Criticism,' Josh Harris Takes Down His Deconstruction Course," ChurchLeaders.com, August 16, 2021, https://churchleaders.com/news/403209-joshua-harris-deconstruction-course.html.

22. In a tweet critical of writer Joshua Harris, author Jamie Lee Finch wrote, "One more thing: Joshua Harris has told me privately how much my book meant to him + to other people he knows who read it. He recently assembled a 'deconstruction starter pack' as marketing material for his course. My book isn't in it. Someone isn't citing their sources," August 13, 2021, https://twitter.com/jamieleefinch/status/1426208616290390021?s=20&t=45P8gxNaR8WIzKJMwljy2A.

23. Odogwu Na The Spender, @TruthBy_JN, Twitter, 10:55 a.m., August 12, 2021, last retrieved November 2, 2023, https://twitter.com/TruthBy_JN/status/1425833229722947594.

24. Tyler Huckabee, phone interview with the author, February 15, 2022.

25. For a more detailed treatment of gender, particularly masculinity, in evangelical culture, see *Jesus and John Wayne* by Kristin Kobes Du Mez or *The Making of Biblical Womanhood* by Beth Allison Barr.

26. "Modeling the Future of Religion in America," Pew Research Center, September 13, 2022, https://www.pewresearch.org/religion/2022/09/13/modeling-the-future-of-religion-in-america/.

27. Russell Moore, "My Dad Taught Me How to Love the Exvangelical," *Christianity Today,* October 21, 2021, https://www.christianitytoday.com/ct/2021/october-web-only/russell-moore-dad-taught-love-exvangelical-pastor-church.html.

28. Ibid.

29. Promise Enlow Councill, phone interview with the author, July 8, 2021.

30. Tom Gjelten, "A 'Scary' Survey Finding: 4 in 10 Republicans Say Political Violence May Be Necessary," NPR, February 11, 2021, https://www.npr.org/2021/02/11/966498544/a-scary-survey-finding-4-in-10-republicans-say-political-violence-may-be-necessa.

31. "Ahead of Anniversary of 1/6 Insurrection, Republicans Remain Entan-

gled in the Big Lie, QAnon, and Temptations Toward Political Violence," Public Religion Research Institute, January 4, 2022, https://www.prri.org/spotlight/anniversary-of-jan-6-insurrection/.

32. Gregory A. Smith, "More White Americans Adopted than Shed Evangelical Label during Trump Presidency, Especially His Supporters," Pew Research Center, September 15, 2021, https://www.pewresearch.org/fact-tank/2021/09/15/more-white-americans-adopted-than-shed-evangelical-label-during-trump-presidency-especially-his-supporters/.

33. Gushee, *After Evangelicalism,* 8.

34. Abraham Piper (@abrahampiper), "Here's why I appreciate fundamentalists . . . ," TikTok, July 1, 2022, https://www.tiktok.com/@abrahampiper/video/7115482992109407534?is_copy_url=1&is_from_webapp=v1&item_id=7115482992109407534&lang=en.

35. Nadia Bolz-Weber, "You Can Take the Girl Out of Fundamentalism, but . . . ," *The Corners,* Substack, October 17, 2022, https://thecorners.substack.com/p/you-can-take-the-girl-out-of-fundamentalism?r=3gbb4&utm_medium=ios&utm_campaign=post.

### 17: INTO ALL THE WORLD

1. Josh Scott, in-person interview with the author at GracePointe Church in Nashville, Tennessee, July 24, 2022.

2. For more from the day I visited, see Josh Scott, "What About Baptism?," GracePointe Church YouTube channel, YouTube video, July 24, 2022, https://www.youtube.com/watch?v=3_WCe2yDrTg.

3. Mel Kulenski, phone interview with the author, October 27, 2022.

4. Cantor Deborrah Cannizzaro, "A Brief History of the Kol Nidrei Prayer," ReformJudaism.org, September 17, 2018, https://reformjudaism.org/blog/brief-history-kol-nidrei-prayer.

5. "What Is a Mezuzah? Why and How Do We Use It?," ReformJudaism.org, last retrieved March 19, 2023, https://reformjudaism.org/beliefs-practices/lifecycle-rituals/what-mezuzah-why-and-how-do-we-use-it.

6. Deuteronomy 6:4–9 (NIV).

7. Smith, "More White Americans Adopted."

8. Charla Arnold, phone interview with the author, September 12, 2022.

9. Diane Bolme, "The Evangelical Church Taught Me Abortion Was Murder. I Changed My Own Mind," *Jezebel,* July 11, 2022, https://jezebel.com/ex-evangelical-pro-choice-abortion-1849163842.

10. Ibid.

11. Diane Bolme, phone interview with the author, July 18, 2022.

12. "PRRI 2021 Census of American Religion, Updates and Trends: White Christian Decline Slows, Unaffiliated Growth Levels Off," Public Religion Research Institute, April 27, 2022, https://www.prri.org/spotlight/prri -2021-american-values-atlas-religious-affiliation-updates-and-trends-white -christian-decline-slows-unaffiliated-growth-levels-off/#:~:text=Both%20 white%20mainline%20Protestants%20and,much%20of%20the%20 fall%2Doff.

13. David Dark, interview with the author in Nashville, Tennessee, July 24, 2022.

14. Diana Butler Bass, "Evangelical Wreckage," *The Cottage,* Substack, October 19, 2022, https://dianabutlerbass.substack.com/p/evangelical-wreckage ?utm_source=substack&utm_medium=email.

15. Ibid.

16. Ibid.

17. Matthew 7:15 (Good News Translation).

18. Abraham Piper (@abrahampiper), Twitter, 6:59 a.m, October 18, 2022, last retrieved March 19, 2023, https://twitter.com/abrahampiper/status /1582325477179416576?s=20&t=T2xbouRt-YtaZJ-8JB5jPQ.

19. Ibid.

# INDEX